Still Letting My People Go

Still Letting My People Go

An Analysis of Eli Washington Caruthers's Manuscript against American Slavery and Its Universal Application of Exodus 10:3

Jack R. Davidson

FOREWORD BY
Kathy Ehrensperger

◆PICKWICK *Publications* • Eugene, Oregon

STILL LETTING MY PEOPLE GO
An Analysis of Eli Washington Caruthers's Manuscript against American Slavery and Its Universal Application of Exodus 10:3

Copyright © 2018 Jack R. Davidson. All rights reserved. Except for brief quotations in critical publications or reviews, no part of this book may be reproduced in any manner without prior written permission from the publisher. Write: Permissions, Wipf and Stock Publishers, 199 W. 8th Ave., Suite 3, Eugene, OR 97401.

Pickwick Publications
An Imprint of Wipf and Stock Publishers
199 W. 8th Ave., Suite 3
Eugene, OR 97401

www.wipfandstock.com

PAPERBACK ISBN: 978-1-5326-0086-9
HARDCOVER ISBN: 978-1-5326-0088-3
EBOOK ISBN: 978-1-5326-0087-6

Cataloguing-in-Publication data:

Names: Davidson, Jack R., author. | Ehrensperger, Kathy, 1956–, foreword.

Title: Still letting my people go : an analysis of Eli Washington Caruthers's manuscript against American slavery and its universal application of Exodus 10:3 / Jack R. Davidson ; foreword by Kathy Ehrensperger

Description: Eugene, OR : Pickwick Publications, 2018 | Includes bibliographical references.

Identifiers: ISBN 978-1-5326-0086-9 (paperback) | ISBN 978-1-5326-0088-3 (hardcover) | ISBN 978-1-5326-0087-6 (ebook)

Subjects: LCSH: Caruthers, E. W. (Eli Washington), 1793–1865. | Slavery—North Carolina. | Presbyterian Church—North Carolina—History. | Presbyterians—North Carolina—History.

Classification: E446 .D26 2018 (print) | E446 .D26 (ebook)

Manufactured in the U.S.A.   07/06/18

Contents

Abstract | vii
Foreword by Kathy Ehrensperger | ix
Introduction | xi

Chapter 1: The Manuscript and Author | 1
    Manuscript | 1
    The Author | 5
    Outline of the Book | 11

Chapter 2: The Claim of Exodus 10:3 | 15
    Creation and Preservation | 15
    Redemption through the Covenant | 24

Chapter 3: The Demand of Exodus 10:3 | 34
    Scripture | 35
    Providence | 46

Chapter 4: The Purpose of Exodus 10:3 | 57
    Christianity and the Laws of Slave States | 57
    Slavery Hinders Service | 63
    Progress of Emancipation, Colonization, and Conclusion | 68

Chapter 5: Presbyterians and American Slavery | 77
    American Presbyterians | 78
    Caruthers and Recent Consideration of the Slavery Question | 89

Chapter 6: Caruthers and the Enlightenment | 92
    Sources of the Antislavery Argument | 92
    Interpreting Caruthers's Use of the Declaration
        of Independence | 101

CONTENTS

Chapter 7: The Similarity of Caruthers to Other Antislavery Literature | 107
Noah's Curse | 107
Abraham's Servants | 113
Moses and Slavery | 116
The Christian Era | 119

Chapter 8: The Exodus Text in Nineteenth-Century Discourse | 124
Exodus Text Conspectus (1807–1865) | 126
Evaluation and Implications | 158

Chapter 9: Caruthers's Method | 162

Chapter 10: Caruthers and Recent Studies | 175
Modern Commentaries and Slavery Texts | 175
Complementary Studies to Caruthers | 178
Keesmaat and Exodus in the Writings of Paul | 186

Chapter 11: Review and Conclusion | 194

Appendix: Evaluating Former Slave Testimony | 201
Bibliography | 217

Abstract

WITHIN THE THEOLOGICAL AND historical context of nineteenth-century America, Eli Washington Caruthers's unpublished manuscript, *American Slavery and the Immediate Duty of Southern Slaveholders*, is an authentic alternative to the nineteenth-century hermeneutics that supported slavery. On the basis of Exodus 10:3—"Let my people go that they may serve me," Caruthers argues that God was acting in history against all slavery. Unlike proslavery or antislavery arguments guided largely by the New Testament, Caruthers believes the Exodus text is a privileged passage to which all thinking on slavery must conform. Permeation of nineteenth-century antislavery literature with the Exodus text gave divine impetus to the struggle against slavery and a genuine social dimension to the Christian faith. As the most extensive development of the Exodus text within this field of literature, Caruthers's manuscript is an invaluable primary source, especially relevant to historians' current appraisal of the biblical sanction for slavery in nineteenth-century America. It does not correspond to characterizations of antislavery literature as biblically weak. For example, historians Elizabeth Fox-Genovese and Eugene Genovese assert that the proslavery argument is based upon scripture and the antislavery argument is less biblical, dependent on the ideals of the Enlightenment. To the contrary, the analysis of Caruthers's manuscript reveals a thoroughly reasoned biblical argument unlike any other produced during the nineteenth century against the hermeneutics supporting slavery.

Foreword

It is with great pleasure that I see the fruits of this important research reach the point where they embark on the journey to a wider academic and interested readership. Jack Davidson embarked on a challenging journey himself when he decided to research the manuscript *American Slavery and the Immediate Duty of Southern Slaveholders* and its author Eli Caruthers. He made the life-changing decision to leave his position as the successful pastor of his congregation and to dedicate several years of his life to a project he was passionate about. It was this passion that led to his search for a supervisor for his dissertation project, and I was lucky enough that he made inquiries at the University of Wales, Lampeter, UK, where I was teaching at the time. I was impressed by the project and the depth of engagement Jack demonstrated, and being involved in research about the relevance of hermeneutical presuppositions in biblical interpretation myself there was obviously a deeply shared concern for the role of the Bible in society past and present. That we both as pastors were also deeply concerned about the role of the Bible in our respective church traditions rendered the cooperation on this project all the more fruitful and personally important also for me.

With the publication of the remarkable manuscript of a remarkable pastor from Greensboro, NC, and its theological analysis, Jack makes the largely forgotten manuscript *American Slavery and the Immediate Duty of Southern Slaveholders* by Eli Caruthers accessible to the public. But not only that, he presents a succinct introduction and analysis of this remarkable piece of work, highlighting its historical and, to a greater extent, its theological significance as a voice from the South that, based on biblical texts, had not tuned into the majority pro-slavery argumentation. Through his careful historical contextualization and theological analysis of the manuscript Davidson is able to demonstrate that specific hermeneutical presuppositions lead Caruthers to a firm argument against slavery. He demonstrates that Caruthers was informed by contemporary philosophical and ethical literature from which anti-slavery arguments generally drew but that his primary hermeneutical key was firmly rooted in biblical texts. By recognizing the passage of Exodus

10:3 as the key theological parameter over against which the Bible as a whole, including the New Testament, had to be read, Caruthers established a theological-hermeneutical key that unlocked the liberating potential of the Bible with regard to the question of slavery. This hermeneutical move appears very modern in that Caruthers claims that a specific narrative of the Bible was the core over against which all other texts had to be evaluated. He thereby acknowledged that a text does not speak for itself but that the reader is conditioned by hermeneutical presuppositions, which guide his or her reading of the Bible. There are analogies to this move in feminist and liberationist interpretations beginning in the 1970s, but also to the core role the Exodus narrative plays in Jewish tradition. There is probably no direct connection, but it is noteworthy that Abraham Lincoln had close connections to Jews, who were involved in the abolitionist cause and he was the first to appoint Jewish army chaplains to serve the thousands of Jewish soldiers fighting for the Union during the Civil War. With Lincoln, Caruthers shared the love for the Old Testament prevalent in many Protestant traditions inspired by Calvin, but Jack demonstrates that although Caruthers had earned his theology degree from Princeton Seminary he was very likely inspired by a combination of thought traditions, with the Exodus narrative providing the decisive structure and argument for his *American Slavery and the Immediate Duty of Southern Slaveholders*. This anti-slavery stance rooted in the Exodus narrative as the hermeneutical key to the Bible is without precedent. Jack Davidson's publication of Eli Caruther's manuscript and his excellent theological analysis demonstrate that the awareness of the hermeneutical framework, now something that is required of biblical interpretation generally, is in nuce already present in this remarkable text of the nineteenth century.

Although it is now several years since the thesis was successfully defended, Jack had to prioritize other tasks in his life, but I had always hoped that he would one day be able to get the time and space to get his excellent dissertation ready for publication. That this has happened now is fantastic and I am sure it will be invaluable on many levels of biblical interpretation and theological discussions, but above all for the debate on the role of the Bible in the pro-and anti-slavery debates of the nineteenth century.

Kathy Ehrensperger

Research Professor of New Testament in Jewish Perspective
Abraham Geiger College,
University of Potsdam, Germany

Introduction

My research in the Bible, Eli Caruthers, and American slavery originated during a two-year period beginning in late 1998 while I was the pastor of a Presbyterian congregation in Eugene, Oregon. A booklet circulating in the church and throughout other congregations in the Pacific Northwest had created a stir. *Southern Slavery As it Was*, published by Canon Press in 1996 was authored by two ministers, one of them a member of my own denomination at the time. The title of their booklet was a play on the abolitionist work published anonymously in 1839 by Theodore Dwight Weld, *American Slavery As it Is: Testimony of a Thousand Witnesses*. In his book Weld presents multiple compilations of the statements of slaveholders about their slaves or slavery culled from more than twenty thousand copies of Southern newspapers sorted by him and his wife, Angelina, and her older sister, Sarah Grimke. Weld's book presents and catalogues the punishments, maiming, branding, and scars resulting from a variety of tortures that were routinely mentioned in the personal descriptions of runaway slaves published in newspaper advertisements by owners hoping to recover their human property. The overall effect is a crushing indictment of American slavery.

Douglas Wilson and Steve Wilkins, the authors of the booklet, replace Weld's negative portrait of slavery with a substantially different and positive view of slavery they believe found in selected slave narratives. They also incorporate elements of the biblical defense offered by proslavery Presbyterian ministers in the run up to and during the war. In their view American slavery was not only biblically sanctioned, but also a social arrangement of divine beauty when purged of its racism and abuse. As a pastor, I felt a responsibility to educate my congregation, but I knew very little. My alarm over modern proslavery belief and its antecedents was then and is now the same: If the Bible sanctions slavery then there can be no biblically based objection to current forms of slavery or to the establishment or continuance of a modern slave state.

INTRODUCTION

I began reading some of the sources cited in the booklet and soon found myself buried in antebellum literature related to the Bible and slavery such as Weld and countless others. I also met with Jack Maddex, a historian of nineteenth-century America, highly regarded for his knowledge of the Presbyterian Church in Antebellum America. In one of our conversations Maddex made reference to Eli Caruthers, a Presbyterian minister and the author of an unpublished manuscript against slavery completed during the 1860s in Greensboro, North Carolina. He encouraged me to look into Caruthers and his manuscript as a unique example of Southern clergy dissent in the slavery controversy.

In 2000, with the help of friends and colleagues, I organized a seminar as a public venue responding to the proslavery booklet mentioned above. During this period I contacted Special Collections at Duke University about Caruthers's manuscript. I wanted to select portions of it and use the voice of a nineteenth-century Presbyterian minister from the South to critique the proslavery sentiment of the booklet. Without a transcription, however, it was not possible to do this. Later on, I was still intrigued by Caruthers's manuscript and worked with the staff of Special Collections to create a microfilm version that I began transcribing. Citations of Caruthers's manuscript throughout this book refer to my completed transcription.[1]

Before the episode with the proslavery booklet and my study of Caruthers, I was predisposed to think that my own evangelical and Reformed view of the Bible suppported an antislavery position. To the contrary, I came to realize that my training in hermeneutics, faithfully applied, led more readily to proslavery conclusions and resisted antislavery convictions. The method of biblical interpretation I had acquired in my theologically conservative seminary training and applied for over fifteen years of preaching in my congregation could not lead to antislavery conclusions. My approach to Scripture was very similar to Presbyterian ministers of the nineteenth century. Because the authors of the proslavery booklet were also shaped by the same theological tradition, our disagreement was a miniature reenactment of the crisis among Presbyterians that presaged the Civil War, a war that powerfully demonstrated the problems of our theological forefathers' interpretive method as well as our own.

The following analysis of Caruthers's prophetic manuscript is merited by the ongoing controversy over the biblical roots of American slavery.

---

1. *American Slavery and Immediate Duty of Southern Slaveholders*, Pickwick Publications.

INTRODUCTION

Years after my encounter with the proslavery booklet mentioned above, I was not surprised to see the same booklet as the subject of an article in *Harpers* magazine in June 2005, entitled, "Let My People Stay." The ironic title illustrates not only the historical and continuing importance of the Exodus text it comically perverts, but also the essence of Caruthers's manuscript. He argues almost exclusively from Exodus 10:3—*Let my people go that they may serve me,* expanding its application universally to every case of enslavement. By this time, my extended consideration of the antebellum debate and interaction with modern day proslavery arguments had destabilized the approach to the Bible I had embraced from my earlier training. To put it another way: Prolonged exposure to the Bible and the American slavery controversy may be hazardous to your hermeneutics. I found myself thinking in new ways and much more cautiously about the Bible and what constitutes a biblical argument. The impetus for the change in my own outlook was the work of this minister whose views on the slavery question were determined not only by his commitment to Scripture but also by the ethical convictions that burdened his conscience and made him a kind of stranger, a sojourner living in a proslavery land.

Chapter 1: The Manuscript and Author

It is strange that a Christian and protestant people, who profess to value liberty above every other consideration on earth and to regard it as indispensable to the welfare of mankind should exhibit to the world such a legalized and systematized course of downright despotism.

Although the subject may have been discussed by a thousand writers and speakers, men of learning and eloquence, it is not exhausted and the discussion ought to be continued without let or hindrance until the question is finally settled.[1]

Manuscript

ELI WASHINGTON CARUTHERS (1793–1865), author of the quotes above, was the pastor of Alamance Presbyterian Church in Greensboro, North Carolina from 1821 until 1861. A disparaging public prayer for the Confederacy is the remembered cause of his retirement after forty years of service. The 1964 bicentennial poster for the Alamance congregation recalls the event that occurred shortly after the bombardment of Fort Sumter in April of the same year and the beginning of the war:

> One Sunday in July 1861, he prayed that the soldiers of the congregation might "be blessed of the Lord and returned in safety, though engaged in a lost cause." A congregational meeting was held, his resignation was requested, and soon the ties were dissolved that had united loving pastor and people for 40 years. Dr. Caruthers was now infirm, and died four years after. He was buried at Alamance where a monument over his grave and a memorial tablet

---

1. Caruthers, *American Slavery*, 68, 369.

. . . attest the esteem of his people for a pastor faithful, honored and beloved.[2]

During the four years that preceded his death in 1865, Caruthers completed a manuscript, over 400 pages in length, based on the text of Exod 10:3, *Let my people go that they may serve me*. It portrays slavery anywhere as a violation of God's will because "slaves cannot make that entire surrender of themselves to the Lord which the gospel required and to which renewed nature prompts them."[3] Dated 1862 and entitled, *American Slavery and the Immediate Duty of Southern Slaveholders*, it was never published and is now in the custody of Special Collections at Duke University.

The following analysis of *American Slavery and the Immediate Duty of Southern Slaveholders* augments the current understanding of the American slavery controversy's significant roots in a biblical debate. Caruthers's manuscript is unusual for a nineteenth-century document of southern origin because it presents a scripturally based argument against slavery. This book attempts to explicate the manuscript's arguments and their relationship to the greater slavery debate of nineteenth-century America. The following analysis also seeks to demonstrate the contribution of the manuscript to a larger conversation within which this research should be heard: the continuing historical and theological assessment of the controversy over the biblical sanction for slavery in nineteenth-century America.

American Slavery and the Immediate Duty of Southern Slaveholders is important because it is a theological work of southern origin against slavery, emerging from the North Carolina Piedmont. Shortly after its discovery in 1898 John Spencer Basset wrote that "it is doubtful if a stronger or clearer anti slavery argument was ever made on this continent."[4] The antebellum struggle to theologically resolve the antithetical impressions resulting from the Bible's regulation of slavery alongside its emphasis on the dignity and equality of human beings is a quest usually attributed to northern theologians, especially those of the Presbyterian Church. Mark Noll's account of conservative Presbyterians' failed efforts to "rescue the Reformed hermeneutic from proslavery," as exemplified in the arguments of Charles Hodge, focuses on the prominent theologians of the North.[5] He has argued that their relationship with their southern counterparts, theological ability, and public influence, best situated

2. Murray, *A History of Alamance Church 1762–1918*, 16.
3. Caruthers, *American Slavery*, 313.
4. Basset, *Antislavery Leaders of North Carolina*, 60.
5. Noll, *America's God*, 413–17.

CHAPTER 1: THE MANUSCRIPT AND AUTHOR

northern Old School Presbyterians for developing a theological alternative to the literal, Reformed biblicism underlying proslavery arguments. Despite Hodge's brilliance and influence, however, reviews of his thinking on slavery have called it "poor enough to invite sarcasm" or like "listening to a phonograph record with the needle stuck."[6] Hodge's response to slavery was, in fact, like the rest of his colleagues at Princeton Seminary: "timid, conventional, and unremarkable."[7] Caruthers, a largely unknown Presbyterian minister in a proslavery state, arguably surpasses Hodge and other Old School colleagues, presenting a biblical alternative to the hermeneutics of slavery practiced in American Presbyterianism.

Caruthers's manuscript is also significant because it does not correspond with the characterization of antislavery literature as biblically weak. The proslavery appeal to the Bible is determined by Elizabeth Fox-Genovese and Eugene Genovese to be the foundation of the convictions of southern whites on the issue of slavery during the American Civil War era. In their view the defenders of slavery are the champions of Scripture citing "chapter and verse," demonstrating "impressive scholarship, close textual analysis, and skillful argumentation." Antislavery writers, on the other hand, "failed to demonstrate that the Bible repudiated slavery" and "primarily ... appealed to the ideals of the Enlightenment and Declaration of Independence."[8] The extensive development and application of the Exodus text against slavery by a southern Presbyterian pastor in North Carolina during the nineteenth century does not fit this assessment. Caruthers's manuscript is an important overlooked primary source in these and other appraisals of the Bible's role in the question of slavery in nineteenth-century America.

As indicated by the manuscript's table of contents, a three-part division is used by Caruthers to develop the universal application of Exod 10:3. In this text Caruthers sees a claim, a demand, and a reason that reflect the broader redemptive theme of the Bible. The three-part structure of the manuscript corresponds to each of these points. For clarity each point in the document's table of contents is emphasized in bold print below.

I. *The claim; My people:* founded,
On creation and preservation—natural differences
among men furnish no justification of slavery. | 9

---

6. Guelzo, "Charles Hodge's Antislavery Movement," 299–326, 324; Barker, "The Social Views of Charles Hodge," 5.

7. Calhoun, *Princeton Seminary,* 328.

8. Fox-Genovese and Genovese, *The Mind of the Master Class,* 7, 490.

1. The deep and long continued degradation of the Africans in their own land—no reason why they should be enslaved. | 13

   The alleged ambiguity of slavery furnishes no justification of this practice. | 29

   Slavery in Egypt | 34

   Slavery, if there was such a thing, in Babylon | 41

   Slavery in Ancient Greece | 45

   Slavery in the Roman Empire | 53

   The orderings of Providence furnish no justification of slavery | 57

2. The Lord's claims on the Africans and all other races and portions of mankind is founded on Redemption | 61

   Differences between servants and slaves | 65

   Noah's prediction | 69

   Servitude during the patriarchal age | 77

   Servitude under the Mosaic dispensation | 87

   Servitude under the Christian dispensation | 103

   The opinions of learned and good men in the favor of slavery is no proof it is right | 125

   Slavery originated in avarice, falsehood and cruelty | 129

II. *The demand:* Let my people go

   The demand enforced by Providences | 157

   Human beings cannot be held as property | 197

III. *The reason* of the demand or the purpose for which it is made. Their powers can never be developed while in a condition of slavery. | 257

   Slave Code of the South | 261

CHAPTER 1: THE MANUSCRIPT AND AUTHOR

According to the present laws and usages of the land, slaves cannot make that entire consecration of themselves to the Lord which the gospel requires and to which the renewed nature prompts them. | 313

Under the existing laws and in the present state of society slaves cannot have that equality of rights and privileges which in the New Testament accorded to all believers. | 325

Progress of emancipation | 345

The influences which the abolition of slavery in these southern states would probably have upon the African Slave trade upon slavery in other parts of the world and upon the future destiny of the whole African race.

What we should now do for them | 393

The sweeping structure of Caruthers's argument as seen in the table of contents has prompted some historians to describe the manuscript as "one of the most thorough condemnations of slavery written by a southerner" or "as sophisticated a polemic against slavery as could be found in the United States, North or South, in the middle years of the nineteenth century."[9] It presents the clearest and most persuasive biblical alternative to the hermeneutics of slavery practiced in nineteenth-century America, North or South.

The Author

Eli Washington Caruthers was born on October 26, 1793, to James and Elizabeth Caruthers, on the family's farm west of Salisbury, North Carolina, three miles west of Thyatira Church in Rowan County. He had five sisters and one brother. His father is mentioned as "a very effective and efficient elder" in the Thyatira congregation. As a young boy he studied for several years with the Rev. Joseph Kirkpatrick, pastor of Black Creek Church, before entering Hampden-Sydney College in 1813.[10] He left Hampden-Sydney and served in the War of 1812 for a short time before

---

9. Chesebrough, *Clergy Dissent in the Old South 1830–1865*, 65; Troxler, "Eli Caruthers," 95.

10. Brockman, *Adams-Caruthers-Clancy-Neely,* 66–67.

reentering school at New Jersey College, receiving a Bachelor's degree in 1817.[11] Caruthers then pursued the traditional course of study to prepare for the Presbyterian ministry, entering the newly founded Princeton Seminary in 1817, graduating in 1820.

Caruthers was ordained by the Orange Presbytery of North Carolina on November 21, 1821, as an associate pastor to the yoked ministries of Buffalo and Alamance Presbyterian churches near Greensboro, North Carolina. He served under the guidance of Dr. David Caldwell until the senior minister's death in 1824 at the age of ninety-nine. An indication of his early attitude towards slavery is revealed in a letter he wrote at this time. Written at the close of 1824 to a minister friend in Ohio, the letter mentions his interest in leaving North Carolina "to go to some of the western states especially to some state where there are no *slaves*."[12] Written at such an early date, the letter may corroborate John Spencer Bassett's opinion that Caruthers became antislavery during his training at Princeton perhaps under the influence of George Stroud whom he met there.[13] Caruthers would never leave North Carolina, but remain as the pastor of the two congregations until 1846 when the combined ministry was dissolved, and he would then continue as pastor of Alamance until 1861.

Over the course of his ministry Caruthers gained a reputation as a respected pastor, educator, and historian.[14] Several published accounts remember a thorough and careful ministry to a congregation that included slaveholders. The more than two hundred of his sermons found in Special Collections at Duke University, written in a variety of booklets or ledgers, show studious preparation. Described as "a thorough scholar, an authority on theological questions, and an earnest and instructive preacher,"[15] he was granted an Honorary Doctorate of Divinity in 1854 by the University of North Carolina. With two nephews as his namesakes, it is likely that Caruthers was held in high regard by his family.[16]

In conjunction with his ministerial work he also taught or performed administrative duties at Greensborough Academy, the Caldwell Institute,

---

11. Troxler, "Eli Caruthers," 95.

12. *Eli Caruthers to Reverend Joseph Merriam*, 30 December 1824 (photocopy from private collection).

13. Basset, *Antislavery Leaders*, 60.

14. Ibid., 56; Troxler, "Eli Caruthers," 101.

15. Murray, *A History of Alamance Church*, 16.

16. Brockman, *Adams-Caruthers*, 69.

CHAPTER 1: THE MANUSCRIPT AND AUTHOR

and Greensboro High School where he taught Greek and served for two years as president.[17] In 1846 he ended his pastoral relationship with the congregation at Buffalo. Soon after, at the request of the Alamance congregation, he resigned from his responsibilities with the high school to devote himself solely to his pastoral responsibilities. Having lived since 1838 in Greensboro at an inn owned by his sister Catherine and her husband, G.C. Townsend, he now moved closer to the Alamance congregation. In his new location he organized classes for yet another school that would later become the Alamance Classical School.

Caruthers's views on slavery were probably known and tolerated by his slave-holding congregation, but when his dissent from the Confederacy became a matter of public knowledge his retirement from the pastorate in 1861 was hastened.[18] He explains his resignation as being "on account of bad health and for other reasons."[19] An early history of the Alamance congregation states that his prayer for the troops "was too much for the people who had risked all for a cause which they hoped to win" and that the congregation met requesting his resignation.[20] No congregational meeting for such a purpose is recorded in the minutes of Alamance church but Caruthers's letter of resignation mentions a proposed meeting for some business." He writes to the elders of the Alamance congregation on July 5, 1861,

> Partly in conformity with a purpose formed more than six months ago, as you and the congregation are well aware and partly on account of my health which is such a[t] present that I shall probably not be able to preach much for some time, I would through you, request of the Alamance church and Session to unite with me in asking a dissolution of my pastoral relation. I understand that the congregation are to have a meeting on some business tomorrow, but I am too unwell to attend. Please bring my request before the church that the application may be made to Presbytery as soon as possible and oblige
>
> your friend and servant.[21]

---

17. Troxler, "Eli Caruthers," 98, 100.
18. Ibid., 95.
19. Caruthers, *Richard Hugg King and the Great Revival in North Carolina*, x.
20. Scott, "A History of Alamance Church," 92–93.
21. Minutes, Session of Alamance Presbyterian Church, 30 July 1861, Greensboro, North Carolina.

Caruthers's signature ends the letter. While not conclusive, the timing and content of the note implies a connection between his public prayer for the troops and the proposed meeting. He may have sensed trouble when he learned of the meeting and ended the conflict with a resignation. If a meeting had been planned it could have then been cancelled. Described as one who had "no sympathy with the Southern Confederacy or anything connected with it," the life-long bachelor now became reclusive, according to his contemporaries "a sort of wanderer" and "little understood." During the last years of his life even longtime "friends were estranged from him in consequence of his unwavering devotion to the American Union."[22]

Caruthers has been described as a dissenter but one whose lack of action contributed to a culture of conformity within the south.[23] Like many of his colleagues, until the war he had probably hoped for a peaceful resolution of the slavery issue and considered the abolitionist movement incendiary and extreme. The views of the Reverend Erasmus D. MacMaster, a well-known antislavery minister, published in an appendix to his speech made before the General Assembly of Presbyterian Church in 1859, might be applicable to many of his colleagues including Caruthers.

> It is with extreme reluctance and profound regret, that I bring out, in the form I here do, opinions, and sentiments, and practices, on this subject of slavery, which I think are not honorable to the Church. I have known these things, as from time to time, through ten years past, they have come to light, with other things of like bearing of earlier date. I have known these things and I have kept silence. I have kept silence, because I have always deprecated violent agitation over particular forms of evil, which is so apt to run into exaggerations and extremes, damaging alike to personal character and to the best interests of truth and righteousness. I have kept silence, because I have no aptitudes and no taste for such conflicts. I have kept silence, because I have known something of the manifold complications and difficulties of this whole problem of slavery and the slave population, and because it has long been my settled conviction, that men living in the midst of slavery, and to whom immediately and chiefly it belongs, alone are competent to deal wisely with it, and to devise and execute measures for abating its evils, and effecting ultimately its abolition.[24]

22. Wilson, *The Presbyterian Historical Almanac*, 6, 350.
23. Chesebrough, *Clergy Dissent in the Old South 1830–1865*, 64.
24. McMaster, Appendix to General Assembly Speech, May 30, 1859 (n.p., n.d.), 33.

CHAPTER 1: THE MANUSCRIPT AND AUTHOR

Some of those "manifold complications and difficulties" in Caruthers's region would have been the sudden and severe reaction to antislavery sentiment in North Carolina. The stories of two other natives of the Salisbury region of small farmers where he grew up and who were also antislavery are well-known. Benjamin Hedrick, dismissed from his faculty post at the University of North Carolina for his political views and born near Salisbury like Caruthers, believed "the majority of the people among whom I was born and educated" opposed slavery.[25] Hedrick was chased out of the state, "savagely driven beyond the borders of his native state," but his ordeal made a lasting impression on the author describing his flight, another Salisbury native, Hinton Rowan Helper.

Helper's controversial polemic, *The Impending Crisis*, accused slavery of undermining the economic development of southern farmers, reducing them to abject misery, ignorance, and poverty. His book's demand for emancipation played upon southern fears of slave insurrections provoking hysteria throughout the south. "Do you aspire to become the victims of white non-slaveholding vengeance by day," he asks the slaveholder, "and of barbarous massacre of the negroes by night?" He warns them," You must emancipate them—speedily emancipate them or we will emancipate them for you!"[26] As throughout the entire south, the book was banned in North Carolina, and Helper was described by one of his state's senators as " a dishonest, degraded, and disgraced man," an "apostate son" of North Carolina who was "catering to a diseased appetite at the north, to obtain a miserable living by slanders upon the land of his birth."[27]

Not far from Caruthers's Greensboro church, Daniel Worth, a Wesleyan Methodist minister and native of Guilford County was charged with the circulation of Helper's book in 1859. A mob surrounded the Greensboro jail holding him and it was feared he would be lynched. He eventually went to trial and was found guilty but skipped bail, fleeing to the North where he earned the money to repay his bondsmen.[28]

The response to Hedrick, Helper, and Worth is indicative of what awaited those who were publicly critical of slavery in North Carolina during the war. Unlike them Caruthers was not an agent of change, but he may have

---

25. Cited in Brown, *Southern Outcast*, 78; cf. Johnson, *Ante-Bellum North Carolina*, 566; Basset, *Antislavery Leaders*, 29–44.

26. Cited in Johnson, *Antebellum North Carolina*, 568.

27. Ibid.

28. Johnson, *Antebellum North Carolina*, 580.

been an agent of the acceptance of change. He must have believed he could do more good if he remained in North Carolina, and he was probably right. He did not make change possible or certain, but the presence and stature of people like him may have made it more acceptable. When emancipation finally came many members of his congregation or others in the Greensboro community, who had conversed frequently with him over his forty years of ministry and with whom he had probably discussed the slavery question, were able to receive emancipation with an attitude otherwise unattainable were it not for the influence of people like Caruthers.

A minister with ecclesiastical and historical interests, Caruthers authored several books focusing on the American Revolution period in North Carolina. His biography of David Caldwell, *A Sketch of the Life and Character of the Reverend David Caldwell, D.D.*, was the first of several installments on Revolutionary history. Caldwell was Caruthers's predecessor in ministry, a self-taught doctor, and perhaps the most famous educator of his era in the South. An essential figure in any history of North Carolina, Caldwell was the courageous proponent of independence whose reputation was only heightened by the burning of his library by British troops in 1781. In this work Caruthers created the singular resource for the study of this remarkable minister, "among the most illustrious of American citizens."[29]

Another two volumes, *Revolutionary Incidents and Sketches of Character Chiefly in The "Old North State,"* and *Interesting Revolutionary Incidents and Sketches of Character Chiefly in The "Old North State," Second Series* are Caruthers's presentation of the strife between the Tories and the Whigs in what can be described as North Carolina's first civil war in the context of America's bid for independence. These volumes record history that would be lost apart from Caruthers's research involving interviews of veterans and those who remembered them, numerous accounts of cowardice and courage, and a detailed vindication of the actions of the North Carolina militia in the Battle of Guilford Courthouse.

When Caruthers died in November of 1865 at the age of 71, he left behind two manuscripts. *Richard Hugg King and His Times*, subsequently published in 1999, recounts the story of King, a farmer turned evangelist, and his role in the revivals of Western North Carolina. The other manuscript, *American Slavery and the Immediate Duty of Southern Slaveholders*, remained unpublished and is now considered.

---

29. Caruthers, *A Sketch of the Life and Character of the Reverend David Caldwell*, iii.

CHAPTER 1: THE MANUSCRIPT AND AUTHOR

Outline of the Book

Using my transcription of the manuscript,[30] the second, third, and fourth chapters assess those aspects that distinguish it from other antislavery literature, highlighting the more salient aspects of Caruthers's work. The three main headings under which his argument is presented indicate the content of these chapters. The remaining six chapters explore corollary issues raised by the manuscript's arguments and their relationship to the greater slavery debate of nineteenth-century America.

Chapter 2, "The Claim," examines creation, preservation, and redemption, which he conceptualizes under the claim of Exod 10:3: "My people... are *mine and not yours*: for you have no right to them."[31] He applies the slavery of the Hebrew people to the plight of the black race in America on the basis of creation and its preservation. God has created the Africans along with all humanity and preserved them throughout history. Slavery contradicts the order of creation, exploiting inequalities that exist within humanity. Utilizing the Bible and ethnographical theories of the nineteenth century, Caruthers argues that the supposed innate racial inferiority of the African does not fit with their larger history, and is, in fact, a mistaken conclusion drawn from their mutable circumstances. This chapter also shows that Caruthers's association of the claim of Exod 10:3 with biblical redemption was understood within the framework of a covenant. The whole world was ruined by sin and under God's judgment but Christ's death has redeemed a people who include the Africans.

Chapter 3, "The Demand," examines the typological and providential arguments made by Caruthers which he associates with the demand of Exod 10:3—"Let my people go." For Caruthers the demand of the Exodus passage cannot be ethically understood or applied to nineteenth-century slavery apart from a typological understanding of the Old Testament. Caruthers's understanding of Isa 61:1–2 and other corroborative texts illuminate this method. Divine providence also enforces the demand of Exod 10:3. Belief in divine guidance or providence as the supreme power controlling the nation was the expression of most nineteenth-century Americans belief in the relationship between their virtue as a people

---

30. *American Slavery and the Immediate Duty of Southern Slaveholders*, Pickwick Publications.

31. Caruthers, *American Slavery*, 4.

and their well-being as a nation.³² Borrowing categories of judicial and historical providentialism as articulated by Nicholas Guyatt, Caruthers's interpretation of the North's "greater prosperity" as God's "providential government of the world enforcing his demand for the unreserved and speedy surrender of our whole slave population" is shown to be a judicial use of providence that opposes the historical providentialism typically used to defend slavery. This chapter demonstrates that in Caruthers's thinking the Civil War is a manifestation of judicial providence and the ethical demand of Exodus coming in full force upon the slaveholders of the south.

Chapter 4, "The Reason," examines the purpose behind the deliverance advocated by Exod 10:3. According to Caruthers it is the indispensable service of all people in God's "merciful designs upon them and for the world." The fulfillment of service to God, however, requires freedom. The laws regulating the life of slaves and freed slaves stand in the way of service and are an obstacle to the fulfillment of God's purpose for them. Specifically, the purpose in view was a missionary enterprise to the continent of Africa. After emancipation, like most people of his time, Caruthers thought that some form of African colonization was a solution to the American slavery crisis.

Chapter 5, "Presbyterians and American Slavery," assesses Caruthers's theological depth among a few of the more prominent mid-nineteenth-century Presbyterians of the South, specifically, Robert Lewis Dabney, James Henley Thornwell, and George Armstrong. The public exchange between Armstrong and Northern theologian, Charles Van Renssaleur, on the slavery issue and the close correspondence between Caruthers's interpretive approach with the ideas of Van Renssaleur in this correspondence is also examined in this chapter. Van Renssaleur stressed that the issue of slavery required a hermeneutic or interpretive guideline not limited to the mere word or letter of the Bible. Caruthers's development of Exodus fills such an opening, and his manuscript is the singular example of this approach in biblical hermeneutics among Old School Presbyterians.

Chapter 6, "Caruthers and the Enlightenment," examines Caruthers's intertwining of biblical argument with the political principles of his era. Appeals to the Declaration of Independence such as occur in antislavery-literature and in Caruthers's manuscript have been described as primarily derived from the Enlightenment.³³ This chapter argues that Caruthers, like

---

32. Hood, *Reformed America, 1783–1837*, 9.
33. Genovese and Fox-Genovese, *The Mind of the Master Class*, 7, 490.

others from his Reformed and Presbyterian tradition, utilizes aspects of the Enlightenment or the Declaration of Independence because he believes such political ideas enshrining equality and liberty are, in fact, biblically derived from the doctrines of creation and redemption.

Chapter 7, "Similarity of Caruthers to Other Antislavery Literature," assesses the similarity of Caruthers to other biblically based arguments against slavery in antislavery literature. The curse of Noah, the servants of Abraham, the slavery of the Mosaic and Christian eras were the familiar ground of the slavery debate. The well-worn arguments examined in the chapter and Caruthers's own views provide a glimpse into various and fragmented interpretive tendencies that marked antislavery literature, the sum of which signaled frustration with, and a departure from, the standard Reformed hermeneutics of the era.

Chapter 8, "The Exodus Text in Nineteenth-Century Discourse," is a review of Exod 10:3 in antislavery literature. Caruthers was not the only writer to depend upon the text although his treatment is the most expansive. The examination of Exod 10:3's use in antislavery literature shows how the text lent divine impetus to the cause of slavery's abolition. Borrowing from the categories assigned to antislavery writers by Robert Forbes, the examples reviewed in this chapter suggest that Forbes' Providentialists found the text highly adaptable because it moved the debate over slavery away from the rights of slaveholders to the perspective of the oppressed and that the nameless character of pharaoh provided an unambiguous identity to their oppressors.

Chapter 9, "Caruthers's Method," compares Caruthers's method of interpretation to that of James Henley Thornwell, giving attention to the differing roles of reason in their arguments. Thornwell's thinking exemplifies a restrained use of reason, prompted by the Evangelical Enlightenment, allowing for a more narrowed focus on a defense of a traditional practice of slavery through deductive, flat, and literal readings of slavery texts in the Bible. In contrast, Caruthers's argument against slavery allows reason a greater role, showing a more deliberate tendency to an inductive and theological reading of texts that draws inferences from certain passages, personal experience, and sees larger themes that eclipse the isolated proof texts for slavery offered by the institution's defenders.

Chapter 10, "Caruthers and Recent Studies," examines the similarity of current opinion regarding New Testament slavery texts to nineteenth-century antislavery arguments. The theological approach of modern commentaries to the slavery issue is foreshadowed in these same arguments. Caruthers is set apart from both his contemporaries and their modern day counterparts by his dependence upon the Exodus text, a dependence this chapter demonstrates was prescient in the light of general trends in current scholarship that assert the importance of Exodus and its role in the life and literature of Israel as well as in the teaching of Paul.

Chapter 2: The Claim of Exodus 10:3

CARUTHERS HEARS GOD'S CLAIM upon American slaves expressed in the words, "My people." He divides the claim under two subheadings: "On the Creation and Preservation" (pp. 5–60) and "Redemption" (pp. 61–136). A similar division is found in Caruthers's undated sermon on First Samuel 15:29, where he describes God's character and the "corresponding affections towards him as our Creator, Preserver, and Redeemer."[1] Using this same division, *American Slavery and the Immediate Duty of Southern Slaveholders* develops lines of argument under each of these headings. In this chapter the content subsumed under the headings of the Exodus claim is examined in two parts, the first part covers creation and preservation and the second, the covenant of redemption.[2]

Creation and Preservation

The claim—"My people"—of the Exodus text is based on creation. The unity of the human race guarantees that if the Hebrews are God's people then so are the Africans. God's claim upon Israel or any nation is based first on his relationship to them as their creator. We can understand God's absolute right to creation, Caruthers argues, by way of our own feelings about the imperfect but legitimate claims of people to their possessions, inventors to their inventions, or farmers to their crops. God "has made everything out of nothing and has given to all men their existence" thus he has "a perfect right to employ or dispose everything as he pleases."[3] If the creator has made humanity "of one blood" then "for one to compel others

---

1. Caruthers, "First Samuel 15:29."

2. The section on the covenant of redemption is the analysis of pp. 61–64 in the manuscript. Because Caruthers's understanding of the covenant's bearing on the question of slavery is unique in the nineteenth century, the entire second part of the present chapter is given to its explanation. Excised for separate consideration because they are more typical of antislavery literature, pp. 65–136 are examined in chapter 7 below.

3. Caruthers, *American Slavery*, 5.

... to serve him all their life without compensation, and to entail that compulsory service upon his unborn posterity, is unjust, inhumane and criminal before high heaven."[4] The claim of Pharaoh or American slaveholders is "no right that can be made good in the court of heaven, nor at the bar of reason or before their own consciences . . . but God's claim is valid and cannot be disputed."[5]

Moreover, in the creation of humanity God has already given "everything which makes existence comfortable or desirable."[6] The explicit declarations of Gen 1:28–30 and their alteration after the flood in Gen 9:2–3 are in view. "The fruits of the earth, the beasts of the field, the fowls of the air and fish of the sea, with the earth itself as the source from which the means of subsistence for man and beast are to be obtained include all that has been granted to the children of men by the Creator," he writes, warning, "and all they can claim as their property."[7] "You may have the earth and its products," he warns again, "but on your fellow man you must not lay your hand unless it becomes necessary in self defense or for the prevention of a crime."[8] From creation Caruthers deduces a " fundamental principle, that we can have no right to hold any thing as property without an *express* grant from the Creator," which he makes, " the basis of all my arguments."[9] Everything that humanity should or ought to possess was expressly given by their creator but "all the rest, the world of intelligent beings, he has reserved for himself."[10] No allowance was made at creation for human beings to possess their own species. Humanity is not made to rule over humans, only the lesser creatures. As such life and labor is marked by a measure of freedom, self-sufficiency, and self-determination which ought not be encroached upon by others. From the creation of humanity, Caruthers sees "great principles . . . distinctly given which are easily comprehended and are applicable at all times and in all circumstances."[11] In its historical context the text is God's counter claim to the illegitimate demands of Pharaoh upon the Hebrews but ethically it applies to all situations of similar circumstances in the

4. Ibid., 6.
5. Ibid., 4.
6. Ibid., 5.
7. Ibid., 202.
8. Ibid., 207.
9. Caruthers, Preface to *American Slavery*.
10. Caruthers, *American Slavery*, 202.
11. Ibid., 207.

CHAPTER 2: THE CLAIM OF EXODUS 10:3

created order. It is on this foundation that Caruthers asserts the universal claim of the Exodus text.

Caruthers casts American slaveholders in the mold of Pharaoh. Just as his claim to the Hebrews usurps God as their creator, "so is the claim of all slaveholders to the services of their slaves," Caruthers writes, " entirely false and consequently sinful." Because the slaveholders' have no such authorization from God, their claim, like Pharaoh's, is "utterly unfounded."[12] Humanity is in the image of God, created to enjoy God's favor, and his possession alone. Because there is no allowance for slavery at creation, American enslavement of Africans is a criminal action against God, "robbing them of their birthright and invading the prerogative of God."[13]

Nor does the slavery generally found in antiquity justify American slavery. Speaking of slavery's advocates, he finds it "strange that men of talents, extensive learning, and hopeful piety, would, in this nineteenth century and in this land of boasted freedom, science and general intelligence" attempt to justify slavery because it is found in antiquity.[14] Since "every conceivable abomination" and "every possible form of injustice and oppression" and "every atrocity" and "every wrong" and "every species of vice" could be justified by its alleged antiquity with this line of reasoning, then the advocates of slavery are only demonstrating by this assertion "a conscious want of more substantial arguments or a careless indifference in regard to truth."[15] If the slavery issue " can not be settled by a fairer process of reasoning" than this, then "it had better be given up."[16] Caruthers then devotes twenty pages of his manuscript to an examination of the histories of Egypt, Babylon, Greece, and Rome in order to prove that American slavery has no parallel in the ancient world. Not even in Egypt, he insists, did Israel's situation reach such a height of inhumanity because there was "no intimation of an edict that their bondage should be upon them forever." Pharaoh, he writes, probably "thought of nothing more than holding them under authority while he lived."[17] Finding no parallel to the perpetual racial slavery of Antebellum America, he argues that the "alleged antiquity of slavery furnishes no justification of the practice." And even if "slavery

12. Ibid., 4.
13. Ibid., 6.
14. Ibid., 30.
15. Ibid., 29, 30.
16. Ibid., 30.
17. Ibid., 36.

always has existed in the world and . . . always will exist," he writes, still "it would be no proof that slavery is right and that we or any other people can perpetuate it without woeful criminality."[18]

Joined to creation is the category of "preservation," which describes the stability of creation under God's continuing care. For Caruthers and his contemporaries, "Preservation" is the first part of a two-fold concept of "providence" formulated in chapter 11 of the *Westminster Confession of Faith* and elsewhere as God's "preserving and governing all his creatures and all their actions." Charles Hodge explained preservation as "the omnipotent energy of God by which all created things . . . are upheld in existence, with all the properties and powers with which He has endowed them."[19] William Sherlock reasons similarly, citing Acts 17:28 and Heb 1:3 to support the division of providence into "preservation and government," the former emphasizing "that God upholds all things in being from falling back into their first notion, and preserves their natural virtues, powers, and faculties, and enables them to act, and to attain the ends of their several natures."[20]

Slavery violates God's ongoing relationship with creation because it interprets perceived differences between ethnic groups for the purpose of exploitation, undermining the unity and equality of humanity established at creation. Any physical, mental, or external inequalities that might exist between people or races "subserve his own wise and beneficent purposes" but the "inequalities which man has made . . . immensely increased the degradation and wretchedness of our race."[21] The use of "inequalities in physical strength, in mental capacities and external advantages" to justify slavery, in Caruthers's view, is only "subserviency to personal and local interests."[22] To the contrary, inequalities in the "variety of phenomena and uniformity of design" in the natural world constitute an instructive analogy for similar variations in humanity. He writes:

> The hills are as important in their place as the lofty mountains, the rivulets as the majestic rivers and the lake as the mighty oceans, but must not be removed nor arrested in their course. The smallest asteroids have an important purpose to answer in the solar system

---

18. Ibid., 29.
19. Hodge, *Systematic Theology*, 1:581.
20. Sherlock, *A Discourse concerning the Divine Providence*, 22.
21. Caruthers, *American Slavery*, 8.
22. Ibid.

as well as the mightiest orbs but must be left free to revolve in their appropriate spheres.[23]

Caruthers's intends all this as an analogous illustration: It is the Africans who have been "removed" from their home, "arrested in their course" and so the universe has been plunged into chaos. The supremacy of human freedom cannot be empirically proven but is instinctively perceived and supported by heuristic arguments drawn from the creator's ongoing relationship with the world. Just as God "has made every planet and asteroid in solar system the right size," he writes, "so he has made the earth and every thing on it—every continent, sea, and river, every man and everything else of the right proportions; but has given man no authority to meddle with his arrangements."[24] Just as the "mightiest orbs" move along their course undisturbed, so all humanity "must be left free."[25] Caruthers deduces from both the creation and preservation of humanity that the "inequalities which the Creator has made to subserve his own wise and beneficent purposes" must never be used as the basis of the wrongful inequalities in the realm of "civil and religious rights."[26]

Caruthers believes that "if left to the unrestricted operation of those laws which the Creator has established the inequalities would not be of long duration in any one line of descent but soon change . . . " due to a process of "unceasing alternations of depression and elevation . . . indispensable to the progress of society."[27] Specifically, "an unvarying law" of human society is that "those who have acquired or inherited wealth and favor and high position gradually lose their intellectual enterprise and are left behind in the race of improvement and of social advantage."[28] Such a law accounts for the experience of the African people. " In the early ages of Christianity," he writes, "the gospel had quite an extensive and thorough influence along the Nile and over all the northern part of Africa," a region populated by "flourishing churches", and the "most learned pious and useful ministers" but now they are treated "with contempt and rigor."[29]

23. Ibid., 9–10.
24. Ibid., 250.
25. Ibid., 10.
26. Ibid., 8.
27. Ibid., 9, 11.
28. Ibid., 12.
29. Ibid., 21, 24.

According to Caruthers not only were the early ages of Christianity times of flourishing for the Africans, but the larger history of the African race reveals the working of this "unvarying law" mentioned above and contradicts the presuppositions of racism. The creation and preservation of the African race is not without change or "vicissitude" that is found in "all the works and operations of the divine Being."[30] Caruthers's thinking on this point is best understood in the larger context of the battle against nineteenth-century racism waged by nineteenth-century Afrocentrism. Determining the degree to which he was in agreement with or influenced by the tenets of nineteenth-century Afrocentricism—a universal history of humanity in which blacks are the founders and leaders of all cultures—is beyond the scope of this book. Regarding the debate over the world-wide significance of the ancient African culture, he might have concurred with Wilson Jeremiah Moses' conclusion that "certain aspects of the so-called Afrocentricism have been sensibly argued" but are "unrelated to the fanciful exaggeration that African Americans are, in some exceptional or exclusive way, heirs to the civilization of the ancient Nile."[31] There is not enough information to know what Caruthers actually thought on the matter. Nevertheless, his emphasis on the change or "vicissitude" that is found in "all the works and operations of the divine Being"[32] and the elaborate ethnography found in his manuscript are both elements typically associated with Afrocentrism.

Caruthers's use of "vicissitude" or change is a version of the Afrocentric emphasis on the "mutability of human affairs." The phrase initially appears in an article published in the *African Repository and Colonial Journal* in 1825 and later becomes the title of a three part series in *Freedom Journal* in 1827. The first issue of the monthly journal, published by the American Colonization Society in March, 1825 includes "Observations on the Early History of the African Race." The author, identified only as "T.R.," describes the once great Ethiopian civilization as the people "who brought the arts and sciences of civilization to the world" and who were once the pinnacle of world culture but who are now diminished because of the "mutability of human affairs."[33] In the appeal to "mutability," antislavery literature employs

---

30. Ibid., 9.
31. Moses, *Afrotopia*, 6.
32. Caruthers, *American Slavery*, 9.
33. Dain, *Hideous Monster of the Mind*, 105.

CHAPTER 2: THE CLAIM OF EXODUS 10:3

history in the racial debate.[34] The state of the African, according to this line of reasoning, is due not to presumed innate inferiority, but to changing historical circumstances.

Bruce Dain has noted the dependence of this article and much of this kind of literature on *Travels through Syria and Egypt*, the reflections of Constantine Volney published in 1784. Samuel Stanhope Smith, successor to John Witherspoon as head of Princeton College, demonstrates Volney's influence in early America recalling in one of his lectures "a remark made by Mr. Volney when contemplating the head of Sphinx in Egypt." Smith recounts Volney's belief that the Sphinx "exhibits a type of the countenance of the ancient inhabitants of the country who resemble more the natives of tropical Africa than the present population."[35]

The travels of Volney, a recognized skeptic and critic of religion, convinced him that it was "to the race of negroes, at present our slaves, and the objects of our extreme contempt, we owe our arts, sciences, and even the very use of speech."[36] T.R.'s "Observations on the Early History of the African Race," bundles Volney's research together with studies on the decipherment of the Rosetta Stone, the history of Herodotus, and the Bible. All are combined to prove the divine role of the once great Ethiopia in the universal salvation of Africa, and all in fulfillment of the champion verse for T.R. and the American Colonization Society, and even Caruthers, Psalm 68:31: "Princes shall come out of Egypt and Ethiopia shall soon stretch forth her hands."[37]

Caruthers utilizes such history against the formidable pretense of African inferiority in his era. By the 1850s the craniology studies of Samuel George Morton had become foundational for scientific racism. Utilizing skull size and capacity it was argued that the African was incapable of having the intelligence of a Caucasian thus rendering African inferiority an unalterable and indisputable fact. Morton's research methods were seriously flawed but his conclusions were embraced by many and used by some proslavery advocates to justify belief in the Africans' inferiority.[38]

---

34. Rael, "A Common Nature, A United Destiny," 193; Dain, *Hideous Monster of the Mind*, 112–48.

35. Smith, *The Lectures Corrected*, 1:43; Smith, *An Essay on the Causes of the Variety of Complexion*, 119.

36. Dain, *Hideous Monster of the Mind*, 77.

37. Ibid., 106.

38. Ibid., 197–99.

Against this background Caruthers's counters: "For long generations they appear to have been the superior race and . . . long buried monuments of their greatness have been brought to light on the Nile, the Tigress, and the Euphrates."[39] He presents an account of an ancient Africa far more capable and accomplished than their nineteenth-century circumstances indicated. The achievements of their past were proof of the Africans' capacity for greatness. The race of Ham is the "intrepid, earnest, and successful" forerunners in human improvement and development, "building cities and establishing governments" or engaged in commerce, ship building, and fine arts, while the other races displayed only "idleness and indifference about the future."[40]

Drawing historical and ethnographical facts from the Bible in order to demonstrate the greatness of ancient African culture was also a preoccupation of Caruthers's era, and his manuscript reveals strong similarities to this aspect of Afrocentrism.[41] He utilizes place names of the Old Testament to construct an account of these descendants, piling up famous personages of the black race, heaping up their accomplishments, while dismissing the rest of humanity as simple, pastoral, and unmotivated. He assumed, along with T.R. and the rest of the antebellum world, that the Africans were, in fact, the descendants of Ham.

T.R. presents the ancient Ethiopians as "invincible in war and yet preeminent in all the arts of peace, distinguished above other men for learning, enterprise, and valour—at once tyrants and instructors of mankind!"[42] Likewise, Caruthers tells his reader of " a galaxy of men who were celebrated for their enterprise and generalship" or of "six African generals" who "were more than a match for the ablest of the Roman commanders" or of another African "who was certainly one of the ablest generals of this age to which he belonged" as well as many " other names of note in history to which we cannot now refer."[43] The ancient Africans "became famous in arms and carried on a world wide and most profitable commerce, while all the rest of mankind were engaged in hunting, or tending their flocks, or whiling away the hours in idle amusements."[44] Once the Africans "were the superior race;

39. Caruthers, *American Slavery*, 17.
40. Ibid., 22.
41. Shavit, *History in Black*, 47.
42. Dain, *Hideous Monster of the Mind*, 105–6.
43. Caruthers, *American Slavery*, 20.
44. Ibid., 19.

CHAPTER 2: THE CLAIM OF EXODUS 10:3

but, owing to a variety of secondary causes . . . they gradually deteriorated and became dispersed."[45]

Not only are the enslaved Africans the descendants of a once-great race but the Americans who now oppress the Africans are themselves the descendants of the "Anglos and Britons and the Germans" who were "exceedingly ignorant, superstitious" and believed inferior by their Roman conquerors.[46] The enslavers of the Africans descend from those who "believed in signs and portents, in fairies, witches, ghosts, and hobgoblins" and "were frightened out of their wits by an eclipse of the sun, the appearance of a comet, or a play of meteors in the heavens."[47] Only through the "humanizing influences of Christianity" over the past fifteen hundred years have they been elevated to their current position.[48] "That the Africans or any other race," he writes, "are of an inferior grade, as to natural capacities and powers is mere slang, the flimsy pretext of slaveholders, to conceal their pride and avarice."[49]

Caruthers's tendentious account powerfully contradicts the claim of southern slaveholders to their slave property. Such a claim "rests not on any origin or express grant from the Creator but entirely on . . . the pretended inferiority of the race."[50] His ethnography sweeps away the basis for American slavery founded in racial superiority. Carl Degler has called it "an ethnological defense of black equality that is unusual anywhere in antislavery thought in the United States, North or South."[51]

Summary

American slaveholders are like Pharaoh, asserting a claim to people who belong only to God. American slavery denies God's order and the sufficiency of his creation. It wrongfully exploits differences and inequalities intended to serve his own purposes in the history of humanity. American slavery is attempting to subvert the course of his creation, presuming the innate inferiority of the African. Borrowing elements of Afrocentrism and

---

45. Ibid., 249.
46. Ibid., 25.
47. Ibid., 26.
48. Ibid.
49. Ibid., 249, 403.
50. Ibid., 249.
51. Degler, *The Other South*, 30.

general history, Caruthers argues that the capabilities and intelligence of races, including his own, are not static but dynamic. Assumptions of slaves' inferiority and their own superiority by slaveholders are thus shown to be self-serving. The exploitation of the African's current circumstances is an injustice not only against them but against God, himself: "He who will rob another who has not strength to resist him . . . is unjust, not only to him," Caruthers emphasizes, "but to God."[52]

Redemption through the Covenant

God's "claim on the Africans and all other races" is not only based on the creation and preservation of humanity but also on their redemption in Christ who "gave himself a ransom for all to be justified in due time."[53] In pages 61–64 Caruthers explains Ps 2:7-8: "I will tell of the decree of the Lord: He said to me, You are my son today I have begotten you. Ask of me, and I will make the nations your heritage and the ends of the earth your possession." The nations, according to Caruthers, have been given to Christ, they are his "inheritance." He explains that because "all nations were included in the cov't [covenant] of redemption."[54] "It was promised to Abraham," Caruthers tells his reader citing Gen 22:18, that "in his seed all the nations of the earth should be blessed."[55] Thus, Africa and all other "heathen nations . . . stand pretty much," the southerner writes, "in the same relation to Him in which the descendants of Abraham, so far as they were included in the promise, stood to Him before their deliverance from Egypt."[56] American slavery is therefore a violation of the "covenant of redemption." Caruthers's distinctive covenantal understanding and its relationship to the Exodus text consists of just four pages but its fuller explanation is warranted because it is the only antislavery argument from a covenantal perspective.[57] Before looking more closely at Caruthers's "covenant of redemption," some general background on the covenant concept and its development in the Westminster Confession of Faith is needed.

52. Caruthers, *American Slavery*, 28.
53. Ibid., 61.
54. Ibid., 61, 62.
55. Ibid., 62.
56. Ibid., 63.

57. The analysis of the remaining portion of this section of the manuscript, pp. 65–136, is found in chapter 4 below.

CHAPTER 2: THE CLAIM OF EXODUS 10:3

The term, "covenant," a fundamental concept in the world of the Old Testament, signifies an agreement between two equal parties by which they obligate themselves to certain responsibilities, such as a marriage or political agreements. See, for example, the description of marriage in Mal 2:14 and Prov 2:18; the agreement between David and Jonathan in 1 Sam 23:18 or the description of treaties between nations in Hos 12:1 and Ezek 17:13. It is also more broadly and frequently used to describe God's relationship to the Hebrew patriarchs and the nation of Israel (Gen 6:18; 9:9–17; 15:18; 17:2–21).

In Covenant Theology or Federal (from the Latin term *foedus*, meaning "compact" or "covenant") Theology the concept of covenant structures God's relation to the world and the Bible's redemptive plan. The multiple types of covenants or covenantal forms and their varying conditions prompt Diarmaid MacCullough's portrayal of it as "a fertile concept that is full of hope and reassurance" resulting in an "idea that can take off in a various directions."[58] The accuracy of his description is verified by the ubiquity of the covenantal form as a central doctrine for theologians within the ranks of Presbyterianism as well as their disagreement over its exact meaning and role. Robert Godfrey's understanding of the covenant of works, "as a key foundation for understanding the work of Christ and justification by faith alone"[59] or Geerhardus Vos' declaration of covenant theology as "a truly universal phenomenon, emerging everywhere where theology is done on the basis of the Reformed principle," as well as Gerard Van Groningen's summary of the Bible as the "written record of the revelation of two covenantal relationships" are representative of the prominence given to Covenant Theology in Reformed and Presbyterian thinking.[60]

The domination of Scottish and British confessions by the covenant concept is accounted for not only because of its biblical roots but also because of its prevalence in legal and political thought as democratic ideas emerged in the early seventeenth century. Arguably, the prevalence of the covenant principle in the Reformation is proof of its adaptability to a unified state and church society.[61] The emergence and development of Covenant Theology during the social crisis in sixteenth-century Zurich was

---

58. MacCullough, *The Reformation*, 174.

59. Cited in Koo Jeon, *Covenant Theology*, xii.

60. Vos, *Redemptive History and Biblical Interpretation*, 238; Groningen, *Messianic Revelation in the Old Testament*, 61.

61. Redding, *The Prayer and Priesthood of Christ*, 149.

actually precipitated by the rejection of the state church by some of Ulrich Zwingli's more radical followers.

After Zwingli's reforms in the early 1520s those who later would be known as anabaptists, disputed the biblical legitimacy of a state church as well as the practice of baptizing infants into its membership. Zwingli's response was to defend the baptism of infants as the Christian equivalent of the Old Testament's practice of circumcision and as the sign of the new covenant now been made in Christ. The linking of baptism with a covenant was particularly successful among the Swiss cantons for whom the '*Bund*' or 'covenant', was already a familiar and useful political structure. Zwingli used the theme of covenant only in relation to infant baptism, but his successor in Zurich, Heinrich Bullinger, organized his entire discussion of Christianity around it.[62]

As a Presbyterian minister Caruthers subscribed to the Westminster Confession of Faith, a Reformed and Puritan confessional document produced in Seventeenth-century England by the Westminster Assembly. With the exception of the seven Independents, the assembly of 121 theologians were Presbyterians. The assembly was convened by the Parliament at Westminster Abbey in 1643 to revise the doctrinal standards of the English church, the Thirty-Nine Articles. A newspaper's reference during the opening week of the assembly to "the drooping spirits of the people of God who lie under the pressure of Popish wars and combustions" typifies the common sentiment during this extended period of political and religious strife between Charles I and Parliament.[63] When revision of the Thirty-Nine Articles proved unworkable, the assembly instead produced several new documents of theological doctrine including a confession of faith for the Reformed churches of Great Britain, Scotland, and Ireland.

Completed by the assembly with proof texts in 1647, the Westminster Confession of Faith never fulfilled its intended role, but still retains an historic place in the doctrines of the Church of Scotland. It was subsequently adopted by American colonial Presbyterians in 1729 with the exception of its chapter on the civil magistrate. It continues to embody the doctrinal standards of Presbyterians in America and throughout the world, but in varying degrees. Berkhof's complaint that "Presbyterian scholars . . . take due account" of covenant doctrine "in their theological works" but "in the

---

62. MacCullough, *The Reformation*, 145; McGrath, *Christian Theology*, 48, 429, 442; Kempla, "The Concept of Covenant in Sixteenth and Seventeenth Century," 94–107.

63. Mitchell and Struthers, *Minutes of the Sessions of the Westminster Assembly*, xi.

Churches which they represent it has all but lost its vitality" is arguably true of the entire confession's present day influence within all but the most conservative Presbyterian congregations.[64] Nevertheless, the Westminster Confession remains the most important embodiment of Covenant Theology because of its arrangement of all redemptive history into a covenantal framework of works and grace.

Vos' description of the Westminster Confession as "the first Reformed confession in which the doctrine of the covenant . . . has been able to permeate at almost every point" suggests the overarching importance of the confession's seventh chapter, *Of God's Covenant with Man* for the Presbyterians of the assembly.[65] As found in the seventh chapter, six sections in the confession explain their understanding of the "voluntary condescension on God's part which he has been pleased to express by way of covenant." Vos notes the appearance of John Ball's *Treatise on the Covenant of Grace* in 1645 during the sitting of the Westminster Assembly as well as Archbishop James Ussher's formulation of the covenant published in the *Irish Articles* in 1615, as probably constituting the direct influences of the confession's seventh chapter.[66]

The Westminster Confession of Faith's seventh chapter presents the "covenant of works," as " the first covenant made with man . . . wherein life was promised to Adam, and in him to his posterity, upon condition of perfect and personal obedience." It was broken by humanity represented by Adam and Eve making them "incapable of life by that covenant" but "the Lord was pleased to make a second . . . the covenant of grace wherein he freely offers to sinners life and salvation by Jesus Christ, requiring of them faith in him." The covenant of grace was "differently administered in the time of the law, and in the time of the gospel," in the former time of the patriarchs and Mosaic era "by promises, prophecies, sacrifices, circumcision, the paschal lamb, and other types and ordinances delivered to the people of the Jews" and in the latter time under the gospel by "the preaching of the Word, and the administration of the sacraments of Baptism and the Lord's Supper."

Not appearing in the Westminster Confession of Faith, but a further development of the concept, the "covenant of redemption" designates for Caruthers and Presbyterian theologians from the eighteenth century onward

---

64. Berkhof, *Systematic Theology*, 217.
65. Vos, *Redemptive History*, 239.
66. Ibid., 241.

"the agreement between the Father, giving the Son as Head and Redeemer of the elect, and the Son, voluntarily taking the place of those whom the Father had given Him."[67] Even those who did not adopt this particular formulation nevertheless spoke of "that eternal agreement between the Persons of the Godhead, on which the whole dispensation of mercy to mankind is founded."[68] Psalm 2, cited by Caruthers, is seen as a particularly persuasive proof of such an agreement between God and Christ. It is a psalm ostensibly written for the immediate Davidic monarchy of its era, but which is also attested as Messianic prophecy by the New Testament implying a compact between the Father and the Son with conditions and promises, after the pattern of a covenant.[69] While in the Old Testament the covenant and its conditions between God and Israel are explicit,[70] other implicit covenantal forms like Psalm 2 can also be found in which a covenant is implied such as in the conditions and responsibilities given to Adam.[71]

Charles Hodge, a nineteenth-century contemporary of Caruthers and the leading theologian of Princeton believed the covenant of redemption is "entirely beyond our comprehension" but "we must receive the teachings of Scripture in relation to it without presuming to penetrate the mystery which naturally belong to it." He realized it is not "expressly asserted" in the Bible but many texts are "equivalent to such direct assertions."[72] As a Reformed and Presbyterian minister Caruthers would have been in agreement with Hodge's following criteria for a covenant:

> When one person assigns a stipulated work to another person with the promise of a reward upon the condition of the performance of that work, there is a covenant. Nothing can be plainer than that all this is true in relation to the Father and the Son. The Father gave the Son a work to do; He sent Him into the world to perform it, and promised Him a great reward when the work was accomplished. Such is the constant repetition of the Scriptures. We have, therefore contracting parties, the promise, and the condition. These are the essential elements of a covenant.[73]

---

67. Berkhof, *Systematic Theology*, 271.
68. Dick, *Lectures on Theology*, 1:489.
69. E.g., Acts 13:13; Heb 1:5, 5:5; Isa 53:10.
70. E.g., Exod 19:5; 24:7; 34:27–28.
71. E.g., Gen 2:15–17.
72. Hodge, *Systematic Theology*, 2:360.
73. Ibid.

CHAPTER 2: THE CLAIM OF EXODUS 10:3

The lack of biblical grounds for the covenant of redemption and its implied agreement between the Father and Son was eventually questioned more directly by Karl Barth: "This is mythology for which there is no place in a right understanding of the Trinity."[74]

As shown above, Covenant Theology or Federal Theology was a central heading under which a large amount of biblical material was organized and interpreted by Caruthers and his nineteenth-century Presbyterian contemporaries. The consensus of the Westminster Assembly regarding covenantal theology, however, was not successfully transmitted to all of its theological descendants. James Torrance's objections to Covenant Theology have been described as "deep-seated and passionate."[75] Citing various sources of federalism, Torrance demonstrates that its adherents confuse a covenant with a contract and thus move the focus away from what Christ has done for us to what we do for ourselves. He also traces elements of anxiety and Pelagianism in Reformed congregations to the Westminster Confession of Faith's doctrines of limited atonement, and complains of its failure to comprehend the meaning of Christ's headship over all humanity by its imposition of a "radical dichotomy between the sphere of Nature and the sphere of Grace, of natural law and the Gospel, so that the Mediatorial Work of Christ is limited to the covenant of grace and the Church, the sphere marked out by the covenant of grace."[76]

Rejection of Covenant Theology from within the ranks of Presbyterianism such as Torrance's is rare but not only recent. In Caruthers's own era Scottish pastor and theologian, John McLeod Campbell, one of Torrance's influences and subject of his research, rejected Covenant Theology.[77] Campbell was deposed from his ministry in the Church of Scotland in 1831 on the charge of heresy and eventually published his views in his major work, *The Nature of the Atonement* in 1856, to explain his views and restore an emphasis upon the fatherhood of God and his universal and unconditional love.[78]

---

74. Barth, *The Doctrine of Reconciliation*, 62.

75. MacCleod, "Covenant Theology," 217.

76. Cited in Redding, *Prayer and Priesthood of Christ in the Reformed Tradition*, 152; cf. Redding, *Prayer and Priesthood of Christ*, 150–57, for Torrance's objections to covenant theology Donald MacCleod's critique of Torrance, and Redding's evaluation.

77. Torrance, "The Contribution of McLeod Campbell to Scottish Theology," 295–311.

78. Torrance, "New Introduction" 2.

In its role for Presbyterians as an "architectonic principle" of federal theology, the covenant has prompted an interminable debate, charitably described by its proponents as "historical development."[79] The continuing variation and disagreement within the reformed ranks over Covenant Theology substantiates MacCullough's observation that the Old Testament speaks a great deal about the covenant between God and Israel as an agreement to keep his law, but that it also develops the idea in various ways, and it talks about covenants in different contexts, and with different implications.[80]

Although Reformed Presbyterians and others committed to federalism have not developed a consensus among themselves with regard to the covenant's soteriological role, the legitimacy of the covenant form is mostly agreed upon within broader biblical studies. The amount of scholarly energy expended on the study of the covenant is impressive with varying results. Studies have tended to seesaw between the early twentieth-century judgments that the covenant did not become a working idea in Israel's literature until the later Deuteronomic traditions and the later twentieth-century views of George Mendenhall, Walther Eichrodt, as well as others who view the covenant as "an early and constitutive notion in Israel."[81] Recent work generally tips in favor of the latter. The covenant's place of importance seems certain in the earliest period of Israel's worship of Yaweh. As such, for Mendenhall, the covenant concept embodies and represents Israel's underlying conviction that its social, religious, and even global aspirations, are important lawful expressions of the nation's relationship to Yaweh.[82]

The lawful dimension of the covenant can be seen as especially prominent in Caruthers's emphasis upon God's rightful claim upon the Africans. Caruthers sees Exodus as an expression of the covenant that authorizes not only God's relationship with Israel but with all the nations of the earth. In her study of the covenant concept in Qumran literature Bilhah Nitzan utilizes aspects of Eichrodt's work that views the covenant as both an early and "revolutionary factor in the relationship between human beings and their deity." In her opinion, Eichrodt correctly understood that Israel's "covenant detached religious faith from the feelings of anxiety and insecurity that characterized pagan religions" and established the more secure "covenantal relationship," capable of regulating human life "according to fixed laws of

---

79. MacCleod, "Covenant Theology," 217; Jeon, *Covenant Theology*, 3.
80. MacCullough, *The Reformation*, 172.
81. Brueggemann, *Theology of the Old Testament*, 418.
82. Mendenhall, "Covenant," 714–23.

retribution given by a single divine authority thereby providing hope for peace and security to those who kept the laws of the covenant."[83]

Similar legal and binding overtones of divine authority are sounded in Caruthers's use of the covenant promise against slavery. When he writes that "it was promised to Abraham," and reminds his reader citing Gen 22:18, that "in his seed all the nations of the earth should be blessed," Caruthers is drawing upon the legality of God's claim not only upon Israel but all nations.[84] Thus Africa and all other "heathen nations . . . stand pretty much," he writes, "in the same relation to Him in which the descendants of Abraham, so far as they were included in the promise, stood to Him before their deliverance from Egypt."[85] Caruthers sees the Exodus text as an expression of the covenant that authorizes not only God's relationship with Israel but with all the nations of the earth. God's covenantal claim upon the enslaved African in the nineteenth century is thus no less legitimate than his claim upon the enslaved Hebrews in the Exodus account.

In Caruthers's thinking enslaved Africans are "My people" because the claim of the Exodus text applies to all nations.[86] The covenant is singular without temporal boundaries, lawful over all of redemptive history, and Africa is among the nations included in the Abrahamic promise as reiterated in Psalm 2. For Caruthers "the whole world was under condemnation and led captive by the devil at his will" but since "all nations were included in the covenant of redemption" in which Christ ransomed his people, then "no man and no act of men have a right to claim the services of any portion of his purchased inheritance."[87] This includes Africans and Anglo Saxons because "both were given him in the covenant of redemption and he has redeemed both by the same price."[88]

Summary

For "the Christian reader," Caruthers writes, "it is unnecessary to multiply quotations" from the Bible in proof of his point, but not before he has cited Psalm 72 and its prediction of "universal homage." Caruthers sees the

---

83. Nitzan, "The Concept of Covenant in Qumran Literature" 86–87.
84. Caruthers, *American Slavery*, 62.
85. Ibid., 63.
86. Ibid.
87. Ibid., 61, 62.
88. Ibid., 312.

Hebrews' redemption from slavery as the pattern for the redemption yet to come in the person of the Messiah, to whom "every knee shall bow . . . and every tongue confess," and from whom "the church, in its ministry and membership, received a commission . . . to go and carry the light of the gospel to them that are sitting in darkness" and to "proclaim an immediate and eternal deliverance to all who were in bondage to sin and Satan."[89] Thus the claim—"My people"—is now doubled in its justification.

First, as shown above, it is justified because it is based on God's role in the creation and preservation of Israel and all other nations. The unity and equality of humanity from the dawn of creation was grounded in their common creator. God's claim upon the Hebrew slaves of Exodus extended to the African slaves of the South. The enslavement of Africans, or any nation, is a violation of the Exodus text and in defiance of the creator's claim. God was the creator and preserver of all humanity and, therefore, the only rightful superintendent of the black race.

Secondly, it is based on the covenant of redemption. In the covenant, deliverance in Christ's name is proclaimed to the Africans because their nation is also his inheritance. As a Presbyterian minister Caruthers was committed to the expression of Covenant Theology developed throughout the Reformation and its expression in the Westminster Confession of Faith. Although that expression has provoked critical dissent and substantial differences among adherents that will not be resolved any time soon, there is general agreement upon the biblical covenant as structurally circumambient, encompassing the relationship between humanity and God in an atmosphere of lawfulness, regulation, and security. For Caruthers, American slavery pollutes and clouds this atmosphere with its illegitimate claims. If the Africans belong to God through creation, and to their Messiah through redemption, they belong to no one else.

Instead of acknowledging God's claims and "bringing them to the knowledge of salvation through the mercy of our God," American slaveholders have enslaved and kept the Africans "in ignorance, degradation and wretchedness, from generation to generation, without any crime alleged and without any authority whatsoever from the Lord whom they profess to serve."[90] American slaveholders are therefore acting criminally towards God. They are violators of creation, preservation, and the covenant of redemption, claiming ownership of people who belong only to Christ

---

89. Ibid., 63.
90. Ibid., 64.

through creation and through a pact with roots in the ancient bond God made with Abraham, reiterated throughout the Mosaic and Davidic eras, celebrated in the psalms of Israel, fulfilled in the appearance of the Messiah, and carried to the ends of the earth.

Chapter 3: The Demand of Exodus 10:3

GOD'S DEMAND REGARDING THE American slaves is to "Let My people go" and it is "made by express communication and enforced by his Providence."[1] The call for Israel's freedom and the miraculous deeds that providentially accompany the demand are applied by Caruthers to American slavery. The manuscript's heading of this section, *The Demand: Let my people go*, is explained scripturally (pp. 137–156), and providentially (pp. 157–256). In his approach to scripture Caruthers employs typology. Apart from a typological understanding of the Old Testament the demand of the Exodus passage cannot be ethically understood or applied to nineteenth-century slavery. Caruthers's understanding of Isa 61:1–2 and other corroborative texts illuminate this method.

Divine providence also enforces God's demand for the freedom of Israel. Belief in divine guidance or providence as the supreme power controlling the nation was the expression of most nineteenth-century Americans belief in the relationship between their virtue as a people and their well-being as a nation.[2] Borrowing categories of judicial and historical providentialism as articulated by Nicholas Guyatt, I will show that Caruthers's interpretation of the North's "greater prosperity" as God's "providential government of the world enforcing his demand for the unreserved and speedy surrender of our whole slave population" is a judicial use of providence that opposes the historical providentialism used to defend slavery. In Caruthers's thinking the entire Civil War is judicial providence, the ethical demand of Exodus coming in full force upon the south: "Now what is all this for? . . . it is a war for the defense and perpetuity of slavery on the part of the South and for its abolition on the part of the North."[3]

---

1. Caruthers, *American Slavery*, 137.
2. Hood, *Reformed America*, 9.
3. Caruthers, *American Slavery*, 157, 195.

CHAPTER 3: THE DEMAND OF EXODUS 10:3

Scripture

The application of the Exodus passage to American slavery might be doubted by those who "don't see how a demand made upon Pharaoh... more than four thousand years ago can have any bearing upon slaveholders at the present day."[4] He counters that if the passage was "recorded by the pen of inspiration" then it cannot be treated "merely as a historical fact." In supporting this part of his argument, in addition to other passages, he cites Rom 15:4 and 1 Cor 10:11, passages that intimate an important connection between ancient Hebrews and Gentile Christians. The use of these particular texts indicate that Caruthers sees a typological origin for God's demand upon American slaveholders. Because a continuing correspondence exists between the church and ancient Israel, God's demand for the release of the Hebrews by Pharaoh must guide the evaluation of slavery for all time. Underneath Caruthers's comprehension of the demand of the Exodus text for American slavery, there is a conviction about the coherence of Jewish and Gentile experience. God "never does anything in vain and the whole transaction in Egypt is fraught with the most important instruction."[5]

Typology is concerned with " the fundamental analogy between different parts of the Bible" and "the consistent working of God" in the lives of people. It seeks to identify the correspondences and parallels in which the Old Testament illuminates the New Testament or vice-versa.[6] Typology describes the correspondence between a type and its antitype as well as intensification or escalation in the latter.[7] The type involves or exhibits certain aspects which can be found with heightened significance in the antitype. The exact nature of correspondence may be difficult to determine. It might be said that typology focuses on the metaphoric role or possibilities of an event, institution, or person, beyond the immediate historical setting to realms of correspondence or prefiguration.[8]

Typology is distinguished from allegory by its reliance on factual or historical elements. Whereas it is permissible for allegory to derive spiritual truths from the slightest details or even the mere words of a text, typology

---

4. Ibid., 140.
5. Ibid.
6. Baker, "Typology and the Christian Use of the Old Testament," 154, 155.
7. Goppelt, *Typos*, x.
8. Ibid., 16.

must transmit, in some way, a similar meaning or structure of meaning. According to Leonard Goppelt allegory "goes its own way regardless of the literal interpretation" but typology "begins with the literal meaning."[9] Typology has a particular concern for understanding the Old Testament's relationship to Christianity. Specifically, it is concerned with "an institution, historical event or person, ordained by God" which "effectively prefigures some truth connected with Christianity."[10] Most importantly perhaps, as Richard Hays has pointed out, typology "is before all else a trope, an act of imaginative correlation" and that "if one pole of the typological correlation annihilates the other, the metaphorical tension disappears, and the trope collapses."[11] Hays's observation cautions against the minimizing or diminishing of the Old Testament that sometimes results from typology, the importance of which is especially seen below in the treatment of the Jubilee.

As a central text for the typological relationship between ancient Israel and the Christian church, the passage cited by Caruthers from First Corinthians is especially significant. Paul calls the Gentile Corinthians "brothers" and refers to ancient Hebrews of Exodus as "our forefathers." What is "a crucial rhetorical maneuver" for Paul, as he identifies his Corinthian readers as Israel's descendants, is also further proof that he thinks of them not simply as Gentiles, but as now identified with Israel.[12] The use of the terms "typoi" and "typikos" in 1 Cor 10:6 and 11, could be translated "examples" or "patterns" or "types."[13] The terms assert a correspondence between the nation of Israel along with their particular circumstances in the Old Testament, presumed the "literal" or "type," and the Corinthians of the New Testament and their circumstances, the "spiritual" or "antitype."[14] The escape of the Hebrews through the Red Sea or Noah's flood are also types that are fulfilled in the antitype of Christian baptism (1 Cor 10:1–2, 1 Pet 3:20–21). The relationship between the type and antitype may be by way of contrast, as in the case of Adam and Christ (Rom 5:12–21, 1 Cor 15:22), or

---

9. Ibid., 1–20.

10. Baker, "Typology and the Christian Use of the Old Testament," 139.

11. Richard Hays, *Echoes of Scripture in the Letters of Paul,* 100.

12. Hays, *Echoes,* 95.

13. The use of this particular word group can be found in the Old Testament (LXX), in Exod 25:40; Amos 5:26; and in the New Testament in John 20:25; Acts 7:43; Acts 7:44; Acts 23:25; Rom 5:14; Rom 6:17; 1 Cor 10:6; 1 Cor 10:11; Phil 3:17; 1 Thess 1:7; 2 Thess 3:9; 1 Tim 4:12, Tit 2:7; Heb 8:5; Heb 9:24; 1 Pet 5:3; 1 Tim 1:16; 2 Tim 1:13.

14. Berkeley, "Typology" 792.

a more exact comparison as in Christ on the cross and the "lifting up" of the bronze serpent in the wilderness (John 3:14).

As mentioned above, it is difficult to determine the exact correspondence intended when passages indicate a typological relationship. The reader may only know that a typological connection exists because of the text's claim. For example, John 3:14 does not tell the reader in what exact way Jesus is like the bronze serpent of Israel's wilderness experience. Patrick Fairbairn speculates in *The Typology of Scripture* that the precise point of correspondence between the lifting up of the bronze serpent and Jesus on the cross is the deceptive appearance they share. A man suffering the death of a convicted criminal on the cross seems as unlikely a help to humanity in need of moral salvation as the image of a despised and poisonous snake to those bitten and in need of a cure.[15]

Caruthers's particular view of typology is not systematically set out as it was not his intention to write a theological treatise, but his comments on the use of Isa 61:1–2 in Luke's Gospel provide an outline from which a reliable construction of his understanding is made possible. Because Caruthers's application of the Exodus passage is guided by his typological understanding of the Old Testament, his explanation of Isa 61:1–2 (pp. 154–56) warrants special attention.

In Luke 4:20 Jesus declares in the synagogue of Nazareth that Isa 61:1–2 is fulfilled by his appearance. The Isaiah text makes reference to Israel's year of Jubilee, the fiftieth year of sabbatical cycles when land is returned to its original owner (Leviticus 25). The forgiveness of debt and the release of all enslaved is a necessary part of Jubilee's program to equalize ownership of the land. In Luke's gospel Jesus applies the words of the prophet to himself, proclaiming "liberty to the captives" thus magnifying the Jubilee beyond the limits of its historical meaning so that it encompasses his own life and work. Caruthers believes that like other "prophecies which related to the Christian age" the passage has "a progressive import and fulfillment." The Jubilee's "general release of all debts and obligations, of all bondmen and bondwomen and of all lands and possessions which had been alienated from the tribes and families to which they belonged," had " a much more important meaning." Jesus's application of the Jubilee year to his own coming "declared plainly enough that the Jubilee had a typical [typological] import."[16]

---

15. Fairbairn, *The Typology of Scripture*, 1:66.
16. Caruthers, *American Slavery*, 155.

In contrast to his contemporaries and many modern commentators, Caruthers believes the Jubilee has meaning that continues to be both literal and spiritual. He calls these same categories "lower" and "higher." Interestingly, he focuses attention on the continuing importance of the lower or literal level of the Jubilee's meaning. Jesus's application of the Isaiah text to himself indicates spiritual liberation from sin but also and equally important, a widening declaration of freedom for those in captivity. When Jesus "applied the prediction to himself he declared plainly enough that Jubilee had a typical import but that only gave it a much more important meaning *without changing in any respect its literal significance*."[17] For Caruthers, the Jubilee typologically foreshadows "spiritual" freedom for those who are captive to the power of sin, but not to the exclusion of its continuing literal meaning. Ongoing fulfillment requires an ongoing experience of liberty.

To support his argument, Caruthers recalls the predictions that "the blind should see, that the deaf should speak and that the lame should walk" in the Messianic era, and that "during the personal ministry of Christ on earth, all the predictions ... received both a literal and spiritual accomplishment." The higher or spiritual sense continues to be fulfilled "every day and everywhere throughout Christendom, in the case of all who are brought out of the darkness of nature into the marvelous light of the gospel" but also "in the lower sense they are receiving a partial accomplishment by the skill of physicians and other friends of humanity." For now, "by various contrivances the lame, the halt, the maimed are enabled to walk, the deaf, the dumb, and the blind are taught to read the Bible and to transact the usual business of life but," Caruthers insists, "they are yet to receive a more literal and full accomplishment by higher attainments in medical skill and by the discovery of means which are yet unknown."[18] In the same manner, the literal implications of the Isaiah passage have already been fulfilled to a "very gratifying extent" but it "*will yet have a universal fulfillment in its fullest extent of meaning.*"[19] A measure of contemporary corroboration of Caruthers's view is found in Michael Green's comment "that Jesus's mission is directed to the poor—defined not merely in subjective, spiritual, or personal, economic terms, but in the holistic sense of those who are for any of a number of socio-religious reasons relegated to positions outside the

---

17. Ibid.
18. Ibid., 156.
19. Ibid., 156; italics added.

CHAPTER 3: THE DEMAND OF EXODUS 10:3

boundaries of God's people."[20] Caruthers is certain that the Jubilee declaration implies not only spiritual liberty but also real freedom:

> Jesus Christ came *to preach liberty to the captive and the opening of the prison to them that are bound* and he will deliver his people who are so unjustly and so cruelly held in bondage here, either by the power of his grace on the hearts of their owners or by such judgments as will make them learn righteousness.[21]

In Caruthers's thinking the distinct but related concerns for spiritual and physical well-being are viewed under the image of the Jubilee. Isaiah 61:1–2 is traditionally understood as a typological use of the Jubilee. The ancient institution of Jubilee is prophetically pulled from the Torah to describe the greater realities of God's forgiveness of Israel and their imminent release from exile and restoration to Zion. The Year of Jubilee image is used to hold together the importance of Israel's forgiveness by God alongside the nation's political freedom to return and restore their land, two distinct but related concerns. Sharon Ringe has noted that "human needs often experienced as competing for attention are brought together onto the single agenda of the Jubilee."[22] Luke's use of Isaiah's text characterizes yet another, even greater era of forgiveness and release to be accomplished by the Messiah. Caruthers's approach understands and upholds these distinctions without diminishing the importance of either.

Conversely, for the nineteenth-century contemporaries of Caruthers and many current commentators, the distinctive social reforms of the original Jubilee are diminished and transcended by the greater spiritual realities they prefigure. J. C. Ryle's commentary on Luke states that Messiah's "victories were not to be over worldly enemies, but over sin" and that he is "the Friend of the poor in spirit, the Physician of the diseased heart, the Deliverer of the soul in bondage."[23] More recent commentators express the meaning in terms of spirituality, such as "deliverance to those who were captives in the power of sin and spiritual wretchedness" or giving back "to the spiritually blind the power of sight" or "freedom from guilt and the effects of sin."[24] Darrel Bock emphasizes "release from sin and spiritual captivity" and the "spiritual overtones" of exilic identity. The Old Testa-

20. Green, *The Gospel of Luke*, 211.
21. Caruthers, *American Slavery*, 376.
22. Ringe, *Jesus, Liberation, and the Biblical Jubilee*, 94.
23. Ryle, *Expository Thoughts on Luke*, 117.
24. Geldenhuys, *Commentary on the Gospel of Luke*, 168; Liefeld, "Luke," 8:867.

ment "viewed the exile as the result of sin."[25] For I. Howard Marshall Jesus's announcement in Luke is an allusion is to the Old Testament Jubilee "appointed by Yaweh . . . and now made symbolic of his own saving acts in order to show his salvation."[26] Joseph Fitzmyer's conclusion is similar: "The Isaian description of a period of favor and deliverance for Zion is now used to proclaim the period of Jesus, and the new mode of salvation that is to come in him."[27] An emphasis on the spiritual fulfillment of Jubilee and a muting of its social reforms in Protestant literature goes back to the earliest views of Martin Luther and John Calvin.[28]

Caruthers's appreciation of the Jubilee's distinctions and their literal fulfillment mirrors another and more influential nineteenth-century Presbyterian minister. The highly regarded Patrick Fairbairn, a theologian in the Free Church of Scotland, exemplifies the Reformed perspective in *The Typology of Scripture*. At nearly a thousand pages in two volumes, Fairbairn's magnum opus remains a standard text on the topic of typology for evangelicals since its publication in 1845. He is considered by some to be "the spokesman for the Reformation tradition" on typology.[29] In line with traditional typology Fairbairn speaks of the "littleness" of historical types, "exhibiting on a comparatively small scale what was afterwards to realize itself on a large on" or of "historical personages and events being related to some higher ideal, in which truths and relations exhibited in them were again to meet, and obtain a more perfect development."[30]

For Fairbairn, as for Caruthers, the concrete social realities of the Jubilee continue to have application as its antitype escalates, and his understanding of the Jubilee's application is very similar to his unknown colleague. The Jubilee addresses sin and effects, not simply as an individual issue that "still causes innumerable troubles and sorrows" but also as political and societal. "Even in the best governed states," he writes, "the true order of absolute righteousness and peace is to be found only in scattered fragments or occasional examples." The purpose of the Jubilee should be seen "as one of deliverance—deliverance from trouble, grievance, and oppression" so that

---

25. Bock, *Luke 1:1—9:50*, 409.

26. Marshall, *The Gospel of Luke: A Commentary on the Greek Text*, 183–84.

27. Fitzmyer, *The Gospel According to Luke I-IX*, 533.

28. Luther, "Lectures on Isaiah Chapters 40–66," 17:331; Calvin, *Harmony of the Evangelists*, 17:229.

29. Van Groningen, *Messianic Revelation*, 161.

30. Fairbairn, *Typology*, 1:65–67, 73.

CHAPTER 3: THE DEMAND OF EXODUS 10:3

the "the aspect of society might reflect" the "well-ordered condition of the heavenly world." Fairbairn envisions specific social imperatives arising from the event of redemption. As he describes it: "When all in a manner, being set right between them and God, it became them to see that every thing was also set right between one person and another."[31]

The sequence of reconciliation noted above by Fairbairn, from God to others, requires continuation of the Jubilee's fuller meaning. He observes that the year of Jubilee's emphasis on the restoration of property and freedom from captivity is united to the restoration of the people's relationship to God. It commences not at the beginning of the year, but follows immediately after the Day of Atonement (Lev 25:9) in which reconciliation with God is dramatically symbolized in the prescribed rituals, the same rituals that foreshadow the Messiah's death for the sins of the people.[32] Isaiah's incorporation of the Jubilee follows the same pattern. Its declaration in Isaiah 61 follows after the "Redeemer" comes and ends the separation of the people from their God (59:16—60:1). Forgiveness and reconciliation precede their release from Babylonian captivity, the end of their oppression, and the restoration of Zion. The typological understanding of the Jubilee involves certain social imperatives or events that result from its redemptive antecedent and without which severely diminished its meaning.

A few current studies corroborate the perspective of Caruthers and Fairbairn. Speaking of what Jesus actually did in his ministry, Paul Hertig observes that "Luke will not allow us to interpret this jubilee language as flowery metaphors or spiritual allegories . . . Jesus literally fulfilled the Jubilee that he proclaimed."[33] Samuel Aborgunrin complains that within traditional theology "the problem of the poor and justice, receive very little attention' because it "does not regard poverty, justice, and other similar social issues as central to the mission of Jesus." Jesus came not only to proclaim a solution to inner dimensions of sin "but also to bring about total deliverance from all forms of power that have held people in bondage" and "this means that the ministry of the Church, like that of its Lord, must always focus on the whole person."[34] The Jubilee's emphasis on concrete social change cannot be diminished by its spiritual overtones and applica-

31. Ibid., 2:404–5
32. Fairbairn, *Typology*, 2:404.
33. Hertig, "The Jubilee Mission of Jesus in the Gospel of Luke," 172.
34. Aborgunrin, "Jesus's Sevenfold Programmatic Declaration at Nazareth," 226, 235.

tion. Although the implementation of the specific reforms of the Jubilee is not intended by Luke's Gospel, David Pao stresses that "the Jubilee connection does highlight the social, economic, and political impact of the arrival of the eschatological era" and observes that, as in Isaiah 61, "this Jubilee theme is one among many that contribute to the wider prophetic paradigm of the second exodus."[35]

Like Fairbairn, his contemporary, and these more recent studies, Caruthers insists that the antitype of Jubilee remains characterized by its literal type. The fullest extent of meaning is achieved only when spiritual redemption is coupled to the Jubilee's literal and universal application for the poor and oppressed of the earth. In his era there was no more obvious example of Jubilee's application than American slavery. The Messiah had brought redemption, now it was the responsibility of a Christianized humanity to bring freedom to the slaves.

In Caruthers's view not only does Luke's use of the Isaiah passage confirm his own use of the Exodus text but the "whole tenor of the Bible is a demand on all who are holding others in bondage and oppression to give them up and leave all free to serve God." He singles out specific "passages which may be cited as corroborative."[36] Throughout the range of biblical literature Caruthers hears the echoes of God's initial demand for the release of Israel from Egypt and argues for its continuing moral implications.

Within the parameters of existing biblical interpretation practiced by American Evangelicals, proslavery advocates argued that slaveholding could not be identified as a sin because it was not expressly forbidden in the Bible. Donald Mathews has observed that "the Evangelical emphasis upon the necessity of a conviction of sin, . . . led a person into psychic confusion, from which he was saved by conversion and reintegrated into society through the church."[37] Because slavery was not expressly forbidden in the Bible, there could be no experience of specific conviction with regard to it. The institution of American slavery was not identifiable as a specific sin so it should not be expressed or experienced as such. Here, in the words of one historian, "was southern evangelicalism's first, essential, and constant proslavery position."[38]

---

35. Pao and Shnabel, "Luke," 290.
36. Caruthers, *American Slavery*, 143.
37. Mathews, *Religion in the Old South*, 74.
38. Crowther, *Southern Protestants Slavery and Secession*, 74.

CHAPTER 3: THE DEMAND OF EXODUS 10:3

Antislavery writers responded by moving away from the description or regulation of slavery found in the Bible to texts they believed more clearly reflected the divine will. In his explanation of the demand of Exod 10:3, Caruthers briefly discusses eight other texts that corroborate his understanding, specifically that "every one must be left free to act on his own responsibility."[39] In the order they appear in the manuscript the texts are Ezek 18:4, Rom 12:1, Rom 6:1, Jer 34:8–22, Neh 5:1–12, Isa 58:6, Ps 72:4–14, and Ps 68:31.

The first text touched on by Caruthers is Ezek 18:4: "*All souls* that is all persons, all men and women, *are mine*" and "*the soul* the man or the woman, *that sinneth shall die.*" In Caruthers's view, slavery confuses the accountability envisioned. If a master commands a slave do things which are "palpably wrong and injurious to the interests of vital piety" and especially in the case of an ongoing repeated violation ordered by "impenitent masters and mistresses" such as "desecrations of the Sabbath" that become "inseparable from the institution as it now exists" then their accountability to God no longer makes complete sense. The passage can only make ethical sense if "all men and all women, all human beings are his and woe to those who infringe upon his rights or dare to interpose, in whole or in part, between any of them and his authority."[40]

Similarly slavery does not allow compliance with the consecration of Rom 12:1 and 6:13. The passages urge readers to "present your bodies a living sacrifice" and "neither yield your members as instruments of unrighteousness." If a slave is a Christian and "their masters claim the whole of their time and strength it is impossible" for them to be consecrated and devoted in the manner "and to the full extent of the . . . requirements" prescribed by the Apostle Paul. What about the plain New Testament teaching that servants are to serve their masters? According to Caruthers those passages were addressed to servants "who were rendering a voluntary service and therefore had the disposal of their time" or to slaves "who belonged to . . . unchristian masters." He does not allow for the possibility of a Christian owning a slave. A slave who is a Christian in the south, and of "any intelligence" cannot comply with the teaching of Romans "as he wishes to do" because "his time and his physical powers are all at the disposal of another."[41]

---

39. Caruthers, *American Slavery,* 144.
40. Ibid.
41. Ibid., 145, 146. Caruthers returns to Romans in his manuscript, beginning at p.

Jeremiah 34:8–22 is singled out by Caruthers as providing "the clearest proof that there could be no such thing as slavery among the Jews" like that of America. Jeremiah condemns the failure of "the king, the nobles, and all who were able to employ servants" for not keeping their covenant to set them free as they had said they would do. Instead they "forced them back into service" and this was "an act of cruelty and a violation of their solemn engagements." Soon after they broke their word, Caruthers points out, "the city was taken and burned, the king, the nobility and all the better classes of people were seized and carried captives to Babylon." In these events, Caruthers sees "God's abhorrence" of slavery.[42]

Nehemiah 5:1–12 demonstrates that "in the mind of all pious Jews" there was "an invincible opposition to *slavery* as we understand the term."[43] Nehemiah is "indignant" upon learning about the bondage imposed on some of the Israelites and requires a "solemn oath of the nobles that they would no more oppress their brethren."[44] All of the teaching of the major and post-exilic prophets "was in constant and direct hostility to anything like an entailed or perpetual enslavement of each other or strangers."[45] The "explicit and comprehensive" language of the Isaiah 58:6—"undo the heavy burdens and let the oppressed go free"—exemplifies their attitude.[46]

Psalm 72:4–14 is "a most animated and glowing description of the Messiah's universal reign." Surely, Caruthers figures, "the slaves of our country must certainly be included among the poor, the needy and the oppressed" whose rescue by the Messiah is announced therein. And if Psalm 68:31, "Ethiopia shall stretch forth her hands to God," does mean that the "African race will believe in Jesus Christ," then a slave's rightful claim upon such a deliverance is undeniable. Caruthers specifically identifies American slaves as included in the psalm's messianic vision of the future. Strictly understood, this is a Messianic interpretation of Israel's earthly king and empire presented by the psalmist. However, Caruthers's identification of the psalmist's local vision for the needy and oppressed of Israel with universal freedom for all in bondage further demonstrates the

---

313, to explain its larger importance for the slavery controversy, the importance of which is considered in chapter 3 below.

42. Ibid., 147, 148.
43. Ibid., 150.
44. Ibid., 149.
45. Ibid., 150.
46. Ibid., 152.

role of typology which underlies Caruthers's application of the Exodus passage to American slavery.

Summary

For Caruthers there are no limits to the application of the Exodus text: "God is demanding the surrender of them to his service. All men and all women, all human beings are his, and woe to those who infringe upon his rights or dare to interpose, in whole or in part, between any of them and his authority." It cannot be restricted to the realm of history. "The passage which we have placed at the head of this discussion . . . " he writes in reference to the Exodus text, " has no condition or limitation and makes no allowance for the interest or convenience of those on whom the demand is made." There can be "no time . . . to sell them off or to make the best arrangements" since "all nations, the Africans included, were given to Jesus Christ in the covenant of redemption and they belong to him." Slaveholders are "to give them up and leave all free to serve God with whatever powers he has given them."[47] "You," he says to slaveholders, "have no valid claim to them and must *let them go.*"[48]

Although Caruthers probably would have appreciated Goppelt's understanding of typology and its emphasis on "the church's place in redemptive history," he does not allow the political liberation of the Exodus event to be diminished, as Goppelt's understanding tends, by the "new people of God, a new humanity, which is distinct from the Jews and no longer needs their shadowy means of redemption because it possesses the reality."[49] To the contrary, Caruthers hears in Exodus a continuing echo of "the whole tenor of the Bible" which is "a demand on all who are holding others in bondage and oppression."[50]

If the Exodus text "has been overlooked, in its true import, for more than two hundred years, it is not the only important one that has shared the same fate." Important texts on the doctrine of justification were overlooked or misunderstood "for a thousand years." Romans 3:28 and Galatians 2:16 along with "scores of others teaching the same doctrine, were "misapplied by the whole Christian world" except by " a little handful" who are "now

47. Ibid., 139, 143.
48. Ibid., 139.
49. Goppelt, *Typos*, 151.
50. Caruthers, *American Slavery*, 143.

known as witnesses for the truth."⁵¹ The larger meaning of the Exodus text has suffered a similar fate but now it should be recognize that, as all of the above passages confirm, the "demand which was first made on Pharaoh, king of Egypt by Moses and Aaron and is now made by the lively oracles of God on all, here in America and every where else, who are holding their fellow men in bondage."⁵²

Providence

God's demand regarding the American slaves is to "Let My people go" and it is also "enforced by his Providence."⁵³ Caruthers asserts God's demand for the "unreserved and speedy surrender of our whole slave population."⁵⁴ The deteriorating economic and intellectual conditions of the slave states are cited as providential evidence of God's demand. Caruthers understands "providence" as the "constant and absolute good which God exercises over this world and all that it contains," including "humans and all other agencies and his employment of these agencies to accomplish his own purposes." In the distinctive national providentialism of nineteenth-century America, providence demonstrated God's favor on the nation as it carried out its divine purpose. While Caruthers probably embraced such a form of providentialism, he also challenged providence as a justification for slavery. "There are few words in our language," he writes of providence, "that are in more frequent use and few that are more oftener perverted or misapplied."⁵⁵ In a longer passage on providence he writes,

> It is strange how inconsiderately and unmeaningly the term is generally used; for Providence is made to favor every successful undertaking whether right or wrong. If a man has prospered in his efforts to accumulate property, tho' it has been been by taking advantage of those who are ignorant of business or less crafty than himself, Providence has certainly favored him; . . . Slave holders talk very fluently about the wise and kind Providence which brought the negroes into this country to be civilized; but as an army when unsuccessful in battle has nothing to say about

---

51. Ibid., 141–42.
52. Ibid., 156.
53. Ibid., 137.
54. Ibid., 157.
55. Ibid., 57.

CHAPTER 3: THE DEMAND OF EXODUS 10:3

Providence, they have no notion of giving them up or of thanking Providence for taking them away.[56]

Caruthers challenges the assertion of God's benevolence toward the institution of slavery often made by slavery's proponents in the name of providence by focusing on a judicial interpretation. As explained by Nicholas Guyatt, historical providentialism interprets providence in terms of a nation's imagined and future significance on the world stage. The rewards or punishments of providence unfolding in history are thus supportive of and tending toward that nation's special role in the overall improvement of the world. A judicial interpretation views providence as a negative assessment of national virtue. The rewards or punishments of God's providence are thus related to a nation's ethical conduct rather than some larger scheme or plan.[57]

Both these forms of providentialism and their variations intermingle in American religious discourse and in Caruthers's manuscript. In some parts of his argument Caruthers's asserts his belief in the larger divine purposes for America, but in this section of his manuscript the Exodus text summons a judicial interpretation of providence in which the South is punished for slavery. The declining and poor industrial record of the South, along with its lack of contributions to literature, art, and technology, are contrasted with the North resulting in clear evidence that Providence is blessing the North and pressuring the South. From such punishments the demand of God for the freedom of the Africans can be heard.

The Five Cotton States and New York: Remarks upon the Social and Economic Aspects of the Southern Political Crisis, a lengthy pamphlet published in 1861, is cited by Caruthers at the beginning of this section, and in a few pages he offers a providential interpretation of the pamphlet's theme. Its author, Stephen Cowell, contrasts the growing population and commercial prosperity of the Northern states with the stagnate conditions of the South. Cowell is not against slavery—it "has more friends in the Northern States than it has in all the world beside" and constitutional protection –but he details the decline of South Carolina.[58] In "her colonial days . . . South Carolina stood in the front rank in point of wealth, education, and aristocratic style of living," he writes, and the state enjoyed "high distinction in many other respects, in comparison with her sister colonies and States." "Charleston"

---

56. Caruthers, *American Slavery*, 59–60.
57. Guyatt, *Providence and the Invention of the United States, 1607–1876*, 4–6.
58. Cowell, *The Five Cotton States*, 6.

he says, "enjoyed a like distinction among the cities of North America, its inhabitants being in high repute for their intelligence, refinement, and liberal style of giving" but now the "State and city have fallen far behind many others in the race of population, wealth, and power."[59]

Caruthers characterizes these and similar findings along with other aspects of Southern society as evidence of God's providential demand for the release of the slaves. The divine operations of providence are enforcing the demand of Exod 10:3: "The greater prosperity of the free than of the slave states first occurs to us an important fact in God's providential government of the world enforcing his demand for the unreserved and speedy surrender of our whole slave population."[60] The industrial, literary, and intellectual accomplishments and contributions of the north are providential signs indicating God's blessing on the absence of slavery in the northern states. The stagnation and decline of the South is providential evidence of God's disapproval of a slave society. Even though "southern men have as good minds as northern men,"[61] the South is "indebted to the North for everything we have worth having."

> for all our valuable works on mathematics, science, and on natural, mental, and moral philosophy; on law and medicine, theology, government and jurisprudence; for all our histories, poetry, and works of taste and general literature, for our books of surveying, navigation, and improvements in farming and farming implements; for our improved breeds of horses, cattle and sheep; for our household furniture . . . In the South we may have invented a pretty good straw cutter and a bedstead that affords little or no harbor for bugs, but nothing, I believe, of more importance.[62]

Mark Noll has described the "flourishing of providential reasoning" during the American slavery controversy and the war that accompanied it in which Caruthers and many others of his era understood their world, its influences, events, circumstances, and "how the moral balance sheet should be read" with greater certainty. Such reasoning made "it easy to reduce the complexities of the war to simple, if sharply contrasting, providential calculations."[63] By Caruthers's calculations the providence of God made it

---

59. Ibid., 7.
60. Caruthers, *American Slavery*, 157.
61. Ibid., 160.
62. Ibid., 159.
63. Noll, *America's God*, 75, 84.

clear that the south should free the slaves, but like Pharaoh the south was incorrigible and would not comply. Threats of slave insurrections and the massacre of whites prompted the adoption of measures towards emancipation and education by the government however "as the price was high, when the danger seemed to have passed away, all their good feelings and resolutions vanished and, like Pharaoh of old, they resolved again that they would not let them go."[64]

Caruthers reasons that the war is the outworking of the demand of Exod 10:3 now finally coming in full force upon the south: "Now what is all this for? . . . it is a war for the defense and perpetuity of slavery on the part of the South and for its abolition on the part of the North."[65] The South is like ancient Egypt under Pharaoh. Its plagues are the paucity of accomplishment in the various fields of human endeavor. The free North has prospered but within the slave society of the South "the boundaries of science have never been extended and nothing of importance has been added to human knowledge. No great inventions have been made in the useful arts and very rarely has much excellence been attained in music, poetry, painting, or sculpture."[66] The South's deficiencies were God's judgment against slavery according to Caruthers. Judicial providence, the " providentialism of wrath," explained the current economic status and intellectual accomplishments of Southern culture.[67] Until the South met God's demand to free the slaves, its demise would continue.

If the slavery debate generated opposing interpretations of scripture, it did also of providence. As expressed by Mark Noll " providence meant different things to different people at different times."[68] The proponents of slavery use providence to justify slavery, while Caruthers uses providence to judge it. Like their seventeenth-century counterparts, Reformed and Presbyterian theologians of nineteenth-century America understood and emphasized providence as God's "design and control" of all history, an "indefinite number of subordinate ends" or "a vast concatenation of causes and effects, from the first to the last moment of time –a successive flow of events, which none can arrest, but He who first set it in motion"[69] but

64. Caruthers, *American Slavery*, 191.
65. Ibid., 195.
66. Ibid., 159.
67. Guyatt, *Providence*, 232.
68. Mark Noll, backcover to Guyatt.
69. Hodge, *Systematic Theology*, 1:581; Matthews, *The Divine Purpose Displayed*, 25.

there was much more. For the historical or national providentialism of Caruthers's generation, the term "providence" encapsulated more than the belief or fact of God's ongoing involvement in the world. It was a term of positive evaluation in the national discourse.

God's supportive and beneficent involvement in the making of the nation descended from seventeenth-century beginnings through the American Revolution and on into the nineteenth century, but slavery created difficulties in this scheme. America was a favored nation under the providential care of God, and there was confidence in the divine plan for the country, but the plan was largely conceived to be along strict racial lines, without Native or African Americans. The presence of slavery created nationwide confusion. The increasing population of African Americans confronted the nation with the question of how its racial diversity could fit into what was believed to be divine purposes for a nation of single color. "God had placed the United States on an upward trajectory and had shaped its past and future toward the improvement of the world," writes Nicholas Guyatt, but "the extension of slavery . . . confounded this effort."[70]

The proponents of slavery were saddled with the responsibility of providentially defending slavery, in Guyatt's words, "until the mists that surrounded the purpose . . . of this baffling institution finally cleared."[71] For James Henley Thornwell, writing in 1861, providence justifies slavery. It is part of "a vast providential scheme" in which "God assigns to every man, by a wise and holy decree, the precise place he is to occupy in the great moral school of humanity."[72] The capacity and abilities of the Africans suit them for slavery, and until they progress, slavery practiced according to the Scriptures provides them the best possible arrangement for their improvement. It is, in fact, "a gracious Providence" for the slaves whose living conditions were now so vastly better than they had been in Africa. And the prospect of Christianizing the Africans shrinks the problem of slavery to a mere "link in the wondrous chain of Providence, through which many sons and daughters have been made heirs of the heavenly inheritance."[73]

For Caruthers, writing a year after Thornwell, providence did not favor slavery but condemned it. Decisions should be made with "reference to great moral principles, or, which is the same thing, to the inspired oracles

70. Guyatt, *Providence*, 4, 214–58.
71. Guyatt, *Providence*, 4–5, 256.
72. Thornwell, *Ecclesiastical*, 461.
73. Ibid., 460.

CHAPTER 3: THE DEMAND OF EXODUS 10:3

of revealed truth, and not by the permissions of Providence." In Caruthers's thinking, the poor performance of the Southern economy and its slight accomplishments in the arts and sciences were proof. Guyatt describes this kind of critique as the "providentialism of wrath" in which judicial providentialism raises unsettling questions about a providential rationale for slavery.[74] Caruthers sees the South lowered in its circumstances by the providence of God and near destruction unless the slaves are freed.

To further his point Caruthers contrasts the "habits of industry, economy, and enterprise" of young men raised in the North to the "idleness . . . hunting, fishing, gambling, and other frivolous amusements" of the ordinary Southerner. The atmosphere of the North is "like a great bee hive, where men, women, and children are all going from sunrise to sundown, as busy as bees" compared to the South where "one fourth of the population are little better than drones . . . sitting on the benches at every tavern door, some half a dozen . . . white men, generally slaveholders" or their "beardless sons . . . smoking their cigars, cracking the heels of their boots together and talking politics." In the North where slavery is absent "intellectual powers above mediocrity" are directed into "one of the learned professions, for scientific and literary pursuits, or . . . the application of mechanical philosophy to mechanical inventions and improvements" but the presence of slavery in the South stunts similar ability resulting in "so few southerners who have made very great scientific and literary attainments."[75] For Caruthers the providence of God has made clear the "simple and undeniable facts . . . in regard to the condition of the South. "[76] "In a slave country" he writes with unequivocal certainty, "there is nothing to produce . . . a full and complete development of all the human powers."[77]

Whether providence is used to justify the enslavement of two million Africans in antebellum America, the founding of Massachusetts by the pilgrims in 1629, or something as esoteric as the addition of vowel points to the Hebrew consonantal text in the Christian era,[78] or even the invasion of Iraq by the American military in 2003,[79] the absolute government of God over all creation has always provoked questions about human responsibility.

---

74. Guyatt, *Providence*, 173–74, 232–33.
75. Caruthers, *American Slavery*, 161.
76. Ibid., 160.
77. Ibid., 164.
78. Pelikan, *Reformation of the Church and Dogma*, 346–47.
79. Guyatt, *Providence*, 1.

Caruthers's understanding of providence descends from its seventeenth-century Reformed definition as God's "most holy, wise, and powerful preserving and governing all his creatures and their actions" as stated in the eleventh question of the Westminster Shorter Catechism. The latter aspect of government predominates in Caruthers's discussion of providence and the slavery controversy in light of the Exodus passage. God, in the words of the fifth chapter in the Westminster Confession of Faith, "doth uphold, direct, dispose, and govern all creatures, actions, and things, from the greatest even to the least by his most wise and holy providence."

The writers of the Westminster Confession of Faith and Catechisms were guided by John Calvin's view that "providence means not that by which God idly views from heaven what takes place on earth, but that by which, as keeper of the keys, he governs all events."[80] The similarity of the confession on the subject of providence in chapter 5 with the subject of predestination in chapter 3 on "God's Eternal Decree" where "God from all eternity did by his most wise and holy counsel of his own will freely and unchangeably ordain whatsoever comes to pass" is, to state it ironically, not by chance. From the framers' perspective, these doctrines are concerned with God's control of either ultimate goals as in the doctrine of eternal decree and predestination or the more intermediate goals as in the doctrine of providence.[81]

Viewing the will of God as central to both of these doctrines, Calvin's own extensive development of the doctrine of providence was originally united with the cognate doctrines of predestination and evolved over the several early editions of his *Institutes*, breaking the silence preferred by Martin Luther and other reformers who were content with reverence toward the mysteries of divine will, predestination, and providence without development of such topics as reprobation or double predestination.[82] Calvin's comment on Lutheran theology was that "many, as if they wished to avert a reproach from God, accept election in such terms as to deny that anyone is condemned."[83] His decision to treat the doctrines of providence and predestination separately in the final and definitive 1559 edition of the *Institutes* for organizational reasons influenced subsequent reformed confessions including the Westminster Confession of Faith.

80. Calvin, *Institutes of the Christian Religion*, 1:202.
81. Pelikan, *Reformation of Church and Dogma*, 221.
82. Ibid., 227.
83. Calvin, *Institutes*, 1:947.

CHAPTER 3: THE DEMAND OF EXODUS 10:3

The conceptualization of human free agency within the Westminster standards is characteristically formal and somewhat vague. Even Archibald Alexander and Charles Hodge, two of Princeton Seminary and the nineteenth-century's most able defenders of the Westminster Confession's formulation of providence, had to concede that the doctrine was "difficult" to comprehend.[84] According to the fifth chapter of the Westminster Confession of Faith, "Of Providence," God rules over all the creation working ordinarily by and through "the nature of second causes, either necessarily, freely, or contingently." But if God's control is absolute does this imply ethical passivity on the part of human beings or make us less culpable? In answer to such a question, the confession offers an emphatic denial. Regardless of God's decree "the liberty or contingency of second causes" is not taken away. In the section on providence it states that any "sinfulness . . . proceeds only from the creature and not from God." The difficulty of solving how sovereignty and human responsibility fit together, Philip Schaff's "problem of the ages," and other related questions about providence and predestination would be revisited and wrangled over by subsequent generations.[85]

The solution formulated by theologians of Caruthers's era was to make distinctions in God's rule over creation, differentiating providence in the realm of the physical world from providence in the realm of humanity. Charles Cashdollar has remarked that such attempts to articulate more precisely God's manner of working in the world became an "exceedingly complex" ordeal, a "finely spun web of subdivisions and corollaries," that awaited every serious student of the doctrine.[86] The advantage, however, of such treatments was the pronounced recognition of humanity as moral beings distinct from the rest of creation. Humanity was under God's moral government whereas the rest of the universe was figured under natural government.

Originally published in the eighteenth century, the nineteenth-century reprint of William Sherlock's, *A Discourse Concerning Divine Providence*, is representative of this solution in nineteenth-century America, and is important background for any similar literature of the era. Sherlock distinguishes between "God's government of the natural world, of the heavens,

---

84. Matthews, *The Divine Purpose Displayed*, 7; Hodge, *Systematic Theology*, 1:615.
85. Schaff, *Modern Christianity*, 94.
86. Cashdollar, "The Social Implications of the Doctrine of Divine Providence," 265–84.

and earth . . . " and "moral causes or free agents."[87] For Sherlock the latter category of providence with regard to moral causes and free agents is "the great difficulty," or, specifically, "how God can exercise such an absolute government over mankind, who are free agents, without destroying the liberty and freedom of their choice." The difficulty is "removed if we distinguish between God's government of men, as reasonable and free agents, and his government of them as the instruments of Providence."[88] The former considers them "in their own private and natural capacity" where every one is left to the freedom of their own choice, but the latter, as instruments "in relation to the rest of mankind."[89]

John Calvin and the writers of the Westminster Confession of Faith were impatient with such difficulties or even the objections of the church fathers who "sometime scrupulously shrink from a simple confession of the truth because they are afraid that may open the way for the impious to speak irreverently of God's works." For Calvin, Pharaoh, like other enemies of God's people, is "deliberately bent" by God to his purposes.[90] In Sherlock's line of reasoning, however, when the Bible speaks in Exodus of God hardening Pharaoh's heart, God does not "infuse hardness into Pharaoh's heart" for that would be "inconsistent with the holiness of providence." What is meant by such expressions in the Bible is "that men take occasion from what God does . . . to harden themselves" and God, does not "forbear doing what wisdom, and justice, and goodness direct to be done because hardened sinners will harden themselves the more by it."[91] Sherlock's meaning is that God does what is right, human beings respond as they will, and God continues to do what is right regardless of human response. In Terrence Fretheim's more modern way of expressing the same idea: "Human patterns of thought and will may in time become irreversible through continual refusal to respond to God's word. At the same time, God bears responsibility for keeping the word of God coming on and on."[92]

The adjustments of the nineteenth century to the stark and unexplained elements of the Westminster Confession's insistence on human

---

87. Sherlock, *A Discourse Concerning the Divine Providence*, 37, 48; cf. Matthews, *The Divine Purpose Displayed*, 64–65; Woods, *The Works of Leonard Woods*, 2:127.

88. Sherlock, *A Discourse Concerning Divine Providence*, 48.

89. Ibid., 49.

90. Calvin, *Institutes*, 1:311, 313.

91. Sherlock, *A Discourse Concerning Divine Providence*, 163.

92. Fretheim, *Exodus*, 98.

responsibility seem to have influenced Caruthers. Sherlock's reasoning illuminates the nuances of Caruthers's thinking on Pharaoh. As a Presbyterian minister in the nineteenth century Caruthers's views on providence are not simply those of the Westminster Confession of Faith but conditioned and moderated by the questions of the larger theological climate of his era as reflected in Sherlock. On the issue of providence, Caruthers writes, "That the Lord does influence the minds and hearts of individuals, communities, and nations is unquestionable and it must be so; for otherwise he could not govern the world. How he does this we need not inquire."[93]

In the case of the king of Egypt, however, Caruthers attempts to explain how the hardening takes place. Writing of Pharaoh he says that "as he had determined and said that he would not give up what he regarded as his slave property, the Lord hardened his heart" and then he proceeds to offer the following options for how this is to be understood: God either "ordered circumstances so that he hardened his own heart or . . . led [him] to persist in his determination until he was overwhelmed in ruin."[94] Which of these options is preferred by Caruthers? He shows his preference for a view of providence that allows for God's "ordering of circumstances" so that in the case of Pharaoh, he acts "freely in accordance with his selfish designs and his aversion to the truth . . . to persist in his tyrannical purposes." God led Pharaoh to harden his heart by persisting in the demand for the release of the Hebrews. Pharaoh, Caruthers writes, " is said to harden his heart . . . voluntarily making the choice he did, without desiring any other direction than that of his own will."[95] The explanation and language used by Caruthers shies away from asserting an infusion of hardness into Pharaoh, placing emphasis on divinely authored circumstances to which Pharaoh freely responds, a marked refinement of the views found in the Westminster Confession of Faith fitting with the more complex formulations exemplified in Sherlock's work.

Summary

In Caruthers's view, arguments from providence are not exempt from ethical scrutiny, and the doctrine of providence must not be used to mask human responsibility. "Providence," he observes, " has permitted all the fraud

---

93. Caruthers, *American Slavery*, 170.
94. Ibid., 189.
95. Ibid., 171.

and injustice, all the lust and ambition, all the tyranny and oppression, all the crimes and abominations that have been committed in the world or they would not have been committed, but will any Christian say that these crimes are therefore justifiable?"[96] He writes that the "question of duty must always be decided by a reference to great moral principles, or . . . to the inspired oracles of revealed truth, and not by the permissions of Providence."[97] The duty of American slaveholders is made clear from the Exodus text. The Scriptures demand the freedom of the slaves, and the judicial providence of God is demanding the same.

96. Ibid., 59.
97. Ibid., 59–60.

Chapter 4: The Purpose of Exodus 10:3

THE THIRD AND FINAL section of Caruthers's manuscript explains the purpose behind God's demand for the freedom of the slaves. "Let my people go that they may serve me" implies that their service is "indispensable to the accomplishment of his merciful designs upon them and for the world."[1] The "merciful designs" follow the redemption that has come through Christ. People must be free in order to serve their Savior in the fullness of their calling. Relying upon Rom 12:1–2 and other passages, Caruthers argues that the capacity and abilities of a people can never be developed for such a cause if they are in slavery because the service God "requires consists in such a voluntary exercise of all their powers" that would cause "increasing honor upon his wisdom, power, and goodness in their creation."[2]

The following three part division facilitates examination of the more important emphases of the larger final section of the manuscript. The length of the section indicates the importance Caruthers places upon this final point. The first part explores Caruthers's reasons for why slavery is incompatible with service to God on account of the existing laws of the slave states (pp. 257–337). This includes his extensive comments on the Slave Code (pp. 261–85). The second part looks more carefully at Caruthers's biblical and theological thinking on slavery's incompatibility with service to God (pp. 257–60 and pp. 286–333). The final part of this chapter takes up his review of emancipation's progress and his advocacy of African colonization (pp. 338–404).

Christianity and the Laws of Slave States

The final section of Caruthers manuscript includes his criticism of state laws and legislation regarding slaves in North Carolina and other slave states. Entitled "Slave Code of the South" this portion of the manuscript

1. Ibid., 257.
2. Ibid.

sets forth the systemic denial of rights and freedom endured by slaves as revealed in the details of slave states' legislation. Commenting on laws regulating the baptism, selling, apprehension, incarceration, punishment, and emancipation of slaves, Caruthers exposes the variance of state enactments and policies with the principles of Christianity and the American Declaration of Independence.

Elizabeth Fox-Genovese and Eugene Genovese's research has explored and evaluated the intellectual depth and variety of thinking in the slaveholding class, including their benevolence. Regarding the many tombstones of the old south designating the deceased as a "kind" and "affectionate" master they ask, "How often did anyone bother to ask the slaves if they agree and were they in a position to answer frankly?"[3] A better question: Should even a former slave's approval of their master be accepted uncritically? Attempts to use former slaves' charitable assessment of their masters as an argument against the systemic abuse associated with slavery provoke this question and deserve careful scrutiny.[4]

Caruthers downplays charity and kindness shown by masters. His approach to the issue is to present slavery "not as it is in a few indulgent families or neighborhoods; but as it is seen in the slave codes of the south and as it is now viewed in the protestant world."[5] It is the "legislation of a country, especially a free country like ours" that is "an index to the sentiments of the people."[6] Throughout this section Caruthers utilizes *Sketch of the Laws Relating to Slavery in the Several States of the United States of America*, published in 1827 and the work of George Stroud, whom he knew at Princeton—"a college mate of the present writer."[7] He reviews the settled laws of the slaveholding states and their systemic denial of human rights, preferring to "speak not of the kindness which individual masters may show their slaves . . . but of the laws" or "abominable laws" of the states which are the "unerring index to the intelligence, the sentiments, and the moral principles of its people."[8] For Caruthers, "the spirit and character of a

---

3. Fox-Genovese and Genovese, *Mind of the Master Class*, 367.
4. See Appendix, "Evaluating Former Slave Testimony."
5. Caruthers, *American Slavery*, 298.
6. Ibid., 359.
7. Ibid.
8. Ibid., 337, 308, 325.

nation is always judged abroad, not by little acts of humanity on the part of the individuals, but by their laws and general usages."⁹

Caruthers gives particular attention to earlier colonial enactments regarding the baptism of slaves, such as the 1715 Maryland enactment that " 'no negroe or negress by the receiving the sacrament of baptism the holy sacrament of baptism, is thereby manumitted or set free.'" As noted by Caruthers, the perspective that the baptism of a slave implied their freedom was widespread enough to warrant such legislation in other colonies. Concerned that slaves would feign religious convictions in the hope of gaining their freedom the 1711 act of South Carolina stated on the topic of baptism " 'that religion may not be made a pretext to alter any man's property and right.'"¹⁰ Albert Raboteau's study of slavery and antebellum religion points out that by 1706 at least six colonies had enacted legislature denying the freedom of a slave as a consequence of baptism.¹¹ One missionary to South Carolina even required slaves who were candidates for baptism to give assent to the following:

> You declare in the presence of God and before this Congregation that you do not ask for the holy baptism out of any design to free yourself from the Duty and Obedience that you owe to your Master while you live, but merely for the good of Your Soul and to partake of the Graces and Blessings promised to the members of the Church of Jesus Christ.¹²

The colonial legislation regarding the baptism of slaves and requiring oaths like the one above exposed the conflict in slaveholding communities, between "interest and conscience," as Caruthers puts it, or the "uneasiness of conscience . . . which serious thinking people of that day had respecting the lawfulness of slavery, or of holding *Christians* in bondage."¹³

Debate over baptism's association with liberty was not unique to the colonies of America but a reenactment of the Scottish and British question over the status of baptized slaves. Caruthers's own Presbyterian forefathers in eighteenth-century Scotland probed the meaning of baptism and its relationship to society. Caruthers's critique of the slave states' laws on baptism reflects an important element within his own Presbyterian tradition

9. Ibid., 288.
10. Ibid., 263.
11. Raboteau, *Slave Religion*, 99, 356.
12. Cited in Raboteau, *Slave Religion*, 123.
13. Caruthers, *American Slavery*, 263.

descending from the Scottish Kirk. Iain Whyte's study of baptism and black slavery in eighteenth-century Scotland concludes that there is not enough evidence to prove that baptism into the Kirk implied "automatic immunity to re-enslavement" but "the public involvement in such an act . . . meant an exposure to local communities wherein the assumption of fundamental freedoms were growing and against which black slavery jarred."[14] Baptism not only marked the recipient's reconciliation to God but as Whyte observes it was "a significant rite of passage within the local community." He cites several documented cases, most notably that of David Spens. A review of Spens case is helpful for discovering the motivation behind the laws critiqued by Caruthers and approximate his own opinions as a Presbyterian minister.

From an estate in Grenada Dr. David Dalrymple purchased a slave in 1760, naming him 'Black Tom' and bringing him to his Fife estate eight years later. At some point it was planned for the slave to return to Grenada under the ownership of Dalrymple for training as a carpenter. The date of return was to be September 11, 1769. On Sunday, September 10, the previous day and with Dalrymple's consent 'Tom' went to Wemyss Parish Church and was publicly baptized by the Reverend Dr. Harry Spens, taking the name of David Spens. He returned to the Dalrymple's estate, packed his clothes the next morning and moved to the home of a Kirk elder, Mr. John Henderson. Dalrymple had given his consent for his slave to attend Spen's church but he was not prepared for what happened shortly afterwards, when David Spens returned with Henderson to make the following declaration:

> I, David Spens, formerly called Black Tom late slave to Dr. David Dalrymple of Lindifferen hereby intimate to you the said Dr. Dalrymple that being formerly an heathen slave to you and of consequence then at your disposal but being now instructed in the Christian Religion I have embraced the same and been publicly baptized to that faith by the Reverend Mr. Harry Spens, minister of the gospel at Wemyss and so admitted to the Church of Christ established in this Kingdom and of consequence I am now by the Christian Liberate and set at free from my old yoke, bondage, and slavery and by the laws of this Christian land there is no slavery nor vestige of slavery allowed. Nevertheless you take it upon you to exercise your tyrannical power over me and would dispose of me arbitrally at your despotic will and pleasure and for that end you threaten to send me abroad out of this country to the West

---

14. Whyte, *Scotland and the Abolition of Black Slavery, 1756–1838*, 35–36.

Indies and there dispose of me for money by which you subvert the ends and design of the Christian institution which ransoms liberty to all its members but also you would deprive our sovereign Lord the King of a good subject.[15]

Spens goes on to declare that he is leaving the Dalrymple household and is no longer in their service, even warning his former master that he will be liable for "all damages or expenses for any of my Christian Brethren who shall aid and assist and protect" him. The defiant Spens was arrested for his refusal to submit to his owner and held for trial. Significantly, the local Kirk Session of the congregation where he was baptized defended him, and with the assistance of several sympathetic lawyers, Spens was released on bail. Before the Court of Session decided his case, Dalrymple died in 1770 and Spens gained his freedom by default.[16] Whyte does not think baptism in eighteenth-century Scotland was a "passport to freedom" for slaves but the story of Spens and others shows that the horrors of slavery and the slave trade were becoming better known in the country. Even though it was only a comparatively a small number of black slaves whose cases were publicized, those few cases helped slaves to be seen "as individuals rather than as a group who might be a threat to white society," thus, making it "easier to see their plight as an unjust one."[17]

The Spens controversy illuminates Caruthers's convictions on baptism as a nineteenth-century theological descendant of the Kirk and his criticism of state slave codes. As an important public sacrament in the Presbyterian Church, baptism involved a recipient's exposure to, and welcome into, the community of the faithful with declarations of full rights and privileges within the church. Composed with the help of individuals from Wemyss Parish were he was baptized, Spens' elaborate declaration to his owner that having been "publicly baptized" and now "set at freedom from my old yoke, bondage, and slavery," mirrors Caruthers's own conclusions about American slavery. Spens believes his continued enslavement as a Christian would "deprive our sovereign Lord the King of a good subject." As Caruthers saw it, laws enacted to head off similar conclusions in America proved that the distinct impression among early colonists was "that members of the Christian church, like those of the Jewish church could not be lawfully held in bondage" and "in this notion," he concludes,

15. Cited in Whyte, *Scotland and the Abolition of Black Slavery*, 35.
16. Ibid., 9–10.
17. Ibid., 11.

"they were not mistaken."[18] The impression is supported by Albert Raboteau's comment that the "would-be missionaries to the slaves" in colonial Virginia complained that slaveholders refused to catechize slaves because "baptism made it necessary to free them."[19]

Caruthers also reviews the "Revised Code of North Carolina," especially the statutes concerning the selling of slaves imported into the state after the federal government had passed the 1808 legislation prohibiting the transporting of slaves to America. "Contrary to the provisions of the act of congress" they were sold "after twenty days notice, by public practice at the court house door" and rewards were offered for any slaves imported who escaped. He wonders why, rather than selling them, they were not delivered to the federal government. Did the legislature of the state have such "a rabid appetite for the bones and sinews of Africans that all their feelings of generosity and even of compassion were kept in abeyance?"[20]

For more than twenty pages Caruthers denounces various state laws describing all the legislation as " an abject and general submission to the god of this world." Runaway slaves are made to be outlaws even though severe treatment, punishment, separation from families, and other extremities are the cause. As outlaws they can be apprehended by anyone, jailed, and, if not reclaimed by their owner, sold to the highest bidder. Emancipation, accomplished by a slave earning enough to pay an agreed upon price to his owner or by a master's willing benevolence, is theoretically possible but made impossible by legislation that involves "so many difficulties and . . . so much expense and trouble . . . that it amounts to a prohibition and was probably intended by the legislature to have that effect." Caruthers has known "of several instances" in which a slave "relying on the promise of emancipation" managed to earn money "enough to pay the price fixed for his ransom" only to be "sold off to the speculators" and the money pocketed by the "avaricious master or mistress."[21]

If a slave is somehow emancipated he or she must leave the state within ninety days and not return. The violation of either of these provisions allows authorities to sell them again into slavery. The laws forbid any free negro from moving into the state. If they come they must pay a five hundred dollar fine and leave the state within thirty days or they are seized and

18. Caruthers, *American Slavery*, 265.
19. Raboteau, *Slave Religion*, 98.
20. Caruthers, *American Slavery*, 267, 268.
21. Ibid., 273, 282, 285.

sold again into slavery. Beatings of slaves resulting in death or the "right out" murder of a slave are seldom punished for lack of "white witnesses" as required by the law. Of beatings resulting in death, Caruthers says, "I have known a number myself in which nobody in the neighborhood had any doubt that the death of the slave was caused by the severity of his treatment, but no attempt was made to punish the cruel perpetrator of the deed."[22]

Summary

"Our laws on the subject of slavery," Caruthers summarizes despondently, "are denounced by most other nations and by a pretty large and respectable portion of the people here at home." Seen against the background of the "noble" and "ever memorable" Declaration of Independence, so beloved by Caruthers, the existing laws violate the "inalienable rights which the Creator has given to all alike." They "are hostile to the best interests of humanity and the great principles of Christianity."[23] In conclusion of this section he returns to the consideration of individual cases of charitable treatment:

> All the comforts bestowed upon their slaves by the most humane and indulgent masters, while they continue to hold them as slaves and not only as slaves, but as property, is like the partial relief afforded by the physician to his suffering patient when he can't remove the *cause* of his sufferings, or a few kind acts done by a despot on the throne to his subjects, while the despotic government remains.[24]

For Caruthers no act of kindness shown to a slave, short of emancipation, is in true conformity with the purpose of God's demand for their freedom and the entirety of slave state legislation is bent toward the denial of such freedom.

Slavery Hinders Service

The purpose of God's demand for the release of the slaves is service, but if anyone is a slave "they *cannot* render such a service as he requires."[25] In

22. Ibid., *American Slavery*, 282.
23. Ibid., 7, 325.
24. Ibid., 337.
25. Ibid., 257.

an undated sermon on John 8:36 Caruthers says " there is nothing which intelligent and sober thinking people value more than freedom, and nothing which they abhor more and deprecate more than slavery. To all classes of mankind, even the most ignorant and degraded, there is a charm in the very name of liberty and the yoke of bondage is evermore a galling one. If there is one sentiment in the human breast which is instinctive and therefore permanent in its nature and essential to our well being, it is the love of liberty." Liberty "is above all price" and "can never be sold without immeasurable loss nor bought for more than it is worth." Regarding one's freedom he says "there is nothing for which people will make greater sacrifices or in the possession and enjoyment of which they feel greater excitation; and there is nothing by which they are more depressed in spirit or degraded in character than by unwilling subjection to the authority and power of another."[26] Those enslaved as property of another are not free to give themselves to God because they can exercise no real will of their own.

Unless slavery is abolished and such liberty is granted "slaves cannot make that entire surrender of themselves to the Lord which the gospel required and to which renewed nature prompts them."[27] Caruthers emphasizes that the benefits of redemption accrue to both soul and body, not only in the future but here and now. Regarding the effect of the gospel in the life of a human being he writes,

> No man has the shadow of a right to lay an arrest on this progress and to say that their whole time and bodily strength shall be devoted to his interests or his pleasures. Such an enslavement of those whom he [Christ] has purchased with his own blood, whether actually converted or not, is a daring encroachment on his rights and a most unjust and cruel outrage.[28]

The capacity and abilities of slaves cannot be developed because by its very nature the institution of slavery interdicts education, family life, even the basic instincts that drive us to acquire possessions, all of which are vital areas of human volition and critical for human development. In support of these ideas Caruthers cites Romans 12:1 and First Corinthians 6:20, two passages that focus not so much on the benefits of redemption, but on the responsibilities that come with redemption and which cannot be fulfilled in American slavery.

26. Caruthers, "John 8:36."
27. Caruthers, *American Slavery*, 313.
28. Ibid., 258.

CHAPTER 4: THE PURPOSE OF EXODUS 10:3

Slaves cannot serve God because they are denied the assistance and education that "consists in rightly developing all the original instincts of our nature" which includes a desire for immortality and knowledge.[29] If intelligent slaves are dangerous slaves it is only "because they are slaves" and "their knowledge of God and his government" makes them so. For this reason slaves are doomed to "gross and perpetual ignorance" and "if any free person, white or black, shall attempt to teach them the use of letters, or shall sell them or *give* them a book or pamphlet of any kind, he shall be found guilty of a misdemeanor in law; and if they shall undertake to teach one another they shall be severely punished." Elsewhere he writes that "legislature and slave owners have done everything in their power" to prevent education. Attempts "to teach them a sort of child's catechism *orally,* is only salve to conscience" and "a solemn mockery of the whole business."[30] William C. Johnson verifies that even efforts to undertake the religious instruction of slaves by ministers such as William Capers, Charles Cotesworth Pinckney, and Charles Colcock Jones were hindered by a state's legal restrictions on slave literacy.[31]

Conjugal and parental instincts fare little better. Any semblance of legal marriage is "all the time, ignored, trampled on, and set at naught." It is "without sacredness, without durability, and without the beneficial results which usually attend legal and regular marriages." As for the "family of a slave," it is only "a nursery for the slave market."[32] Caruthers relates the story of a black family in his own Alamance congregation whose experience "was sad and painful in the extreme." Upon the death of his master, the slave's daughter, "a fine looking young woman . . . was the first one sold." Caruthers recounts the father and mother's inconsolable grief upon the loss of their daughter: "In some two or three weeks . . . he died of a broken heart and so did his wife." Caruthers writes, " I could fill a volume with similar cases." He asks,

> In the name of high heaven, is there no flesh in man's obdurate heart? How shall such scenes of injustice and cruelty, such sorrow and distress, be enacted almost daily before the eyes of a Christian community . . . without stirring up the compassion of the soul to its lowest depths and without calling forth a united and determined

---

29. Ibid., 286, 287, 291, 295, 299.
30. Ibid., 295–96, 311.
31. Johnson, "A Delusive Clothing," 296.
32. Caruthers, *American Slavery,* 299–300.

effort to drive this intolerable scourge of humanity from the land? How much longer can we expect that justice will slumber and that the divine forbearance will hold out?"[33]

Among the "instincts or tendencies of our nature" Caruthers stresses the primacy of the "possessory instinct" which is one's "sense of possession or *right* to possess what he has honestly obtained."[34] In ecclesiastical and theological literature of the nineteenth century, the "possessory instinct" is explained by Thomas Chalmers as an "original instinct, an ultimate fact in the mental constitution" or "all the advantages which accrue to society from the desire of property and from the respect for it which exists among men."[35] Of course, "fallen from God . . . and under the power of sin, all men, until renewed by grace make this world their portion and grasp as much of it as they can get" and "this is a sad perversion of an original and noble instinct of our nature."[36] A slave cannot develop this instinct. He "has not an hour of time nor a dime of money that he can legally call his own" and his "instinctive desire of possession can neither be developed nor gratified nor made subservient to his higher and more important attainments."[37] The order of development from gratification to subservience is important. In Caruthers's thinking because slavery denies the slaves' right to possessions such as property, they are without the experience of ownership. This threatens a process of maturation designed by God through which one comes to understand and see genuine possessions in this world as indicative of something even greater to be possessed beyond it—"an interest in Christ; a pure and unalloyed friendship with God and man."[38] As slaves "the pious men and women among our blacks" are not "the intelligent, large minded and influential men and women that they would have been if their powers had been properly developed."[39]

Caruthers argues that "there is a sufficiency in the world to furnish all" with enough "for every desirable purpose" and that "the liberality which the gospel requires, if it is so practiced as it ought to be and will be

33. Ibid., 308–310.

34. Caruthers, *American Slavery*, 287.

35. Chalmers, *The Works of Thomas Chalmers*, 297. Cf. the review of Chalmers, *On the Power, Wisdom, and Goodness of God*, 264, 269.

36. Caruthers, *American Slavery*, 289.

37. Ibid., 288.

38. Ibid., 287.

39. Ibid., 294.

someday, would furnish every human being with the means for the full development of all his powers." The condition of slavery, however, makes it "impossible . . . that this instinctive desire of possession can ever be gratified" and amounts to "daring encroachment on the prerogative of God . . . robbing him of the glory which would otherwise redound to his creative wisdom and power."[40]

In order to render true service to God the slaves must be free. Caruthers relies on the Old Testament's interchangeable concepts of "service" and "worship," appealing to background and imagery of Rom 12:1–2—"present your bodies a living sacrifice." The freedom of the ancient worshipper to select the best of his flock for sacrifice to God as worship should be "distinctly noticed." This was a "whole burnt offering, no part of which was allowed to be reserved or put to any other use."[41] Against this background, "the Christian sacrifice . . . must be a *living* sacrifice" characterized by similar volition and free will.

True worship or service for God, Caruthers argues, "taken in its widest sense, does not consist merely in feelings of adoration, love, and praise" but "includes the employment of our time or portions of it in ways which will express the homage of the heart, and free will offerings from the fruit of our labors."[42] The "service he [God] requires consists in . . . a voluntary exercise of all their powers" and with that comes "their increasing enjoyment" and " increasing honor upon his [God's] wisdom, power, and goodness in their creation."[43] Slaves cannot worship or serve God in this way. "Surely no one will undertake to assert that our slaves are thus able to present their *bodies* a living sacrifice . . . as the free will offering of rational beings and moral agents" Caruthers writes, " . . . for they have no command of their time nor their actions, plans, and pursuits."[44] The similarity of Caruthers's reasoning to that of William Edmundson, a seventeenth-century Quaker and forerunner of abolition, deserves mention. From his home in Newport, Rhode Island, Edmundson sent out a letter in 1676 to all Quakers in slaveholding colonies suggesting that slavery and Christian liberty were incompatible and that only with liberty could slaves fulfill the

---

40. Ibid., 290.
41. Ibid., 313.
42. Ibid., 297.
43. Ibid., 257.
44. Ibid., 314.

law of Christ.⁴⁵ Edmundson insists that if all the Friends to whom he wrote would refrain from slaveholding then both they and the slaves would then be able to do God's will.⁴⁶

Caruthers also cites 1 Cor 6:20—"glorify God in your body and in your spirit which are God's." "Both *body and spirit* are here severally and distinctly mentioned and the two include the whole man," he writes, "so that since Christ redeemed the body as well as the soul and both together constitute but one accountable being he [Christ] claims the entire services of the whole man, soul and body."⁴⁷ Not only are there the benefits of redemption by Christ, but there are also responsibilities of the one redeemed, responsibilities that cannot be met in the system of American slavery.

A contemporary of Caruthers, James Henley Thornwell, believed American slavery was "nothing but an organization of labor . . . an organization by virtue of which labour and capital are made to coincide," and thought the "real question is: whether it [slavery] is incompatible with the spiritual prosperity of individuals."⁴⁸ In contrast and in keeping with his understanding of this passage, Caruthers argues that not only spiritual prosperity must be considered in the evaluation of slavery but physical well-being and prosperity as well. The "great design" of "the gospel of God's grace . . . is to deliver us from all the "physical, social, and moral results" of depravity.⁴⁹ Because the "soul and body" of the slave constitute one person—an "intelligent and accountable being"—and because "both were included in the great redemptive act of Calvary" then "both will share in the final results of that redemption." No one, he says, "can prevent them [slaves] without great guilt from sharing in the benefits here to the full extent of their capacity."⁵⁰

Progress of Emancipation, Colonization, and Conclusion

In this final section, "The Progress of Emancipation," Caruthers charts what he believes to be movement toward the recognition of human equality in

45. Davis, 307.
46. Brown, *Moral Capital*, 57.
47. Caruthers, *American Slavery*, 318.
48. Thornwell, *Ecclesiastical*, 539.
49. Caruthers, *American Slavery*, 110.
50. Ibid., 258.

CHAPTER 4: THE PURPOSE OF EXODUS 10:3

the early political documents of the colonies. Caruthers consults "the first Constitutions of all 'the old Thirteen'" as well as "legislative enactments and several other facts of a historical kind" taken from Stroud.[51] Caruthers uses these early constitutions to demonstrate a progression in thought regarding human equality. The outlook of these documents is to be contrasted with those of the slave states who view slavery as a domestic institution, including his own state of North Carolina. Caruthers then finishes out his manuscript with a discussion of African colonization, and his hope for the transformation of the continent into another Christian civilization carried out by the emancipated slaves.

In the different states of the country, various acts of emancipation during and following the Revolutionary War, including Pennsylvania legislation as well as the acts of Massachusetts, Connecticut, Rhode Island, Vermont, New York, New Hampshire, New Jersey, and Maine demonstrate the progression of human equality. In addition, the laws governing Ohio, Indiana, Illinois, Michigan, Iowa, and Minnesota all recognize "the great principle of universal freedom" in legislation that accomplished abolition by either immediate or gradual means.[52] Even Delaware, he remarks, although a slave state, has in its constitution a declaration of universal and equal rights to which, unaccountably, "they have added no explicit qualification."[53]

As for the attempt in slave states to label slavery a "*domestic* institution," it "sounds very pretty and is quite convenient" but it only shows how "people smooth things over as much as possible" like "all wrong doing which can't be justified" when the "love of gain is too strong to give up the practice." He calls it "a mockery of human wretchedness" that "satisfies no man of sense of who is not under the dominion of avarice or hardened by familiarity with suffering." The talk of "Preachers and Christian slaveholders" about "doing their *duty* to their slaves . . . is all a sham."[54]

In responding to the idea of slavery as domestic institution and the "palaver which we so often hear from slave holders about the mild and humane treatment of their slaves," Caruthers turns again to Stroud in a critique of the legislation of the slave states. Utilizing Stroud he criticizes the legislature for the trial and punishment of slaves, regulations for food

51. Ibid., 359.
52. Ibid., 346–56.
53. Ibid., 358.
54. Ibid., 391.

and clothing allowances and various other laws in the states of Maryland, Virginia, Louisiana, Mississippi, Missouri, South Carolina, Georgia, Tennessee, and North Carolina.

In the latter, his home state, masters were required to give slaves "*one quart* of corn per day, but no meat nor anything else; and they were punished severely for even catching *fish* in certain streams . . . And that was kind and humane treatment?"[55] North Carolina did not list as other states the specific crimes for which a slave could be put to death, such as Virginia's "*seventy one* crimes punishable with death if committed by slaves," but "a slave who runs away and hides in the swamps, if he resists or attempts to escape when pursued, may be outlawed, and anyone who can may shoot him, or knock him in the head with a bludgeon or kill him in whatever way he finds most convenient; but," Caruthers sarcastically concludes, "we need not go into any further details for what has been said furnishes sufficient proof of their mild and humane treatment!"[56] Caruthers describes the slave laws as "an outrage on humanity and an everlasting reproach to a protestant people" and "these *croppings* and cruel whippings . . . for their violations of . . . laws, little petty offenses, for a large proportion of which a white man would be subject to no punishment whatever, are deemed a *mild and humane treatment* for Africans who are chargeable with the 'atrocious crime' of having a dark skin."[57] In the case of trials of slaves in which "many an innocent man has been . . . condemned to death" Caruthers writes,

> Now consider the prejudices of the white man against the negro, the contempt with which the latter is treated and the little value put upon his life and happiness compared with that of a white man and judge of the wrong to which he is liable; but all this is 'mild and humane treatment' for human beings, made of the same flesh and blood with ourselves; redeemed by the same sacrifice, regenerated by the same grace and entitled to the same inheritance of everlasting glory and blessedness—because they are of a different color.[58]

Any attempt to sustain American slavery by reforming it is doomed not only because of greed and avarice but also because it fails to meet the Exodus standard:

55. Ibid., 378.
56. Ibid., 381.
57. Ibid., 386.
58. Ibid., 388.

CHAPTER 4: THE PURPOSE OF EXODUS 10:3

> The Lord did not authorize Moses and Aaron to charge Pharaoh with his cruelty to the Israelites nor to urge upon him the necessity of a mild and humane treatment, but positively and absolutely to demand their release. Let them go was reiterated to him with the annunciation of every plague from first to last and as nothing more was required nothing less would exempt him from the terrible inflictions of God's displeasure.[59]

Beyond emancipation, like many of his era, Caruthers believed in some form of African colonization as a solution to the American slavery crisis. In an earlier section Caruthers recounts the efforts of "Dr. Finley and his co-adjutors."[60] In 1816, Robert Finley a Presbyterian minister in New Jersey organized the American Colonization Society with the help of the nation's political leaders believing that "should the time ever come when slavery shall not exist in these states, yet if the people of colour remain among us, the effect of their presence will be unfavourable to our industry and morals."[61] For Finley, "the great desire of those whose minds are impressed with the subject [of colonization] is to give opportunity to the free people of color to rise to their proper level and at the same time to provide a powerful means of putting an end to the slave trade and sending civilization and Christianity to Africa."[62]

The society came into existence along with many other voluntary societies in the early nineteenth century. Fund raising for the manumission of slaves and their transportation to Africa reached a climax with the departure of the first ship for the new nation of Liberia in 1820. Caruthers writes of "the establishment of blacks . . . on the western coast of Africa" whose "prosperity . . . so far cannot be viewed in any other light than as providential events of more importance than we can now estimate." Organized and founded by "men of piety, foresight, and large minded patriotism," the colony has "men of ability at the head of their government, in the army and in all the learned professions" as well as "churches of all the protestant denominations." "Their prosperity," he writes, "has in fact been greater than the first settlements planted in this country attained in the same length of

---

59. Caruthers, *American Slavery*, 392.
60. Ibid., 184.
61. Cited in Fred Hood *Reformed America*, 129.
62. Cited in Saneh *Abolitionists Abroad*, 97.

time."⁶³ But he is also certain that nothing less than a complete emancipation will assure the success of colonization.

> That the free blacks in the North, where there are half a million or not much less could never be persuade, with few exceptions, to immigrate to the colony in Africa, when it was manifestly their interest to do so, ought to be regarded as another significant fact, especially when it is known that they reason which they have always assigned, as stated in the Northern papers a few years ago, was that they did not feel like leaving their native land while their country men were in bondage.⁶⁴

Their reluctance mirrors Moses who "would not forsake Egypt entirely while his people were in bondage and chose rather to suffer affliction with them than to be called the son of Pharaoh's daughter or sway the scepter over subjugated millions."⁶⁵

By 1860 Liberia had failed to become the Christian pilot for the nation of Africa, but was instead in chaos. Few slaves would actually be manumitted or freed over the next forty years, possibly four thousand by 1860.⁶⁶ Belief in the inferiority of blacks probably assured the initial success and establishment of over two hundred local ACS groups in both northern and southern communities. Comprised of abolitionists as well as evangelicals with a millennial vision for a Christian African nation, but requiring the support of slaveholders whose only interest was the removal of the socially unacceptable free Negroes from slave states, the American Colonization Society became an ineffective movement.⁶⁷

In a passage that may indicate Caruthers was somehow involved in appealing to slaveholders to emancipate their slaves, he complains of the excuses given. "Often within the last thirty years" he writes, "when urging upon slaveholders the duty of emancipating their slaves, the question has been asked, what would we do with them? Would you have them remain here among us? Or where would you send them?" Upon hearing of colonization " the reply has generally been that their transportation could never

---

63. Caruthers, *American Slavery*, 181–82.
64. Ibid., 169.
65. Ibid.
66. Ahlstrom, *A Religious History of the American People*, 650–51.
67. For a fuller discussion of the American Colonization Society and its antecedents see Staudenraus, *The African Colonization Movement, 1816-1865*; Shay, "Antislavery Movement in North Carolina Princeton"; Saneh, *Abolitionists Abroad*, 91–97, 182–237.

CHAPTER 4: THE PURPOSE OF EXODUS 10:3

be effected or not in a hundred years and that the attempt would be useless; but this was only the suggestion of avarice and could not be meant as a serious objection. . . . people can always accomplish anything in the world that they ought to do." Caruthers responds, "The money expended and the property already destroyed in this war would pay for every "nigger" in the south, at a moderate wholesale price, and then pay for his transportation to the shores of Africa. The Lord has manifestly a great work for them to do on that widely extended continent."[68]

The American Colonization Society's mission to transport freed blacks back to Christianize the African nation was in part based on the argument that the elevation of Africans required an environment away from the deeply engrained racism of America where the coexistence of two races was believed impossible.[69] Princeton Seminary's support of African colonization is probably an important early influence in the development of Caruthers's views.

The faculty of Princeton decisively favored African colonization as means to the gradual elimination of slavery.[70] As mentioned above, the organization was established in 1816 by Robert Finley, a New Jersey Presbyterian minister. In Finley's *Thoughts on Colonization* he proposed the formation of a national society to utilize free Negroes in the evangelization of Africa. He briefly united future proslavery and future abolition advocates into one impressive national organization.[71] Subscriptions by the seminary to magazines supporting colonization such as the *African Repository and Colonial Journal* and *Freedom Journal* reinforce this impression. The seminary's subscription to *Freedom Journal* was cancelled when its editor began to oppose the colonization movement, prompting one of the professors, Archibald Alexander, to comment, "If I were a coloured man, I would not hesitate a moment to relinquish a country where a black skin and the lowest degree of degradation are so identified that scarcely any manifestation of talent, scarcely any course of good conduct can entirely overcome the contempt which exists."[72]

---

68. Caruthers, *American Slavery*, 364.

69. Rael, "A Common Nature, A United Destiny," 193; Davis, *The Problem of Slavery in the Age of Revolution 1770-1823*, 199; Dain, *A Hideous Monster of the Mind*, 112-48.

70. Calhoun, *Princeton Seminary*, 328; Dain, *A Hideous Monster of the Mind*, 132.

71. Tise, *Proslavery*, 52.

72. Cited in Dain, *A Hideous Monster of the Mind*, 132.

Alexander's comment reveals an outlook that is probably similar to Caruthers's own. "According to our imperfect views," Caruthers writes, "it would not be best for them to turn them loose and let them remain here among the whites, where they would have no certain means of support."[73] In Caruthers thinking, colonization complemented emancipation because it provided a way around the racism of his age. It met the needs of the freed slaves for elevation and furthermore assured the conversion of Africa to Christianity.

In colonization, Caruthers discerned an Exodus pattern in which the freed Africans lived apart from white society as he makes clear in the following description:

> The Israelites must have been all collected, by some means or other, into one place so that all could move off together in one compact and well organized body; and whatever disposal is to be finally made, of the blacks, we presume that some place of *rendevous* will be assigned them by Him who claims their services, watches over their destiny and now demands their release. If they are to have a territory and a government of their own on this continent, the cotton and sugar regions of ? would seem to be the most suitable place for them or if the Lord designs that they shall be returned to their father land, the Gulf of Mexico will be the most convenient place for their embarkation. A large majority of them are there already and in some of the states their relative proportion to the whites is nearly three to one. The remainder can soon be taken thither and then they will be ready to occupy those states or the islands in the Gulf of Mexico, or return to Africa, as *the pillar of cloud and of fire* may direct. When the Israelites assembled at their place of *rendezvous*, they had the promised land in view, the land given to them by the oath of Him who cannot lie; but none of them, not even their leaders, knew by what route they should be led nor how long they would be on the way. Although the Holy One of Israel demands the release of the four millions now held in a degrading and oppressive bondage among us and will not cease to visit us, at longer or shorter intervals, with the judgments of his hand he has not told us [until they are released] where is the land which he has designed for them, nor precisely where nor when nor how he designs to employ them in his service; but our duty is to yield a cordial and prompt compliance with his requisitions and trust him for the results. We are in the midst of great and mysterious movements which we cannot control and the *finale* of which

---

73. Caruthers, *American Slavery*, 363.

CHAPTER 4: THE PURPOSE OF EXODUS 10:3

> is beyond our ken; but we have the sure word of command and we have the Providence of the God pointing out our course as we advance. Pharaoh and his servants would not take the warnings given them by the divinely commissioned leaders of Israel nor yield to the pressure of the calamities which were coming upon them with increasing severity, until it was too late.[74]

Just as Israel went out of Egypt so the slaves would escape their American Pharaohs. America, like ancient Egypt, was in the "midst of great and mysterious movements." Caruthers concludes his manuscript with the familiar hope of African colonization leading to "a moral reformation in that ill fated country."[75] He looks forward to the time when freed slaves "with the invigorated powers of a new and ever increasing life . . . return to the land of their forefathers, carrying with them their inestimable boon of a pure Christianity and all the blessings of civilization."[76] In the future of freed slaves he believes that "emancipation whenever and however it may be effected, will be like a resurrection to the slaves . . . raising them up from the very lowest depths of degradation . . . with invigorated powers of a new and ever increasing life"; returning " to the land of their forefathers, carrying with them the inestimable boon of a pure Christianity and all the blessings of civilization."[77] In the last passage of the manuscript Caruthers mingles his hopes for colonization with Israel's enslavement and exodus.

> If the slaves of this country were returned to their fatherland and the slave trade were abolished and no calamity should befall the noble enterprise now begun we have no doubt that in half a century from this time the hundred millions of Africans there ready for organization and improvement will form one of the most commercial and important nations in the world. The descendants of Abraham were six generations in Egypt, about the length of time that the Africans have been in bondage here and during the latter part of that time . . . they were sent to the lowest depths of degradation and wretchedness; but in a short time they were raised up to be the most prosperous, powerful, and honored nation on earth; and the degradation of the African race for the last two or three centuries we regard as a certain indication of a corresponding elevation to national prosperity and greatness.[78]

---

74. Ibid., 166–67.
75. Ibid., 402.
76. Ibid.
77. Ibid.
78. Ibid., 403.

Summary

In the final section of his manuscript Caruthers has urged the "attentive reader" to "perceive that the slavery question should be considered . . . with more general honesty and thoroughness than it has hitherto been discussed." Using the legislation of the slave states, he proves the "immense wrong which is done to slaves" and "the injury slavery does to society at large" and "the claims of God to their services which can be neither denied, evaded, nor resisted."[79] Unless emancipation takes place, Caruthers fears "the scorn of the civilized world, or at least of the Protestant world will rest upon us and the cry of untold millions whom we now have it in our power to elevate and bless and save will call down the wrath of heaven upon us and upon our posterity."[80] Since emancipation follows the pattern of Exodus, so the freed slaves should follow the example of the Hebrews who left Egypt. The slaves could never expect that once freed, America's racism would allow them to thrive, but they should journey to Africa to Christianize the continent and establish a new society.

If Caruthers had read Albert Barnes' comment that "slavery interferes with the natural right which every human being has, to worship God according to his own views of what is true," he would have thought it fell short.[81] Caruthers believes a wider range of natural rights and instincts, especially the desire for education, family, and possessions, is subverted by slavery. He uses Rom 12:1 to expand the concept of worship by noting its interchangeability with "service" and First Corinthians 6:20 to emphasize the unity of body and soul. He would have agreed entirely with Robert Forbes' statement that "slavery not only constituted an infringement of the enslaved person's inalienable rights; perhaps even more urgently, it rendered him or her incapable of discharging solemn responsibilities to man and to God that could neither be revoked nor delegated."[82] Liberty is the required condition for service to God and such service is the purpose of the Exodus demand for the freedom.

---

79. Ibid., 338.
80. Caruthers, *American Slavery*, 342.
81. Barnes, *An Inquiry into the Scriptural View of Slavery*, 350–51.
82. Forbes, "Slavery and the Evangelical Enlightenment," 73.

Chapter 5: Presbyterians and American Slavery

THE AMERICAN SLAVERY CONTROVERSY was the supreme challenge to the unity of nineteenth-century evangelicals and their moral guidance of the nation.[1] The problem of slavery tested as never before their ability to apply the Bible to a dominant social issue. Previous to the rise of abolitionism, America was increasingly riddled with deep conflict over slavery. As early as 1820 luminaries of the Republic such as John Quincy Adams believed slavery "the great and foul stain upon the North American Union." He envisioned the nation's dissolution over slavery "and a war between the two severed portions of the Union" resulting in the "extirpation of slavery from this whole continent." For Adams the abolition of slavery was "contemplation worthy of the most exalted soul."[2]

The maturing of America's seminal commitment to human dignity as seen in the convictions of Adams is mirrored in the theological turmoil throughout the churches of America. Special attention should be given to the Presbyterians in this regard. Another writer has said that the dispute over slavery in American Protestantism could be characterized as "a fraternal dispute between Calvinist factions espousing different theological views of the human condition, the role of social institutions, and of freedom itself."[3] The following account considers the slavery question within Presbyterian communions and amongst a few of Caruthers's ministerial colleagues during the early nineteenth century. It provides a sample of the national conscience deeply agitated by the slavery issue, at first hoping for a gradual end of the institution and attempting interim compromises, but ultimately drawn into the war prophesied by Adams. In this chapter the early declarations of Presbyterians against slavery before 1830 and the views of both proslavery and antislavery ministers after 1830 are con-

1. Crowther, *Southern Protestants Slavery and Secession*, 57; Noll, *America's God*, 386.
2. Cited in Miller, *Arguing About Slavery*, 187, 193.
3. Hutchison, *The Bible and Slavery, a Test of Ethical Method*.

sidered with special attention to the exchange in 1858 between George Armstrong and Courtland Van Rensselaer. The second part of the chapter considers Caruthers's value for contemporary consideration of the biblical debate over slavery.

American Presbyterians

American religious conflict over slavery within Presbyterianism dates back to the refusal of the Reverend Alexander McLeod to accept a call because slaveholders were in the congregation. The record states "the Presbytery now having the subject regularly before them, resolved to purge the Church of this dreadful evil" and "enacted that no slaveholder should be retained in their communion."[4] In 1802, McLeod, a minister of the Reformed Presbyterian Church in America, serving in New York, published a treatise denouncing slavery as "a manifest violation of four precepts of the Decalogue." McLeod believed "the whole decalogue is violated" by the practice of slavery.[5] His answer to those objecting that slavery was tolerated in the early Church, would be repeated throughout the debate: "If such practices are not formally mentioned and condemned in the New Testament, the principles from which they proceed are reprobated in the strongest terms. The whole system of slavery is opposite to the spirit of *that* religion which is righteousness and peace."[6] For those who could not afford to simply release their slaves because of their investment, he told them to "do justice" and "deal mercifully with your servant." Slaveholders should calculate the wages and "when the wages which might have been annually earned shall have amounted to the purchase money, and lawful interest" the slave should be "set immediately at liberty from your control."[7]

McLeod's reaction to slavery was echoed by Caruthers's own Presbyterian communion, the General Assembly of the Presbyterian Church in 1818. When the assembly dealt with the issue of slavery in America, the following declaration was made:

---

4. "A Historical View of the State of Reformed Presbyterian Church in America, Until the Ratification of Their Testimony in May, 1806" in *Reformation Principles Exhibited by the Reformed Presbyterian Church in the United States of America*, 102–40, esp. 138.

5. McLeod, *Negro Slavery Unjustifiable*, 13.

6. Ibid., 37.

7. Ibid., 37–39.

CHAPTER 5: PRESBYTERIANS AND AMERICAN SLAVERY

> The General Assembly of the Presbyterian church, having taken into consideration the subject of SLAVERY, think proper to make known their sentiments upon it to the churches and people under care. We consider the voluntary enslaving of one part of the human race by another as a gross violation of the most precious and sacred rights of human nature, as utterly inconsistent with the law of God which requires us to love our neighbor as ourselves, and as totally irreconcilable with the spirit and principles of the gospel of Christ, which enjoin that 'all things whatsoever ye would that men should do to you, do ye even so to them.' Slavery creates a paradox in the moral system; it exhibits rational, accountable, and immortal beings in such circumstances as scarcely to leave them the power of moral action. It exhibits them as dependent on the will of others whether they receive religious instruction; whether they shall know and worship the true God; whether they shall enjoy the ordinances of the gospel; whether they shall perform the duties and cherish the endearments of husbands and wives, parents and children, neighbors and friends; whether they shall preserve their chastity and purity, or regard the dictates of justice and humanity. Such are some of the consequences of slavery,—consequences not imaginary, but which connect themselves with its very existence. The evils to which the slave is *always* exposed often take place in fact and in their very worst degree and form; and where all of them do not take place, as we rejoice to say that in many instances, through the influence of the principles of humanity and religion on the minds of the masters, they do not, still, the slave is deprived of his natural right, degraded as a human being, and exposed to the danger of passing into the hands of a master who may inflict upon him all the hardships and injuries which inhumanity and avarice may suggest.[8]

The Assembly's declaration is thorough, calling for "the unwearied endeavors to correct the errors of former times, and as speedily as possible to efface this blot on our holy religion, and to obtain the complete abolition of slavery throughout Christendom, and if possible throughout the world" and "exertions to EFFECT A TOTAL ABOLITION OF SLAVERY."[9] Subsequent assemblies and Presbyterians writers debated the precise meaning and implications of the 1818 declaration, but it stands as typical

---

8. *Extracts from the Minutes of the General Assembly of the Presbyterian Church*, 28–30.

9. Ibid., 30.

of the sentiments expressed among American Presbyterians in the early nineteenth century.[10]

Only ten years later, the peaceful abolition of slavery must have seemed possible because of growing support in the South for its end. In 1827 the abolitionist Benjamin Lundy reported 106 antislaverysocieties in the Upper South with 5,150 members predominantly located in eastern Tennessee and North Carolina, compared to the total membership of 1,475 in similar societies of the North at that time. In Caruthers's own region, the Piedmont of North Carolina, fifty such societies existed, more than double the twenty-four organizations established in the entire North.[11] But any enthusiasm for liberty in the Upper South was not sustained. By 1830, the fear of slave revolts and abolitionist agitation helped to galvanize a strong proslavery consensus throughout the southern states committed to the preservation of slavery in their social order.[12]

The root of the division among evangelicals over slavery, however, was neither a fear of a slave uprising nor disagreement over the tactics of the abolitionists, but a genuine conflict over the meaning of their Scriptures. For those who sought its end American slavery violated ethical and humanitarian principles derived from the Bible. "Slavery is," wrote Theodore Dwight Weld, "the eternal distinction between a person and a thing, blotted out . . . the rational, immortal principle, consecrated by God."[13]

For proslavery thinkers the Bible's regulation of slavery was plain proof that American slavery was acceptable if practiced according to those instructions. The southern dependence on a straight-forward reading of the Bible was the most critical part of its defense of slavery. No views or theories could ever expect a hearing in the deeply religious South unless grounded in Scripture. In their view, Christianity in the northern states was more influenced by personal and romantic notions, whereas, in the South, one's religious ideas were more biblically and doctrinally based. Elizabeth Fox-Genovese and Eugene Genovese have previously provided an account of slavery's defense, charting the shift of Southern slaveholders from their understanding of slavery as a necessary evil and economic precondition of southern prosperity to defending slavery as a positive good under what they believed to be the encroaching shadow of the north's unchristian

---

10. "Slavery in the Church Courts," 516–56.
11. Fox-Genovese and Genovese, *Mind of the Master Class*, 231.
12. Cheseborough, Introduction to *Clergy Dissent*, xii.
13. Weld, *The Bible Against Slavery*, 19.

CHAPTER 5: PRESBYTERIANS AND AMERICAN SLAVERY

culture. The writings of James H. Thornwell and Robert L. Dabney are representative of this defense. What began as a convenient source of labor became, in the southern mind, a divinely sanctioned social order, highly preferable to the increasingly godless and industrialized northern system with its abuse of free labor.

Among Presbyterians, however, belief in American slavery's evolution from a necessary evil to a divinely authorized institution had its skeptics. Albert Barnes' *An Inquiry into the Scriptural View of Slavery* challenged the proslavery argument typified by Thornwell and Dabney, prompting George Armstrong's proslavery defense and pointed rebuttal of Barnes, *The Christian Doctrine of Slavery*. Barnes' affiliation with the New School movement—Presbyterians who were less rigid Calvinists and who favored revivals—and its less traditional identity within Presbyterianism would cause him to be easily dismissed by his more traditional Old School opponents. But as the critique of Armstrong's work by his own Old School colleague, Courtland Van Rennselaer, reveals, the division over slavery could not be reduced to differences between New School and Old School Presbyterians. Even among Old School proponents, considered to be the more conservative and traditional of Presbyterians, significant interpretive disagreements over the Bible and slavery marked the emergence of a larger biblical argument opposed to slavery. A brief look at these Presbyterians and their work provide a sample of their interpretive disagreement and the early stages of an argument that, in the description of Mark Noll, moved "from the literal words of the Bible to biblically normed responses to new or developing situations," one that might even allow for "apparent contradictions between bare words of particular texts of Scripture."[14]

Southern Presbyterian James H. Thornwell wrote that "if men had drawn their conclusions from the Bible, it would no more have entered into any human head to denounce Slavery as a sin, than to denounce monarchy, aristocracy or poverty." Antislavery writers had listened "to what they falsely considered as primitive intuitions, or, as necessary deductions from primitive cognitions, and then ... gone to the Bible to confirm the crochets of their vain philosophy." Thornwell was ready to acknowledge "primitive principals in morals which lie at the root of human consciousness. But the question is, How are we to distinguish them?" A "subjective feeling of certainty" against slavery was "no adequate criterion." One could not know when such "certainty indicates a primitive cognition, and when it does not." The only real

---

14. Noll, *America's God*, 416.

criteria for the evaluation of such certainty would have to be universal. If humanity "has everywhere condemned" slavery and "if all human laws have prohibited it as crime" then slavery is in the "same category with malice, murder, and theft" and "we are willing to renounce it forever. But what if the overwhelming majority of mankind have approved it?"[15]

In Thornwell's thinking antislavery theologians went to the Bible "determined to find a particular result, and the consequence is, that they leave having *made*, instead of having *interpreted* Scripture."[16] It was "the antagonism of Northern and Southern sentiment on the subject of Slavery" that was "at the root of all the difficulties" that had dismembered the nation " and involved us in the horrors of an unnatural war."[17] Slavery was "an existing element of society . . . actually sanctioned by Christ and His Apostles."[18] Because it was part of society and addressed by biblical texts, it was arguably essential.

Robert L. Dabney's vision of slavery "under the restraints of statute law" mirrors Thornwell's similar emphasis on "the real rights of the slave."[19] Although Dabney's views on slavery were not published until 1867 and later, his views are representative of the southern call to acknowledge slavery according to biblical instruction preceding the war. Presbyterians in the southern states knew that the system of slavery had to be more humane in order to comply with the Bible's teaching and believed that when properly located within the Christian household and culture, slavery itself was not only not evil, it was the only biblical hope of their society. Dabney believed that without the familial, organic relationship as existed between masters and slaves, free laborers, as in the northern states, would be exploited, brutalized, and could be left to starvation. But slavery in the care of a deeply Christian people, committed to the hierarchy they found in the Bible, provided the social dependency that would curtail such abuses.[20]

In the context of Old School Southern Presbyterians who defended slavery, Dabney, like Thornwell, was among those who cast a vision for

---

15. Thornwell, *Ecclesiastical*, 462.
16. Ibid., 456–57.
17. Ibid., 454.
18. Ibid., 456–57.
19. Cited in Chesebrough, *Clergy Dissent*, 190; Dabney, *Discussions of Robert L. Dabney*, 3:333.
20. Dabney, *Defense of Virginia*, 297–331.

the institution of slavery based upon the Bible.[21] With a pronounced commitment to the authority of the Bible, they were templates of Presbyterian churchmen, like those envisioned by Charles Colcock Jones in his commencement address to the senior class of the Theological Seminary of the Synod of South Carolina and Georgia: they were "decided men" whose opinions were built upon "the plain declarations of the Bible alone."[22]

For Dabney slavery was biblically established and socially responsible. Blacks were not responsible enough to be free but could be happy, useful, and productive as slaves. The relationship between master and slave was construed paternally. A slave is like a minor child in his mental capacity, but unlike a child, he never matures. He is "deemed by the law unfitted for his own safe control" and placed "in the hands of a citizen supposed by the law to be more competent."[23] Even though slavery was involuntary, to attack such an institution was tantamount to overthrowing the hierarchical nature of relationships taught by the Bible, not unlike an attack on "the righteousness of the parental authority over minors, and indeed every form of governmental restraint of magistrates over individuals not grounded in conviction of crime."[24] Like Thornwell, he recognized slavery as "a social element in all states, from the dawn of history until the present period," asserting that "the slightest caution" against it could not be found in the Bible.[25] He was certain "that the Word is on our side, and the teachings of Abolitionism are clearly of a rationalistic origin, of infidel tendency, and only sustained by reckless and licentious perversions of the meaning of the Sacred text."[26]

Albert Barnes' *An Inquiry into the Scriptural View of Slavery*, however, presented an interpretation of the Bible's teaching on slavery that contradicted his southern colleagues. He argued that the slavery of the South could never be reformed and that it should not be confused with conditions of apprenticeship or serfdom.[27] Rejecting Dabney's assertion that questioning slavery was an attack on the hierarchy of the family, Barnes countered

---

21. Fox-Genovese and Genovese, "The Divine Sanction of Social Order," 211–23.
22. Cited in Crowther, *Southern Protestants Slavery and Secession*, 50.
23. Dabney, *Discussions*, 3:332; cf. Thornwell, "The Rights and the Duties of Masters," 177–92.
24. Dabney, *Discussions*, 3:332.
25 Cited in Anderson, "Presbyterians Meet the Slavery Problem," 9.
26. Dabney, *Defense of Virginia*, 21.
27 Barnes, *An Inquiry into the Scriptural Views of Slavery*, 44.

that "nature not force, has made the condition of a minor." The relationship of the parent and the child is "a natural relation, that of master and slave is not."[28] For Barnes, slavery, because it was a violation of natural law, was plainly "contrary to the spirit of the Bible." Human equality was an absolute truth, and the antislavery mission was "to secure the conviction everywhere, in the church and out of it, that slavery is evil, and only evil."[29]

Dabney and Barnes illustrate a critical difference between proslavery and antislavery thought regarding the relationship of the individual to society. Antislavery thought presented social order as dependent on equal individuals who were free to do as they pleased with their labor or resources. Social order and its institutions all derived from the freedom and equality of individuals. For Barnes the freedom of the individual was an absolute and differences among people, innate or otherwise, did not constitute a basis for the limitation of the freedom that was a fundamental right. For Dabney the freedom of an individual was not a disembodied idea but a particular truth for those who had proven themselves capable of its proper exercise. Freedom was subservient to order, and slavery was the foundation of an interdependent and hierarchal society. People had "different relations to each other in society, corresponding to their differing capacities and fitnesses." There were "different classes of human beings in the commonwealth" with "different grades" and privileges were given "according to their different natures and qualifications."[30]

As a New School Presbyterian, Barnes would count as one of those theologians Thornwell had in mind who did not interpret the Bible but made it conform to their own opinions. The Old School/New School division in 1837 among Presbyterians distinguished less strict Calvinists who favored revivals and a broader evangelicalism (New School) from the more orthodox Calvinists who emphasized adherence to the Westminster Confession of Faith (Old School). Barnes' comprehensive work, *Inquiry into the Scriptural Views of Slavery*, presented an intensive study of slavery in the Old and New Testament that he argued bore little resemblance to American slavery. Barnes himself professed the centrality of the Bible in America in the Presbyterians' debate over slavery as well as any other issue. He believed that "there is not a judge on any bench who would pronounce a decision that would be clearly contrary to a principle laid down in the Sacred Scriptures; there is not

28. Ibid., 42.
29. Ibid., 377.
30. Dabney, *Discussions*, 3:23.

a department of government that would not admit that if the Bible has settled a question, it is final."[31] Barnes would later revise some of arguments and hear other points of his critique of slavery effectively countered by his opponents.[32] His argument against the association of slavery with the hierarchy of the family, however, as well as his insistence on the impossibility of reforming slavery, remained unchanged and convincing.

Barnes also examines the plight of the Hebrew people and their deliverance from bondage.[33] Like Caruthers, he saw the condemnation of slavery in divine providence and appealed to the Exodus account as a pattern. He believed that the "existence of slavery is attended with a series of inevitable calamities" and that God's "sentiments on the subject of slavery" could be discerned from the "remarkable interventions of heaven."[34] He asks whether conclusions can be drawn for American slavery and other forms of oppression from the intervention of God recorded in the Exodus story, and answers that "the divine declarations in regard to Egyptian bondage, and the expressions of disapprobation of what occurred in Egypt, are applicable to the system of things in this country."[35]

> The conclusions which I am authorized to draw from this signal interposition in behalf of an oppressed people, are, that such oppression is hateful to God; that the acts of cruelty and wickedness which are necessary to perpetuate such oppression, are the objects of his abhorrence; that wherever the same system of things exists which did there, it must be equally offensive to him; that it is his will that, if a foreign race have been held in servitude, they should be allowed to go free; and that if those who hold them in bondage will not allow them to go free when he commands it, he will, by his own providence, bring such a series of desolating judgments on a people, that however hardened their hearts may have been towards the oppressed and the down trodden and however much they may be disposed, like Pharaoh, to say, "Who is Jehovah, that we should obey his voice to let the people go? (Ex. v. 2;) he will pursue them their maledictions, as Pharaoh pursued the ransomed Hebrews with his embattled hosts. If we may draw an inference, also, from this case, in regard to the *manner*

---

31. Barnes, *An Inquiry into the Scriptural View of Slavery*, 21.

32. Noll, *America's God*, 390; Harrill, "Use of the New Testament in the American Slave Controversy," 166.

33. Barnes, *An Inquiry into the Scriptural View of Slavery*, 96–104.

34. Ibid., 102, 97.

35. Ibid., 99.

in which God would have such a people restored to freedom, it would be in favor of *immediate emancipation*.[36]

George Armstrong's *The Christian Doctrine of Slavery* typifies southern reaction to Albert Barnes. Armstrong, the pastor of the Presbyterian Church in Norfolk, Virginia, presents an argument, like many works of the era, stating that "it appears to us too clear to admit of either denial or doubt, that the Scriptures do sanction slave-holding."[37] Armstrong's work treats the entire range of New Testament texts. Slavery in the Old Testament was "expressly permitted by divine command, and under the New Testament ... nowhere forbidden or denounced, but on the contrary, acknowledged to be consistent with the Christian character and profession." Like Dabney and others, he agreed the slave trade was wrong because it involved the crime of kidnapping, but considered any condemnation of owning slaves to be "a direct impeachment of the Word of God."[38]

Armstrong's work is important because it was critically reviewed by Cortland Van Rensselaer, another Old School Presbyterian and the editor of *Presbyterian Magazine*.[39] The review of Armstrong's work, quickly escalated into an exchange of letters. Their published correspondence provides a rare glimpse beneath the veneer of consensus among northern and southern Presbyterians prior to the war.

Van Rensselaer, an Old School Presbyterian like Armstrong, was moderately critical of Armstrong's book and believed that " Christians, whose minds and hearts are imbued with the spirit of their Lord, cannot regard with complacency an institution whose origin is wrong, and whose continuance depends upon the inferior condition of a large class of their fellow-men."[40] Armstrong was not moved. At the outset of the exchange spanning over the months of 1858, Van Rensselaer offered to "cordially acquit" him "of any intention to contribute to the propagation of extreme opinions"[41] but at the end of the correspondence he complained, "I fear that, without intending it, you have lowered the tone of public sentiment

---

36. Barnes, *An Inquiry into the Scriptural View of Slavery*, 104.

37. Armstrong, *The Christian Doctrine of Slavery*, 145; cf. Priest, *Bible Defence of Slavery*; Thornwell, "The Rights and the Duties of Masters," 177–92.

38 Armstrong, *The Christian Doctrine of Slavery*, 16, 145.

39. I am indebted to Dr. Jack Maddex, University of Oregon, for bringing this exchange to my attention.

40. Rensselaer, "Dr. Van Rensselaer's Reply to Dr. Armstrong," 24.

41. Ibid., 26.

CHAPTER 5: PRESBYTERIANS AND AMERICAN SLAVERY

wherever your influence extends, and have impaired the obligations of conscientious Christians on this great subject."[42] In Armstrong's opinion "the word of God contains no deliverance, expressly or clearly implied, respecting emancipation."[43] Van Rensselaer countered that a hermeneutic or interpretive guideline for situations not expressly envisioned in Scripture was necessary for dealing with American slavery.

> The Church has a right to expound, and to apply, the word of God, in reference to all the relations of life, and to all the changing aspects of society. The exposition and application must, of course, be consistent with the spirit and principles of the Bible, but they are not limited to the mere word of its letter, nor to any general or universal formula of expression. From the nature of the case, exposition requires enlargement of scriptural statement, and application implies a regard to providential developments and to the varying circumstances of social and public life…The Church has, in every age, the right to expound the sacred Scriptures according to the light granted by the Holy Spirit, and to apply its interpretation to all cases, judged to be within its spiritual jurisdiction.[44]

The correspondence between Armstrong and Van Rensselaer is representative of the chasm that could not be bridged between Presbyterians, as well as the broader movement among Evangelicals away from the "Reformed literal hermeneutic" that had been practiced since the nation's inception.[45] The Bible, the book that had been the unifying central cultural document of the American republic, became the source of opposing forces in the Christian society evangelicals had so successfully forged.[46] Proslavery and antislavery advocates with equal estimation of the Bible's authority espoused contrary interpretations as they faced the ethical question of their era.

Mark Noll believes that an orthodox, non-literal alternative to the reformed literal approach existed that would have soundly condemned slavery but such an alternative could not be embraced by a culture where any compromise on the literalist view constituted an attack on the Bible itself. In particular he believes that conservative and Reformed Presbyterians

42. Rensselaer, "Dr. Van Rensselaer's Second Rejoinder," 553.
43. Rensselaer, "Dr. Van Rensselaer's Reply to Dr. Armstrong," 77.
44. Ibid.
45. Noll, *America's God*, 367–85.
46. Goen, *Broken Churches, Broken Nation*, 127; Crowther, *Southern Protestants Slavery and Secession*, 7.

such as Charles Hodge of Princeton had the insight to see that in America, a "nation influenced by eighteen centuries of Christian development," there could be "biblically normed responses to new or developing situations" unlike the cultural and political contexts of Old or New Testament, but a "move from the literal words of the Bible" was required.[47] Their failure to advance such thinking and adjudicate the slavery question was, like the rest of evangelicals, complete and catastrophic. Led to war by warring interpretations, America would have to decide who was right by the ordeal of bloody combat. Noll correctly assays the agony of many evangelicals over slavery: "Many Northern Bible-readers and not a few in the South felt that slavery was evil. They somehow knew the Bible supported them in that feeling. Yet when it came to using the Bible . . . the sacred page was snatched out of their hands."[48] Mark Noll sums up the outcome of the evangelical debate over slavery: "The supreme crisis over the Bible was that there existed no apparent biblical resolution to the crisis . . . it was left to those consummate theologians, the Reverend Doctors Ulysses S. Grant and William Tecumseh Sherman, to decide what in fact the Bible actually meant."[49]

The disagreements among Presbyterians over slavery exposed interpretive differences that prevented a genuine consensus and contributed to America's sectional crisis. Caruthers, like Van Rensselaer, demonstrated that the issue of slavery required a hermeneutic or interpretive guideline not limited to the "mere word" or letter of the Bible. Caruthers found such a guideline, however, not in the frequently debated texts of the New Testament, but in the Old Testament book of Exodus. J. Albert Harrill has written that "antislavery and abolitionist interpretations of the New Testament during the American slave controversy . . . pushed biblical exegetes toward a critical hermeneutics, preparing the way for the eventual reception in this country of German higher criticism."[50] On the other hand, according to Harrill and "most embarrassing for today's readers of the Bible," the proslavery defense correctly discerned that "the New Testament contained passages that did not merely recommend subjection of slaves to their masters" but also "signaled acceptance of an organic model of civilization for which subjection was essential." Applying Harrill's conclusions, Caruthers, Van Rensselaer, and other evangelicals who turned

---

47. Noll, *America's God*, 416.
48. Ibid., 398–400.
49. Noll, *The Civil War as a Theological Crisis*, 50.
50. Harrill, "Use of the New Testament in the American Slave Controversy," 150.

to the Bible to argue against slavery "constituted an early form of biblical criticism," and demonstrate the abandonment of a literal approach to the Bible in favor of moral intuition.[51]

Harrill's assessment of the slavery controversy and the progression from literalism to moral intuition focuses on the New Testament, however, unlike Caruthers whose opinions are shaped by the Exodus text. In a untitled section preceding the main manuscript's table of contents, Caruthers comments that "it is said that that neither Jesus nor his Apostles denounced slavery, but recognized it as an existing institution ... in force for time immemorial and prescribed the duties which slave owed to their masters and those which masters owed to their slaves." But, he writes, " neither did they denounce despotic governments; but inculcated obedience and specified the duties which subjects owed to their rulers and those which rulers owed to their subjects, although the Roman government was then one of the most despotic, immoral, and persecuting governments of the world." Are they to be regarded then as sanctioning despotism or designing that it should be perfected?" He answers in another place: "surely no intelligent and sober thinking Christian can believe that these inspired men intended by this language to sanction the despotic, cruel, and persecuting government of Rome, or to forbid them who were thus subjected to change it when they could do so without causing some greater calamity."[52] If Caruthers's answer to his own question is not a persuasive exegetical answer it is because the New Testament does not provide a conclusive answer. Instead, it is the Exodus text that "includes the whole subject, in whatever aspect it may be viewed and whatever may be its consequences, proximate or remote."[53]

Caruthers and Recent Consideration of the Slavery Question

David Barrows, a Baptist minister and an opponent of slavery asks an ominous question in an early publication: "Who, or what party among us, really understands the Bible best? This is not with me to say ... future events will determine it."[54] The nation's Civil War was the specific answer

51. Harrill, "Use of the New Testament in the American Slave Controversy," 174.
52. Caruthers, *American Slavery*, 117.
53. Ibid., 3.
54. Barrow, *Involuntary, Unmerited, Perpetual, Absolute, Hereditary Slavery Examined*, 37.

to Barrow's prophetic question but its disinterred spirit still haunts American historical/theological studies. "To this day," write historians Elizabeth Fox-Genovese and Eugene Genovese, "the southern theologians' scriptural defense of slavery as a system of social relations—not black slavery but slavery per se—has gone unanswered."[55]

In this line of thinking southerners were wrong in a defense of slavery on the basis of race, but right about the Bible's sanctioning of slavery as a social order. According to the Genoveses the southern defense of racially based slavery was simply an illegitimate application of a legitimate biblical argument. They believe the proslavery defense was mistaken in making a case for the social necessity of slavery based on the supposed inferiority of the Africans, a view found nowhere in the Bible. Based on a farfetched interpretation of Ham's curse in the book of Genesis, it legitimized oppression of Africans on the basis of their skin color. But the argument that since slavery was in the Bible and nowhere condemned, and therefore part of an acceptable social order, is considered sound.

For Caruthers, however, the acceptance or role of slavery in the societal forms of the New Testament was not decisive in the debate over American slavery. It was overshadowed by the clearer expressions of God's will for humanity expressed in the Exodus text. His manuscript could be construed as a kind of dialogue between his ethical concerns over American slavery and his understanding of the Bible. In that dialogue, as demonstrated above in chapter 2, the deliverance of Israel is a voice that harmonizes perfectly with creation, redemption, and his instincts, a harmonization the proslavery argument could not achieve. He exemplifies a theologian/pastor dissatisfied with the hermeneutics of his day but also convinced that the Bible, specifically the Exodus account as corroborated by aspects of creation and redemption, answers the proslavery argument and condemns slavery everywhere.

Summary

Among his southern contemporaries Caruthers's manuscript is the singular example of a progressive approach to biblical interpretation among Presbyterians in the Old South. The distinctiveness of his manuscript among Presbyterians and evangelicals in general lies in its strong language, abolitionist leaning, and its extensive development of the Exodus text. Caruthers

---

55. Fox-Genovese and Genovese, *Mind of the Master Class*, 526.

understands the Exodus text as a divine word for the American slavery question, one that resonates with Christianity's understanding of creation and redemption. Impressions from the New Testament that the Bible authorizes slavery have mistaken slavery's presence as divine sanction. The Exodus text provides the clearer word. David Brion Davis has written that the problem of the Bible's apparent authorization or sanctioning of slavery was overcome when American writers made "a sharp distinction between Biblical description and Biblical sanction."[56] Caruthers's manuscript reveals many examples of biblical interpretation observing this distinction, rising above the field of his proslavery contemporaries and showing the height to which an antislavery argument could rise, even in an Old South setting.

---

56. Davis, *The Problem of Slavery in the Age of Revolution 1770–1823*, 552, 553.

Chapter 6: Caruthers and the Enlightenment

THROUGHOUT HIS MANUSCRIPT CARUTHERS makes use of the Declaration of Independence and inalienable rights, concepts of human rights born of the Enlightenment era. As David Brion Davis observes, Christianity in America became equated "not only with political liberty but with the rights of mankind."[1] Caruthers's manuscript's embodiment of this same equation is considered in this chapter. Assessments of human rights as understood by antislavery writers usually stress those writers' dependence on the Enlightenment. For Eugene Genovese and Elizabeth Fox-Genovese antislavery writers "failed to demonstrate that the Bible repudiated slavery" and "primarily . . . appealed to the ideals of the Enlightenment and Declaration of Independence."[2] E. Brooks Holifield asserts matter-of-factly that "the antislavery argument depended on assumptions about equality drawn from the philosophies of the enlightenment," and "the Declaration of Independence became, in effect, a glass through which scripture could be read."[3]

Sources of the Antislavery Argument

It is certain that antislavery writers failed to convince the larger public that the Bible was against slavery, but it is less clear how the ideals of the Enlightenment or the Declaration of Independence influenced their arguments.[4] Caruthers's self-conscious commitment to a biblical foundation underlying his thought is obscured if his use of other sources is mistaken for a dependence on them. The principles he drew from the doctrines of creation and redemption were expressed in the era's appeal to human rights, but, in his

1. Davis, *The Problem of Slavery in the Age of Revolution 1770–1823*, 552.
2. Genovese and Fox-Genovese, *The Mind of the Master Class*, 7, 490.
3. Holifield, *Theology in America*, 503.
4. Davis, *The Problem of Slavery*, 527; Noll, *America's God*, 376.

CHAPTER 6: CARUTHERS AND THE ENLIGHTENMENT

thinking, the inalienable rights of the Declaration of Independence are an application of these principles, not their source. Speaking of "civil and religious rights" he reminds his reader that it has only been "a little more than three quarters of a century since these rights were *embodied* in a declaration of independence."[5] As the philospher Michael Polanyi observes in a different context, "by accepting such teaching man testifies to the existence of grounds on which he can claim freedom."[6] In other words, the universal acceptance of such a political statement as the Declaration of Independence suggests an ontological point of reference, and for Eli Caruthers it is the Bible, specifically and as already discussed, the Genesis account of creation. For Caruthers, political truths are first biblical truths.

Caruthers reinforces his arguments from the Bible's teaching on creation and preservation, not only with American political documents but also the "light of nature" which also denies all claims of slaveholders. He appeals to "the original instincts of our nature" or "natural reason, conscience and those feelings of justice and humanity which may be said to be universal."[7] Biblical language and an emphasis on reason are interwoven throughout the manuscript as exemplified in the following passage:

> Mankind, the most important part of the creation, were made in the image of God and were designed especially to manifest his glory and to enjoy his favor. Made of one blood, as they all were, and constituting as they were designed to do and ought to do, one harmonious family living together in mutual sympathy and acts of kindness, for one to compel others, who have not his strength and have not enjoyed his advantages, to serve him all their life without compensation and to entail that compulsory service upon his unborn posterity, is unjust, inhumane and criminal before high heaven. It is robbing them of their birthright and invading the prerogative of God. According to reason, therefore, or the light of nature, no man and no set of men have a right to make slaves of others without an *express* grant from the Creator, which, on the ground we now occupy, no man will be hardy enough to claim.[8]

Caruthers prepared for ministry at the newly founded Princeton Seminary in 1817, and the above quote reflects his Princeton education and the wider intellectual world in which he lived and wrote. His manuscript

---

5. Caruthers, *American Slavery*, 26.
6. Polanyi, *Personal Knowledge*, 389.
7. Caruthers, preface to *American Slavery*.
8. Caruthers, *American Slavery*, 6.

testifies to the assimilation of Enlightenment philosophy and Republican ideals by American Christianity. His training at Princeton presumably followed the catalogue published by the seminary in 1818. The catalogue lists Ashbel Green as President, and two professors, Archibald Alexander as "Professor of Didactic and Polemic Theology" and Samuel Miller, "Professor of Ecclesiastical History and Church Government". A three year program of instruction is outlined in Princton's catalogue as follows:

> First Year: Orginal Languages of Scripture; Sacred Chronology; Sacred Geography; Biblical and Profane History connected; Jewish Antiquities; The Scriptures in the English Translation; Exegetical Theology.
>
> Second Year: Biblical Criticism; Didactick (sic) Theology and Ecclesiastical History.
>
> Third Year: Didactick Theology continued; Polemick (sic) Theology; Ecclesiastical History continued; Church Government; Compostion and delivery of Sermons; Pastoral Care.[9]

The program of Caruthers's study represents the early form of what would become known around the world as "The Princeton Theology": an emphasis on the inerrancy and authority of the Bible, Christian piety, and a theological perspective structured by the Westminster Confession of Faith.

At this period in its history, Princeton's regard of the Bible "in the very highest sense as the Word of God"[10] is generally regarded as the consensus of Christians until the liberalizing influences of the Enlightenment.[11] But, ironically, Princeton stood against the tide by forging a bond between its own theological enterprise and Baconian common sense.[12] Princeton College's first President, John Witherspoon, had arrived from Scotland in 1768 bringing with him Scottish Common Sense Realism. Witherspoon had a lasting impact on William Graham who especially enjoyed philosophy and used Witherspoon's own lecture notes to teach Archibald Alexander and his colleagues Scottish Common Sense Realism.[13]

Caruthers's second year biblical criticism course in the outline above would have provided exposure to common sense philosophy. Taught by

---

9. *Princeton Seminary Catalogue*.
10. Cited in Calhoun, *Princeton Seminary*, 403.
11. Marsden, *Understanding Fundamentalism and Evangelicalism*, 37.
12. Noll, *America's God*, 248–49.
13. Calhoun, *Princeton Seminary*, 48.

CHAPTER 6: CARUTHERS AND THE ENLIGHTENMENT

Archibald Alexander, the course content at Princeton may be deduced from Alexander's previous studies with William Graham under whom he had trained for the ministry. He would later tell his students that "the English ground of faith and common sense instead of the German ground of skepticism and nonsense" was the preferred approach to the Bible.[14]

Alexander's "common sense" is the Scottish Common Sense Realism of Thomas Reid and other Scottish philosophers who were reacting to the skepticism of David Hume. It is by no means certain that Reid correctly understood Hume's arguments but his representation of Hume's thinking as philosophical skepticism was persuasive, and his response influenced subsequent generations of intellectual thought.[15] Although Reid's understanding of Hume is probably incorrect, his reaction provides a point of origin for the philosophical outlook that would permeate American seminaries including Princeton, taking on "unusual theological importance" and shaping what has been described as the "Reformed and literal hermeneutic."[16] Interpreting the Bible in this approach is a straightforward task requiring sole reliance upon the Bible. Conclusions and opinions are matter-of-fact and uncolored by theological perspective or any other principles or presuppositions. The American variety of Common Sense biblical interpretation was, in fact, a product of American republicanism and a Baconian intellectual approach that elevated the right and reason of every individual with respect to the Bible. Anyone who read it properly could easily understand its teaching on any matter under consideration. Just as reliance upon inductive investigation removed the obscurities and the mystery of science and nature, so the difficulties of the Bible were removed if only the light of reason were properly applied.[17]

Interpreting the use of Enlightenment ideals by a nineteenth-century Presbyterian minister such as Caruthers, whose education at Princeton Seminary involved a sustained exposure to a Common Sense approach to the Bible as well as the Westminster Confession and the doctrines of Calvinism, is conditioned by at least three factors. Consideration of these same factors should serve as a precautionary measure in attempts to reconstruct the relationship between the nineteenth-century movement to abolish American slavery and the Enlightenment.

14. Cited in ibid., 85.
15. Nash, *The Word of God and the Mind of Man*, 18–19.
16. Noll, *America's God*, 233, 370.
17. Ibid., 370–84.

First of all, as is well known, the Enlightenment origins of certain political theories about human rights cannot be taken to mean that the era's writers unequivocally condemned slavery, black or otherwise. They did not. Such a conclusion oversimplifies to the point of distorting the complex attitudes of Enlightenment thinkers on the issue of slavery.[18] The era's lack of practical resolution on slavery lessens the likelihood of its role as an impetus for the antislavery arguments of the nineteenth century.

For example, on the issue of chattel slavery such as existed in America, John Locke was "abstract, ambiguous, and cautious."[19] He had no difficulty declaiming the natural rights of man and political liberty on the one hand, but in his work on the charter for the establishment of South Carolina in 1669 asserted the absolute power and authority of a master over his slaves. Locke, in fact, would later have holdings as an investor in the Royal African Company.[20] His acceptance of slavery suggests that the egalitarian abstractions of Enlightenment writers were outmatched by certain exceptions or hierarchal assumptions that justified slavery and shaped their practical sociological outlook. In Locke's case, he viewed slaves from Africa as legitimate captives of a just war subject to their conquerors for life.[21]

The impetus of immediate emancipation in the nineteenth century does not simply originate from the concept of natural or inalienable rights as envisioned by Locke or any other writer of the Enlightenment. With the exception of George Wallace, discussed below, the most the era's writers could do was to define and critique the institution of slavery and urge gradual reform.[22] Even for the early nineteenth-century abolitionists, themselves, emancipation was an ultimate objective. In 1806 Samuel Fox described emancipation as "not now and not soon." In 1818 William Wilberforce still imagined "the almost insensible result of the various Improvements to be Slaves gradually transmitted into a free Peasantry."[23]

Enlightenment writers influenced abolitionists, but, as noted by C. Duncan Rice, abolitionists were greatly affected by "the increasingly

18. Morrow, "The Problem of Slavery in the Polemic Literature of the American Enlightenment," 236.

19. Davis, *The Problem of Slavery in Western Culture*, 118–19; Morrow, "The Problem of Slavery in the Polemic Literature of the American Enlightenment," 237.

20. Davis, *The Problem of Slavery in Western Culture*, 118–19; Morrow "The Problem of Slavery in the Polemic Literature of the American Enlightenment," 237.

21. Davis, *The Problem of Slavery in Western Culture*, 120.

22. Brown, *Moral Capital*, 174.

23. Cited in Turley, *The Culture of English Antislavery, 1780–1860*, 30.

CHAPTER 6: CARUTHERS AND THE ENLIGHTENMENT

evangelical Christianity of their age."[24] Granville Sharp was known for his "preoccupation with Judgment Day" which gave his appeals "distinct urgency," and for loading his speeches with "dark warnings of divine retribution."[25] Thomas Clarkson's award-winning essay at Cambridge emphasized that the national sin of slavery would bring down the "heaviest judgment of Almighty God" who would not "suffer such deliberate, such monstrous iniquity to pass along unpunished."[26] Iain Whyte argues further that a key idea brought to the slavery controversy by evangelical theology of the nineteenth century was "that of fallen humanity and the inevitable abuse of power by sinful humans."[27] The moral certainty of the antislavery movement cannot be traced to the Enlightenment, rather it was, in Whyte's words, "the acceptance of the gravity of the sin of slavery . . . that provided an urgency to abandon it that could not brook delay."[28]

Secondly, antislavery sentiment resists being described as a product of the Enlightenment because antislavery views emerge before the era, quite apart from and preceding nineteenth-century abolitionism. The existence of antislavery convictions or ideas of human equality before the era of the Enlightenment does not rule out its influence in the abolition movement, but the likelihood of it being the primary source is lessened.

In addition to American and British antislavery sentiment, Spanish and Portugese writers, "early protesters," argued against the enslavement of Africans, with "exclamations of moral sentiment" as well as "reasoned deductions on human equality" before the eighteenth century and decades before the British colonial effort was undertaken.[29] Christopher Brown describes a "long history of sincere but inconsequential protest," and the "distant antecedents" of the antislavery literature of the abolitionist era.[30] C. Duncan Rice calls attention to the "individual polemicists . . . presenting a critique of slavery to an unreceptive world" and "the scattering of articles and pamphlets" against slavery dating back to the late seventeenth century, all of them voices against slavery crying in the wilderness.[31] David

24. Rice, *The Rise and Fall of Black Slavery*, 160.
25. Brown, *Moral Capital*, 175.
26. Cited in Brog, *In Defense of Faith*, 137.
27. Whyte, *Scotland and the Abolition of Black Slavery*, 253.
28. Ibid., 254.
29. Brown, *Moral Capital*, 38–39.
30. Ibid., 38.
31. Rice, *The Rise and Fall of Black Slavery* 186–87, 154.

B. Davis' identifies "an increasing number" of antislavery voices who "on both sides of the Atlantic saw modern slavery as a moral contradiction, a force incompatible with natural law, Christianity, the progress of scientific enlightenment, or the mission of American democracy."[32]

Many of the themes of the Enlightenment according to David B. Davis are prefigured in Seventeenth-century British Protestantism. Elements of Puritanism such as "suspicion of unlimited power, indifference toward external distinctions, and faith in individual moral judgment" provide the "essential ingredients of the antislaverymind."[33] One prefiguration that resembles Caruthers's own argument is found in the work of Richard Baxter, the noted Seventeenth-century English Puritan. Baxters' "Directions to those Masters in foreign Plantations who own Negroes and other Slaves," published in 1664, cautions masters to remember their slaves " are reasonable creatures as well as you, and born to as much natural liberty." He believes their could be such a thing as legitimate enslavement—"if their sin have enslaved them to you, yet," he writes," nature made them your equals." Like Caruthers, he stresses "that God is their absolute Owner" and that "they can be no further yours, than you have God's consent, who is the Lord of them and you." It is "God's interest in them and by them" that "must be served first." Within the context of redemption Baxter writes, "remember that they are the redeemed ones of Christ, and that he hath not sold you his title to them. As he bought their souls at a price invaluable, so he hath not given the purchase of his blood to be absolutely at your disposal."[34] This sounds like Caruthers's own sort of objection: "Before we doom four millions of our fellow beings, with their unborn and unoffending offspring, to a condition of ignorance, degradation, and laborious servitude we must have an express grant from the creator to do so, or be chargeable before high heaven with wholesale injustice and oppression."[35] In Baxter's thinking the only real reason for buying slaves was to set them free, and any other reason was "heinous sin." As Davis points out "his rhetoric approached the vehemence of the most militant abolitionists."[36]

Thirdly, identifying antislavery or abolitionist arguments with the Enlightenment suggests a traceable march or flow of ideas from the

---

32. Davis, *The Problem of Slavery in Western Culture*, 25.
33. Ibid., 337–38.
34. Baxter, *A Christian Directory*, 461.
35 Caruthers, *American Slavery*, 369.
36. Davis, *The Problem of Slavery in Western Culture*, 338–39.

CHAPTER 6: CARUTHERS AND THE ENLIGHTENMENT

Enlightenment to antislavery and abolitionist literature. The crisscrossing fertilization of ideas that took place between religious, political, and philosophical writers in America, Scotland, England, and Europe, however, makes such a trace difficult, if not impossible. Regarding the late eighteenth century, Brown urges his reader to "resist the inclination" to view the antislavery movements of the late eighteenth century as a "working out of cultural trends or as the consequence of a series of intellectual steps that ascended to a breakthrough in moral perception."[37] Similar caution is apt for evaluations of nineteenth-century antislavery literature as well. The reconstruction offered by C. Duncan Rice thirty-five years ago illustrates this point.

Drawing on the work of David B. Davis and others, Rice attempts to sort out who contributed what to the "ferment of tortured reconsideration of the religious and intellectual underpinning of slavery indeed of hierarchy in general." The "nature of the abolitionist impulse" is "intensely complex," and its story is an "extraordinarily complex interplay" between Scotland, England, America, and Europe. In his attempt at "unraveling the various influences in play," the Scottish Enlightenment is "a clearing-house for Enlightenment ideas on slavery." As Rice retraces its development, "the germ of the intellectual attack on slavery was taken from Enlightenment writers such a Montesquieu by the scholars of the Scottish Enlightenment" who influenced American writers who would subsequently influence abolitionists in England.[38]

George Wallace is mentioned among several Scots, including Francis Hutcheson and John Millar, but his work merits special attention in Rice's reconstruction. According to Rice, the ideas of Wallace, and other Scottish writers were perfections of the eighteenth century's rational arguments against slavery. Described by Aaron Garrett as "perhaps the most important eighteenth century Scots legal critic of slavery,"[39] Wallace's treatise on the laws of Scotland, published in 1760, describes liberty as a natural faculty and slavery as contrary to nature even though sanctioned by ancient Roman law and "so horrid and so contrary to the feelings of humanity, that it cannot be agreeable to the law of Scotland."[40] Due to their radical nature, Wallace's arguments against slavery played no direct role in the later

---

37. Brown, *Moral Capital*, 40; cf. Davis, *The Problem of Slavery in Western Culture*, 201.

38. Rice, *The Rise and Fall of Black Slavery*, 176, 160–61.

39. Broadie, ed., *The Cambridge Companion to the Scottish Enlightenment*, 88.

40. Cited in Whyte, *Scotland and the Abolition of Black Slavery*, 254.

abolitionist movement of Britain, however, his unclouded vision of emancipation as the first step toward equality resonated with Anthony Benezet, a Philadelphian Quaker, who cited the Scottish author and incorporated passages of his work into his own literature in 1762.[41]

Wallace's work traveled from Scotland to American pamphleteers such as Benezet, whose pamphlets were read in England and reprinted for distribution by Granville Sharp. In an ironic twist Wallace's radical ideas were also plagiarized in a formative French encyclopedia article on slavery appearing in 1765, thus the germination of Montesquieu traveled back to France via Scotland.[42] The stream of antislavery legacy is thus "a dog-leg transfer of ideas" flowing from the Scottish Enlightenment to colonial America and crossing back to the English abolitionists.[43] The transfer of ideas from Scottish philosophers and writers to colonial America includes the corollary influence of Edinburgh upon Princeton College, transmitted through John Witherspoon's leadership and Samuel Stanhope Smith, a future president of Princeton, whose development of the moral sciences descends from Scottish philosophy. Rice draws for the reader "the filaments of an Atlantic intellectual web, at the centre of which sat the philosophers of the Scottish Enlightenment."[44]

Rice's attempt to trace the abolitionist impulse to Wallace and the philosophers of the Scottish Enlightenment, however, is complicated by the introduction of Anthony Benezet who is the center of his own unique web: Quaker antislavery sentiment with its own source dating back to the late seventeenth-century colonial America. Wallace's ideas resonated with Benezet's own, but were not the catalyst. Rice himself notes the "small and premature revulsion" of seventeenth-century Pennsylvania Quakers that produced documents opposing slavery as early as 1688, predating the publication of Joseph Sewall's *The Selling of Joseph* in New England,[45] and forecasting their central role in the antislavery movement in America and England.[46]

---

41. Davis, *The Problem of Slavery in the Age of Revolution*, 269.

42. Rice, *The Rise and Fall of Black Slavery*, 167; Davis, *The Problem of Slavery in the Age of Revolution*, 269.

43. Rice, *The Rise and Fall of Black Slavery*, 166.

44. Ibid., 165–67.

45. Sewall, *The Selling of Joseph*.

46. Rice, *The Rise and Fall of Black Slavery*, 188–89.

CHAPTER 6: CARUTHERS AND THE ENLIGHTENMENT

Rice calls the influence of the Quakers the "most important godly impulse towards British abolition of slavery."[47] Judging from the extended exchange that took place between Sharp and Benezet and between English and colonial Friends, it is likely that the Quaker's humanitarian concern which had harnessed Wallace and anything else that could be used in its service, resonated with Granville Sharp and the English antislavery movement's own developing humanitarian concerns more than anything else. As for Sharp's own moral opposition to slavery, it originates with the legal disputes over status of slaves from the West Indies who claimed their freedom when brought to England. Sharp concluded that holding slaves in England was a violation of the nation's constitution, in Christopher Brown's words, "a violation of foundational rights pregnant with vast and dangerous consequences for English liberties."[48]

Summary

Determining the connection between the promotion of human equality or critiques of slavery in the literature of the Enlightenment and the antislavery views of Presbyterian minister from the nineteenth century influenced by Common Sense, like Caruthers, is problematic. As has been shown, determining the degree or nature of his reliance on the Enlightenment is complicated by the ambiguity of that era's writers on the practical question of slavery, the presence of antislavery ideas and literature previous to the era, and the multiple philosophical, religious, and legal webs that develop from several distinctive centers in the nineteenth century's movement to abolish slavery.

Interpreting Caruthers's Use of the Declaration of Independence

Caruthers's intertwining of biblical argument with arguments derived from political documents is a pattern discernable in the earlier literature of the British movement to abolish the slave trade and slavery itself. An instructive example is seen in Bishop Thomas Burgess' response to the publication in 1787 of *Scriptural Researches on the Licitness of the Slave Trade* by Raymond

---

47. Ibid., 161.
48. Ibid., 215; Brown, *Moral Capital*, 93–97.

Harris. Harris was a pseudonym for Don Raymondo Hormaza, a Jesuit priest expelled from Spain and living in Liverpool. The reasons for the publication present a story of intrigue and need not be reviewed here.[49] Harris sought to show that the "Slave Trade is perfectly consonant to the principles of the law of nations, the Mosaic Dispensation and the Christian Law, as delineated to us in the Sacred Writings of the Word of God."[50]

Among several who responded to Harris, Burgess, an Anglican theologian and founder of St. David's College in Wales, published *Considerations on the Abolition of Slavery and the Slave Trade upon Grounds of Natural, Religious and Political Duty*.[51] Burgess acknowledges the worth of previous responses, but believes Harris requires an answer based not only on Scripture but "reasons of political duty derived from our constitution." Bishop Burgess writes,

> I shall pursue the inferences, which I deduce from the principles of *natural* right and *Scriptural* authority, and endeavor to confirm them by reasons of *political* duty derived from our civil constitution. The inconsistency between Slavery or the Slave Trade, and the general principles of our law and constitution, between the permission of such usages and our high pretensions to civil liberty, appeared to contain arguments for the abolition of Slavery not less powerful on one hand, than the injunctions of Scripture, and the rights of Nature on the other. But while no small share of eloquence has been displayed in asserting the claims of Nature, and the genuine injunctions of God's word, this political inconsistency has been very little insisted on in the many publications, which the present emergency has produced.[52]

David B. Davis describes British antislavery literature as involving a pattern that equates Christianity with political liberty and the rights of mankind, a pattern more fully developed in the American antislavery

---

49. For a review of the Harris episode see Davis, *The Problem of Slavery in the Age of Revolution 1170-1823*, 542-51.

50. Cited in "We Are All Brethren."

51. Burgess, *Considerations on the Abolition of Slavery*. Burgess's is one of several responses to Harris. For further study see James Ramsay, *Examination of the Rev. Mr. Harris's "Scriptural Researches"*; Robinson, *Slavery Inconsistent with the Spirit of Christianity*; Hughes, *Answer to the Rev. Mr. Harris's "Scriptural Researches on the Licitness of the Slave Trade*.

52. Burgess, *Considerations on the Abolition of Slavery*, 8-9.

CHAPTER 6: CARUTHERS AND THE ENLIGHTENMENT

literature.[53] There is support for this equation since certain Enlightenment ideas regarding equality and liberty appropriated by English and American Christianity have roots in early forms of biblical criticism. Quentin Skinner's description of how Huguenot theorists after the massacre of 1572 began "turning away from providentialist assumptions in order to develop an essentially scholastic theory about the origins and character of legitimate political societies" points to the role of Christianity in its own political evolution.[54] For Burgess, it was the *political* inconsistency between the existence of slavery and "our law and constitution" that was overlooked in the response to Harris. He writes,

> The absolute dominion of Man over Man is inconsistent with the rights of Society deducible from Scripture. The extent of these rights may be collected from the God's first commission to Man; and from the concurrence of Hebrew law with the custom of other nations. In God's first commission to Man, which gives him dominion over the *brute* creation, there is no expression, from which Adam or any of his posterity could collect, that they had a right of dominion over their own species.[55]

Similarly, Caruthers saw in Genesis a limitation on the dominion given to humanity. Everything that humanity should or ought to possess was expressly given by their creator but "all the rest, the world of intelligent beings, he has reserved for himself."[56] There is no provision or allowance for human beings to possess their own species. In Genesis, Caruthers sees "great principles . . . distinctly given which are easily comprehended and are applicable at all times and in all circumstances."[57]

Burgess mentions "the concurrence of Hebrew law with . . . other nations." His meaning is made clear when he repeats the phrase and completes the thought a little further on, writing of "the common concurrence in the Hebrews and all nations *in exempting their native subjects from involuntary servitude*." He observes that in the ancient world "it was too repugnant to all natural rights and feelings for any nation to permit the absolute and

---

53. Davis, *The Problem of Slavery in the Age of Revolution*, 552.

54. Skinner, *Modern Political Though*, 2:326; For a discussion of what has been termed the "Evangelical Enlightenment," see Noll, *America's God*, 93–95; Forbes, "Slavery and the Evangelical Enlightenment."

55. Burgess, *Considerations on the Abolition of Slavery*, 48–49.

56. Caruthers, *American Slavery*, 202.

57. Ibid., 207.

involuntary subjection of one fellow subject to another." With the Genesis account in the background Burgess argues that "the exemption bears a clear testimony to the common rights of Society. For it follows by a necessary inference, that a right, which every particular state considers as the privilege of its own subjects, reason and humanity consider as the right of all mankind."[58] Just as Caruthers discerns a biblical background in creation and the Exodus text for human equality as it was expressed in the Declaration of Independence, Burgess' understands that certain political values of England are moored to Genesis.

It is not known if Caruthers was familiar with Burgess. He was certainly familiar with "the laws and statutes of Great Britain" and "the fundamental principle of the British constitution" with respect to labor and slavery. On related issues he knows "of the view taken of this subject by [Thomas] Clarkson and [William] Wilberforce."[59] After the American Revolutionary War, the Church of England in the United States became the American Episcopal Church in 1787. Burgess' book was distributed widely in the North America and found many receptive readers.[60] We do not know if Caruthers was one. Regardless, Burgess believed that human equality embodied in English law was derived from the Bible's account of creation, and if no Englishman could be a slave then no other person should be a slave. Similarly, Caruthers believed that human equality as expressed in the American Declaration of Independence was based in creation and the warrant of political liberty to all humanity.

A further explanation for Caruthers's use of Enlightenment based ideas is also suggested by a closer examination of Anthony Benezet. As pointed out by Davis, Benezet used rationalistic vocabulary but, at heart, he was a Quaker, "an intensely pious, self-effacing man." He did not believe in the progress of humanity as foretold by writers of the Enlightenment such as Wallace. To the contrary, he "held little hope for human happiness or perfectibility in this world," and was very selective in his use of radical antislavery literature.[61] The degree and way in which Benezet incorporated Wallace's work indicates more Quaker than Enlightenment influence. A similar observation is apt for Caruthers, and the entirety of antislavery

---

58. Burgess, *Considerations on the Abolition of Slavery*, 50–51; my emphasis.
59. Caruthers, *American Slavery*, 134.
60. Abrahamsen, "Episcopal Church," 1:259.
61. Davis, *The Problem of Slavery in the Age of Revolution*, 592.

literature by authors of religious conviction: at heart they were religious writers, and their unique beliefs informed and determined what they wrote.

Caruthers is not unlike other Common Sense ministers in his Reformed and Presbyterian tradition who used the language and symbols of the Enlightenment. In his discussion of religious liberty and its relationship to civil liberty and republican government in late eighteenth-century and early nineteenth-century America, Fred Hood has observed that "even when the Reformed used Lockean or Enlightenment language to describe religious liberty they had in mind the affirmation of the Protestant religious article of faith rather than an abstract political or social right."[62]

Among the numerous examples cited by Hood is the Presbytery of Hanover in 1777, affirming certain "unalienable" rights not on the basis of social contract but religious principle. Similarly, in the language of their deliberations over the reorganization of Presbyterianism, the Synod of New York and Philadelphia in 1788 demonstrate that "in Reformed usage the language of the Enlightenment was saturated with conservative theological content." George Washington Bethune, a Dutch Reformed minister in Washington, D.C., speaks of "liberty, like every other blessing" as derived "from Christ." In his Fourth of July speech published in 1835, Daniel B. Barnard comments that the equality of all men stated in the Declaration of Independence is not a new truth but results from "the order of the creation" and "it was proclaimed by Moses and the prophets, and authoritatively taught in the mission of Jesus Christ." It is only "as a political truth" that the Declaration of Independence is new.[63] Hood's general observations of the Reformed movement during this time period could be applied to Caruthers and others like him, who cite the Declaration of Independence:

> The Reformed did not search through the annals of political, social, or technological development to explain the emergence of civil liberty, nor did they consider the intellectual influence of the Enlightenment. Theirs was a holistic approach to reality, and religion was the core from which radiated all that was either good, true, or beautiful. Civil liberty they deemed to be one of their most precious possessions. Could it have any other source but Christianity?[64]

62. Hood, *Reformed America*, 52–53.
63. Ibid., 61.
64. Ibid., 60–61.

Summary

Like others in his Reformed tradition, Caruthers thought certain ideas embodied in the Declaration of Independence might be new political truths, but they were as old as creation. He believed the original source of his argument was Christianity. He clothes his claims with the popular language and concepts of the Enlightenment but biblical truth was the core from which he thought they radiated. Just as a notable Scot's' "dismissal of the very possibility of slavery in Scotland because it was contrary to Christian liberty to make slaves of men in a Christian country," so for Caruthers, "we profess to be a Christian and protestant people."[65] If America is such a nation then slavery cannot exist by virtue of convictions embodied in its Declaration of Independence. Slavery denied the liberty in which humanity was created to live and serve their creator and redeemer as understood from Christianity's doctrines of creation and redemption. Such doctrines were not simply the basis of human rights, but the basis of God's rights, too. Neither slavery nor the laws of the slave states could be reconciled to human rights, American rights or the rights of America's God.

---

65. Whyte, *Scotland and the Abolition of Black Slavery*, 31.

Chapter 7: The Similarity of Caruthers to other Antislavery Literature

THE PREVIOUS CHAPTERS HAVE identified and explained the salient and unique features of Caruthers's understanding of Exod 10:3. The text—*Let my people go that they may serve me*—embodies a logical order of claim, demand, and reason from which he explicates a timeless argument against slavery. It thus serves as a universal construct against the institution or practice of slavery, and stands apart from other antislavery literature of his era. Shifting from the unique to the typical, this chapter evaluates a portion of the manuscript that is similar to other nineteenth-century antislavery literature, specifically, Caruthers's survey of slavery from the various biblical eras (pp. 65–136).

"The advocates of slavery appeal to the Bible," he writes, "and as truth ought to be our only object, some enquiry into the teachings of inspiration" will "prove all things."[1] He dismisses the idea that "slavery in our sense of the term" can be found in the Bible, but there are milder forms of slavery or servitude during the eras of Noah, Abraham, Moses, and Christ. Caruthers uses many of the standard arguments typically associated with antislavery and abolitionist literature in answering those who "find the institution sanctioned in the Bible."[2] Caruthers does not embrace abolitionism, but he employs their arguments to demonstrate the temporal limits, benevolent motives, or voluntary nature of servitude in the Bible.

Noah's Curse

Caruthers examines proslavery's biblical arguments beginning with the curse pronounced by Noah,

> Cursed be Canaan; lowest of slaves shall he be to his brothers. He also said, Blessed be the Lord, the God of Shem! May Canaan be

---

1. Caruthers, *American Slavery*, 64.
2. Ibid., 128.

the slave of Shem. May God extend the territory of Japheth; may Jappheth live in the tents of Shem, and may Canaan be his slave.³

Caruthers's treatment of the Noah's curse is twofold. He both questions the interpretation given to the text by proslavery advocates, and depreciates the text, questioning its importance for the slavery question. Before considering these aspects of his argument, some general observations about the antislavery argument and Noah's curse should be noted. Antislavery literature in America sought to destabilize the proslavery argument by undermining its biblical defense. Many texts of the Bible were used in the proslavery argument but none with greater political or popular power than the curse pronounced by Noah in Gen 9:25–26.⁴

Although the appeal to the curse of Noah in the justification of slavery was challenged in colonial America as early as 1700 and dismissed by some proslavery advocates, it nevertheless provided Antebellum America with its unassailable moral proof of slavery's righteousness against the rising tide of abolitionism in the 1830s.⁵ In his defense of slavery in the House of Representatives on February 1, 1836, James Henry Hammond reminded his listeners that "the doom of Ham has been branded on the form and features of his African descendants. The hand of fate has united his color and destiny. Man cannot separate what God hath joined."⁶ Widely understood by proslavery advocates as the divine establishment of the racial subordination of blacks in the role of Canaan's descendants, its serviceability in their argument has earned its description as the "chief rationale for bondage."⁷

Ancient and modern probes of Noah's curse have yet to penetrate the veil created by the lack of detail and absence of subsequent clarification. The reader is told very little about curse when it is pronounced and nothing later on. Noah becomes drunk after drinking wine from his vineyard. Ham sees his father naked and sleeping off his intoxication. He reports it to his two brothers, Japheth and Shem, who cover him up. When Noah awakens he announces a curse, strangely not on Ham, but on one of his descendants, Canaan. The curse is mysterious in its origins, sparse in its details, and lacks the divine approbation later generations would assign to it. It is not made clear in the text or elsewhere that Noah, awakened from

---

3. Gen 9:25–26.
4. Fox-Genovese and Genovese, *Mind of the Master Class*, 521.
5. Tise, Proslavery, 495.
6. Miller, *Arguing about Slavery*, 139.
7. Haynes, *Noah's Curse*, 85.

his drunken state, utters the divine will, as believed by most and advocated in Thornton Stringfellow's declaration that Noah speaks "in God's stead."[8] Some abolitionists asserted he did not.[9] And if Noah is speaking for God, the Hebrew text is not so straightforward. According to John Sailhamer Gen 9:25 is clear enough, but the introduction of the verse 26 ("He also said") marks it off from verse 25 with language shifting from the certainty of the imperfect tense in verse 25 ("he will be") to the less determined and more wishful mode of the jussive tense in verses 26–27 ("May he be").[10]

The precise nature of Ham's offense is never explained and has provoked numerous proposals and questions. Is the singling out of Canaan a later invention to legitimize Israel's treatment of Canaan's inhabitants? Does the curse come because Ham tells his brothers something or because he saw his father in a disgraceful condition? Did Ham do something known through tradition but not recorded in the text? Does the response of his brothers who walk backward to avoid seeing their father as they covered him indicate that Ham's egregious behavior was that he stared at his father rather than turn away? Is there a rivalry between Japheth and Shem, a rivalry for blessing that necessitates the victimization of Ham? These and other unanswered questions did not curtail the text's role in the explanation of American slavery: the Africans were the descendants of Ham and their enslavement to the European and American descendants of Japheth was biblically sanctioned by the honorable patriarch.[11]

Caruthers's assertion that "if these words were interpreted literally the curse would be exhausted when the Canaanites were all destroyed by the people of Israel" resembles other antislavery literature. If it is not understood literally but includes all the descendants of Ham then "was it a command or simple prediction?" he asks. He doubts it was the former because there is no subsequent record in the Bible of such a command being carried out by the descendants of Shem and Japheth "until the Israelites more than eight hundred years afterwards receive a special injunction to subdue and exterminate the people of Canaan." The idea of slavery practiced in America would probably have been unfamiliar to

---

8. Cited in McKitrick, "A Scriptural View of Slavery," 86.
9. Haynes, *Noah's Curse*, 182.
10. Sailhamer, "Genesis," 1:97n26.
11. For a full discussion of racial hierarchy in the antebellum era based on Noah's curse, see Peterson, *Ham and Jepheth: The Mythic World of Whites in the Antebellum South*.

Noah's sons since "the Hebrew noun *obed* translated "servant" was "never used to designate the Antediluvians" and there were "no servants or slaves in the ark ... all were freemen."[12]

But if Noah's curse really is a prophecy, he asks, then "on what principle are we to aim at its accomplishment?"[13] The fulfillment of every prophecy should not be sought rather "it is our duty to do all the good we can, and of course, to desire and seek and rejoice in the fulfillment of every promise; but it is equally our duty to take the warning given and do all we can to avert from ourselves and others the calamity which it imports."[14] The distinction between command and prediction is an important one because "if Noah's prediction justifies us in the enslavement of the Africans all who acted as agents in executing the great judgments of heaven on a guilty world might make the same plea; for it was *foretold*." The active pursuit of every dire prediction's fulfillment should then be sought as if it were virtuous to do so including, according to Caruthers, the subjection of women, the oppression of Israel, Judas' betrayal of Jesus, the destruction of Jerusalem, and the rule of the Antichrist. "The people of Israel never thought of either destroying or enslaving ... the Canaanites until they were expressly commanded by the God of their fathers to do so; and then they seemed reluctant" but "we, Caruthers says, " have undertaken without warrant or authority to be the executioners of a prophetic malediction."[15]

Caruthers's choice of the term "executioners" is reminiscent of Samuel Sewall's *The Selling of Joseph: A Memorial*, published in 1700. "Of all Offices" or responsibilities one could be given by God, Sewall writes regarding the curse, "one would not begg this ... to be an Executioner of the Vindictive Wrath of God."[16] Caruthers shies away from a direct comparison of the "religious portion of our community who are slaveholders" with Pharaoh or Nebuchadnezzar or even Judas "in moral and religious character" but the parallels of oppression, tyranny, and betrayal of trust are clear enough. It is, he writes, "the blinding influence of self interest" on the part of the slaveholder that prevents "an intelligent and impartial view on this subject." For this reason slavery's advocates should "be very shy of founding a plea

---

12. Caruthers, 70, 71.
13. Caruthers, *American Slavery*, 72.
14. Ibid.
15. Ibid, 72, 75.
16. Sewall, *The Selling of Joseph*, 12.

CH 7: THE SIMILARITY OF CARUTHERS TO OTHER ANTISLAVERY LITERATURE

... on Noah's prophetic malediction on Ham's distant posterity or on any other prophecy in the Bible."[17]

Elsewhere Caruthers doubts the importance of the curse. In a study without proper pagination inserted into this section of the manuscript, he observes "there is no allusion to this prediction in any other part of the Bible." In this line of reasoning Noah's words are viewed as justified by Ham's actions but they carry no greater message than the expression of his anger. Depreciation of the curse was not unique to Caruthers. William Henry Brisbane asks similarly, "Is there any thing about [the curse] that implies that Noah spake as moved by the Spirit of God? Is it anything more than an historical fact in the life of Noah?" In support of this assessment Brisbane goes on to point out that Noah's vision is never really fulfilled. Nimrod is a descendant of Ham, as is Asshur, but neither are made subservient. To the contrary, Shem's descendants are eventually carried in captivity into Egypt were it seems they serve the descendants of Ham.[18] Caruthers takes a similar tack. Noah's words are not programmatic for the ages to come. He does not speak in God's place, and the curse is no more inspired "than where he planted his vineyard."[19]

Although Caruthers's treatment of Noah's curse is brief it is a necessary part of his general survey of the proslavery argument. The historical difficulties caused by casting of Africans as the descendants of the Canaan or Ham were noticed by few Americans and readily overcome by the lure of a divine explanation for the prejudices they felt or the established slave society in which they lived.[20] The rejection of Noah's curse as a justification for American slavery by James Thornwell, Robert Dabney, and other proslavery theologians and intellectuals did not diminish its appeal to the proslavery mindset. Here was a text that supported the subordination of blacks by whites.[21] The place of importance given to the text by Caruthers and other antislavery writers cannot be properly grasped otherwise. In an address after the war, Benjamin Morgan Palmer, the outspoken advocate of secession and pastor of First Presbyterian Church in New Orleans, described the Genesis passage as "the fortunes of mankind presented in perfect outline." In Palmer's thinking the "mental and moral characteris-

---

17. Caruthers, *American Slavery*, 76.
18. Cited in Haynes, *Noah's Curse*, 182.
19. Caruthers, *American Slavery*, 80–109.
20. Haynes, *Noah's Curse*, 11–12.
21. Fox-Genovese and Genovese, *The Mind of the Master Class*, 523.

tics" of the African "have marked them for servitude." "Upon Ham," he declares, "was pronounced the doom of perpetual servitude—proclaimed with double emphasis, as it is twice repeated that he shall be the servant of Japhet and the servant of Shem."[22] Thornton Stringfellow, pamphleteer, essayist, and Baptist minister from Richmond, Virginia summarized his argument for slavery beginning with "God decreed this relation between the posterity of Canaan and the posterity of Shem and Japheth."[23] Commenting on Gen 9:25 and Ham's descendants in *The Christian Doctrine of Slavery* George Armstrong, author and minister of Presbyterian Church in Norfolk, Virginia writes that it was "in consequence of sin, in part actually committed, and yet more foreseen in the future, that the first slave sentence . . . was pronounced by Noah upon Canaan and his descendants."[24] Genesis 9:25–27 was the divine account of slavery's origin and its warrant for all generations prompting abolitionist Theodore Dwight Weld's famous comment that "this prophecy of Noah is the *vade mecum* of slaveholders, and they never venture abroad without it."[25]

Caruthers's insistence that no divine "warrant or authority" existed in Noah's words for the enslavement of Africans contradicted the logic of domination usually drawn from the text. In the Antebellum era the relationship of Noah's sons provided a sought after justification for the relationship between three racial groups—Caucasian, Asiatic, and Negroid. In Stephen Ray's words, "These relations were unsurprisingly a mirror of contemporary relations in the nineteenth century—whites were dominant, indigenous peoples were marginalized, and blacks were subjugated."[26] Donald Mathews has likewise suggested that the advocates of slavery came to the Genesis account of Noah's curse in search of divine legitimacy for views already decided on the grounds of personal experience and prejudice.[27] Stephen Haynes' treatment of southerner and Presbyterian, Benjamin Morgan Palmer, has described Palmer's use of Noah's curse as that of someone "in search of a transcendent warrant for racial hierarchy," a man seeking to "validate the claim that Southern whites had both a right and responsibility

---

22. Cited in Chesebrough, *God Ordained This War*, 203.

23. Cited in Noll, *America's God*, 388.

24. Armstrong, *The Christian Doctrine of Slavery*, 110, 111.

25. Weld, *The Bible Against Slavery*, 46.

26. Ray's review of *The Myth of Ham in Nineteenth-Century American Christianity*, 36–43.

27. Mathews, *Religion in the Old South*, 171.

to master the 'sons of Ham.'"[28] No such right or responsibility could be established from Noah's curse according to Caruthers. "This," he writes, "we have done entirely from motives of avarice."[29]

Abraham's Servants

Proslavery advocates saw the presence of slaves in the household of Abraham and other patriarchs and the regulation of slavery in the Bible as evidence of divine approval for American slavery. In their thinking Abraham was the model and example for slaveholding. Caruthers cites an unidentified source that exemplifies this outlook:

> It has been asserted of late . . . that Abraham was in very deed a slave holder; that "the first organization of the church as a visible society, separate and distinct from the unbelieving world, was inaugurated in the family of a slave holder, that the very first persons to whom the seal of circumcision was affixed were the slaves of the father of the faithful."[30]

Like other antislavery writers, Caruthers answered such arguments by drawing a distinction of "vital importance" within the "gradations of society" of the Old Testament and between a servant and slave, "those terms on which the controversy turns."[31] Abraham had servants but not slaves.[32] "There is between these two classes," he argues, " a radical and essential difference."[33] The Hebrew term, *obed*, is generally a 'servant,' one who serves another freely and usually for a stipulated reward or compensation" but it can also describe "one who labors for another, either for hire or by compulsion," but a 'slave' "renders compulsory service and without any compensation." Even "when the angels of the Lord himself" appear in Genesis they find no "parade of slaves in attendance" within Abraham's clan but only a servant, "a young man, one of his employees" who helps "butcher a calf . . . while Sarah herself made the cakes."[34] Eleazar, one of Abraham's servants

---

28. Haynes, *Noah's Curse*, 145, 158.
29. Caruthers, *American Slavery*, 76.
30. Ibid., 78.
31. Ibid., 65–68.
32. Ibid., 77.
33. Ibid., 79.
34. Ibid., 81.

was designated to be his "*heir* in case he should have no children of his own but has such a thing ever occurred or could it occur in the south?"[35] Nor is there ever mention of slaves being inherited as property or as inventory in the narratives of Abraham, Isaac, or Jacob, "an important and often the most important part" of a southern slaveholder's last will and testament, and the absence of which reveals to Caruthers a vast discrepancy between Abraham's servants and America's slaves.[36] He overlooks the listing of Abraham's servants in Genesis along with his beasts, and other property, including Sarah, his wife.

For Caruthers, the equation of American slaves to the servants of Abraham is a bare assertion, "unsupported by facts or testimony of any kind" and "rendered highly improbable by a number of circumstances mentioned in the history and entirely obvious to the plainest reader."[37] He would have been in agreement with Albert Barnes: "we can ascertain the meaning of the *word* from *the facts* in the case; not the nature of *the facts* from the use of *the word.*"[38]

A densely written twenty-seven page study of slavery's vocabulary and circumstances in the Old Testament prepared earlier on ledger paper by Caruthers precedes his manuscript, and many of his findings are repeated in this section of the manuscript. It includes a review of the multiple uses of Hebrew verb, from which the noun *obed* is derived, ranging from labor for one's self or voluntary wage labor for another to labor enforced on others without wages and the political servitude exemplified in the slavery of the Hebrews recorded in Exodus. He observes the range of meaning for the concept of labor beyond that envisioned by the commandment in Exod. 20:9. This includes its "secondary meaning: to labor for another, voluntary and for wages" as well as "to labor for another by force." The study also contains some of his preliminary conclusions regarding slavery and Abraham. He doubts any correspondence between American slaves and Abraham's servants labeling it " criminal as well as ungenerous to apply modern terms, Greek, Latin, or English, for where there is no Hebrew word or corresponding import to the patriarchal . . . usages."

Moreover, because Abraham lived where there was no civil government capable of enforcing enslavement and "neither he nor any body else

---

35. Ibid., 79.
36. Ibid., 85.
37. Ibid., 79.
38. Barnes, *An Inquiry into the Scriptural Views of Slavery*, 70.

CH 7: THE SIMILARITY OF CARUTHERS TO OTHER ANTISLAVERY LITERATURE

had power to maintain" an institution like American slavery, thus making it "absurd to carry the name or the idea of slavery back into the household of Abraham."[39] Existing over a territory "not half as large as North Carolina," the Canaanite culture in which Abraham lived consisted of numerous tribes, "like our western Indians" or the "Highland clans of Scotland" without "mutual cooperation or settled principles." The patriarch did his best in his circumstances using a "peaceable demeanor" and lending assistance when he could such as in the repulsion of "northern and eastern hordes" recorded in Genesis 14. Within this kind of environment "in the name of common sense, how could Abraham make slaves of three hundred and eighteen armed men and entail that bondage upon the unborn generations?" The patriarch's willingness to arm his servants for the rescue of Lot in Gen 14:14 loomed especially large in Caruthers's thinking. While considering this point, he relates the simultaneous visit of an unnamed fellow minister and their discussion:

> Some conversation ensued about the subject on which I was writing. After stating to him the substance of what I had just written—the impossibility in his circumstances of Abraham's making slaves, in our sense of the term, of three hundred and eighteen armed men and entailing that bondage upon their unborn offspring, he said he thought it was very possible for a man of great moral power, like Abraham, to make slaves of even a greater number of ignorant and superstitious heathen but my reply was and is that ... the cases are not parallel; for assuredly Abraham's servants or employees, were heathen sunk in ignorance, vice, and superstition ... they were converts to his faith in Mesopotamia, having been brought to the knowledge of the truth by his instructions and had followed him to the land of promise ... They knew all he knew; they were acquainted with the revelations which he had received and with the covenants and promises which had been repeated.[40]

The conversation between Caruthers and his colleague is a poignant miniature of the larger stalemate in the antebellum debate over Abraham's servants. Abraham's arming of his servants was also an example utilized in the proslavery argument. Caruthers cannot imagine how Abraham could possibly be a slaveholder in the American sense of the term, but his visitor can. Dating back to George Whitefield, the defense of slavery incorporated this

---

39. Caruthers, *American Slavery*, 81–83.
40. Ibid.

very incident as proof that Abraham had possessed slaves.[41] Time and time again throughout the run up to the sectional crisis, both sides would make their case, both dependent on the texts of the Bible, both equally capable and rigorous, and both unable to persuade anyone beyond conclusions at which they had already arrived.

On another tack, Caruthers cannot allow that Abraham's servants would be anything like slaves since God's disclosure to Abraham of his own descendants' slavery in Egypt in Gen 15:14 is conclusively "reprobatory of compulsory and unpaid service." " Could Abraham," he rhetorically asks, "inflict on another race the bondage, cruelty, injustice and oppression which was here so strongly reprobated when inflicted on his own? What was a crime in others would be a crime in him."[42] Not only is it criminal but insulting, "an act of gross injustice to the memory of those venerable patriarchs, who have received the promises and who looked for a better country . . . to charge them with being slaveholders." For Abraham or any of the patriarchs to be considered as slaveholders "belied the whole tenor of their lives in other respects, their justice and humanity, their kindness and generosity and they would have scorned such a suggestion." Apart from all such arguments, Caruthers makes the familiar concession of abolitionist literature when he offers that even "if . . . Abraham was a *slaveholder* according to the southern import of that term, it would not prove slavery to be right for he did some other things which would not be justifiable at the present day."[43] His relationship with concubines and dissimulation are also recorded, and "surely Christian people will not assert that his example can justify them in the same practice."[44]

Moses and Slavery

For the defenders of slavery, the presence of slaves and the numerous regulations surrounding their acquisition and treatment in the Mosaic era "expressly authorized" American slavery.[45] To this assertion, like Albert Barnes and other antislavery writers of his era, Caruthers insists that slavery " in our sense of the term" was absent "from the first of Genesis to the end of

---

41. Fox-Genovese and Genovese, *The Mind of the Master Class*, 506.
42. Caruthers Papers (w/o pagination).
43. Caruthers, *American Slavery*, 86.
44. Ibid., 77.
45. Armstrong, *The Christian Doctrine of Slavery*, 16.

CH 7: THE SIMILARITY OF CARUTHERS TO OTHER ANTISLAVERY LITERATURE

Revelation."[46] Nevertheless, he thinks there is enough resemblance between the slavery practiced in America and slavery in the Exodus account to argue against slavery based on the Exodus text, and he acknowledges elsewhere a "hard servitude . . . allowed in certain cases by the law of Moses" as "might be expected in that age of rudeness."[47] The acknowledgment of these proximate forms of American slavery is accompanied by numerous qualifications. In the case of the Hebrews' enslavement in Egypt, "there is no intimation of an edict that their bondage should be upon them forever" and he speculates that Pharaoh intended "nothing more than holding them under authority while lived."[48] Unlike American slaves, in the Exodus account the Hebrew slaves' "domestic relations were not interfered with, husbands and wives, and parents and children were not separated and bought and sold to the highest bidder like cattle in the market" and "they were exclusively the property of the government . . . because from the time of Joseph, the lands belonged to Pharaoh."[49] Moreover, the Hebrew slaves, unlike American slaves, could hold property, were highly skilled workers, literate, and with the semblance of their own working government embodied in the elders who first hear Moses. Caruthers goes so far to say that "the bondage of the Israelites in Egypt was greatly preferable to that of our slaves in these southern states, where no sort of respect is paid by the law . . . to the conjugal and parental relations any more than if they were beasts . . . where no negro, however industrious, honest, and meritorious; can legally own a cent's worth of property."[50]

All slaves in the Mosaic era "had some important rights and privileges which are denied to our slaves" but "none of them were in a hopeless condition for there was a way by which they or their children might, in due time—longer or shorter according to the circumstances—regain their freedom and a restoration to all the rights and privileges of citizenship."[51] The permission in the Mosaic law to purchase servants from surrounding nations was a benefit to the slave. A servant "of foreign birth in whatever way he had been obtained, could at any time become a prosletyte to the Jewish religion and consequently be entitled to all the freedom and other

46. Caruthers, *American Slavery*, 68.
47. Ibid., 89.
48. Ibid., 36.
49. Ibid., 37.
50. Ibid., 39.
51. Ibid., 89.

privileges of native born Israelites." Slavery was limited by the Jubilee, the end of a seven year period, and "all the servants or slaves of Hebrew birth and according to many learned men, all others were to be emancipated when their forfeited estates, if they ever had any, were restored to them and they returned to the full and secure enjoyment of all the rights and privileges which had belonged to them."[52]

Regarding those Hebrews who were servants there were "no enactments designed to render the bondage of any class as perpetual, degrading, and absolute . . . provision was made for the improvement of their condition, for the elevation of their character, and for their speedy and full restoration to all the rights and immunities which belonged to the chosen race."[53] The one kind of irreversible servitude for life allowed by Moses outlined in Exod 21:5–6 and Deut 16:16–17 was entered into voluntarily by the servant, "there was no compulsion," because the servant "made his determination freely and in full view of all the consequences."[54]

Altogether, the multiple forms of slavery allowed under the Mosaic code were "essentially milder and far more favorable . . . than the slavery known among the civilized nations of more modern times."[55] Caruthers emphasizes that the time of Moses was a *"peculiar"* era, "designed to be *temporary*," and "confined to that people and to that age of the world."[56] In this same age other things were permitted such as polygamy and divorce "which are forbidden under the more full and spiritual dispensation of the gospel."[57] Generally, Caruthers's emphasizes the "facts and regulations" of the Mosaic era that are "of a favorable kind" rendering servitude nothing like the "cruel and despotic slavery . . . as we have in these southern states."[58] Kidnapping someone into slavery was punishable by death, and although an individual could come into servitude through war or debt or birth there were always important limiting factors. A competent servant could become a steward over other servants, manager of the entire household, or even a teacher of their master's children.[59]

52. Ibid., 92.
53. Ibid., 96.
54. Ibid., 99.
55. Ibid., 103.
56. Ibid., 87.
57. Ibid., 88.
58. Ibid., 93.
59. Ibid., 95.

The Christian Era

Turning from the *obed* of the Old Testament to the *doulos* of the New Testament, Caruthers notes its "great latitude of meaning" and its application to all who were "subservient, submissive, or obedient" to others, voluntarily or involuntarily.[60] He thinks little can be gained by an exhaustive study of the term itself but instead rhetorically asks,

> Would He who came to preach the gospel to the poor and the brokenhearted, then proclaim liberty to the captive and the opening of the prison to them, that are bound, who enjoined it upon all that hear the gospel *to break every yoke* and *to let the oppressed go free*—would he, by his own teachings or by those of his inspired Apostles, sanction such absolute and degrading and hopeless bondage as we have in these southern states?"[61]

Caruthers thinks not. Instead of dealing individually with the usual texts informing the relations between masters and servants that were cited in proslavery literature, he examines "despotism . . . the exercise of absolute power over others," considering it to be more instructive. Whether it is control of a nation or an individual, the absolute nature of despotism is its distinguishing feature "for a number cannot change the nature of the control." American slavery is despotism. Making a greater to lesser argument, from a despotic government of an entire nation to a despotic master of one slave, all forms of despotism are in "direct opposition" to the "spirit and design" of the New Testament.[62] Christ and his Apostles abhor all despotism but treat it "with consummate prudence and discretion." In Caruthers's thinking this explains the similarity in the New Testament's teaching regarding the compliance of Christians to the despotic governments of their era and the compliance of slaves to similar masters. Christians are instructed "to be submissive and obedient" to their government regardless of despotism (Rom 13:17, Titus 3:1, 1 Pet 2:13–14).[63] However, he writes,

> Surely no intelligent and sober thinking Christian can believe that these inspired men intended by this language to sanction the despotic, cruel, and persecuting government of Rome, or to forbid

---

60. Ibid., 106.
61. Ibid., 108.
62. Ibid., 109.
63. Ibid., 117.

them who thus subjected to change it when they could do so without causing some greater calamity.[64]

Caruthers challenges the divine sanctioning of such government. "On the same principle," he asserts that servants or slaves, "of whom there appear to have been a number in the church," are to be submissive and obedient (Col 3:22, 1 Tim 6:1–2, Titus 2:8–9). This however does not mean God sanctions slavery, "the key to the exposition of all these passages" is 1 Cor 7:21 and its encouragement for slaves to get their freedom if they can rightfully do so. "This was as much" as Paul could write "with prudence."[65] In what appears to be a sermon or an earlier version of the document's opening pages that precedes the main manuscript's Table of Contents, Caruthers is more expansive on this point:

> It is said that neither Jesus nor his Apostles denounced slavery, but recognized it as an existing institution . . . in force for time immemorial and prescribed the duties which slave owed to their masters and those which masters owed to their slaves. Neither did they denounce despotic governments; but inculcated obedience and specified the duties which subjects owed to their rulers and those which rulers owed to their subjects, although the Roman government was then one of the most despotic, immoral, and persecuting governments of the world. Are they to be regarded then as sanctioning despotism or designing that it should be perfected? What would have been the consequences to them and to the infant church if they had explicitly and openly denounced the haughty and absolute monarch who was then at the head of the Roman empire? Or that slavery was wrong and must be forth with abolished? . . . They took the wiser course of enjoining upon all concerned such duties as the nature of the case required and leaving it to the silence progress of gospel truth and Christian love to correct the evil; but the very duties enjoined upon rulers and masters, if understood, in their true spirit and practiced in their full import would do away with all despotism whether exercised by one man over a nation or by one man over another man; for they are just the same in nature.

The tactic for the gradual elimination of slavery described in the above passage can be found throughout antislavery literature's treatment of the New Testament. Caruthers follows a well-worn trail traveled by Francis

64. Ibid.
65. Ibid., 118.

Wayland, Albert Barnes, and practically ever other antislavery writer.[66] Increasingly throughout the 1840s and 1850s antislavery writers adopted an approach to the Bible that reflected what they believed to be the meaning of true Christianity.[67] Even though "all tyranny, injustice, and oppression the weak by the strong are the outgrowth of depravity," they must be tolerated while the gospel silently works their overthrow.

Caruthers devotes several pages to a discussion of Onesimus, Philemon's runaway slave. He doubts Onesimus was a slave but a "domestic or hired servant" because the Apostle Paul asks Philemon in his letter to charge him personally for anything Onesimus might owe him. It seems more likely to Caruthers that a servant would owe a debt. Perhaps wages had been paid in advance and the agreement or contract subsequently broken by Onesimus. Even though Onesimus is not a slave, Caruthers seizes on Paul's instruction that in the light of the gospel, Philemon no longer think of Onesimus as a servant but "a *freeman* entitled to share in that equality which was the spiritual birthright of the whole brotherhood."[68]

Summary

Throughout the New and Old Testaments, the regulation of slavery is an irreducible fact. With what was arguably prophetic insight, Caruthers and others contended that this did not give divine sanction to slavery. Nevertheless, Caruthers and other nineteenth-century antislavery writers still believed it was important to expunge the scriptures of the moral offence of slavery by reducing its severity, enhancing its circumstances, or limiting its duration. If their denial of correspondence between the less harsh forms of slavery identified within the biblical eras and the plainly despotic American slavery had a measure of validity, it also revealed their dilemma. Slavery was in their sacred text but not condemned as they believed it should be. Caruthers and others were, in the words of Robert Mullins, "caught between a loyalty to their exegetical method and a personal dislike for the institution of slavery."[69] Mullins' account of the "the almost schizophrenic response" provoked in many readers of Theodore Dwight Weld's *The Bible*

---

66. Barnes, *An Inquiry into the Scriptural View of Slavery*, 283–308; Francis Wayland and Richard Fuller, *Wayland-Fuller Debates*, 4–6.

67. Harrill, "The Use of the New Testament," 154–56.

68. Caruthers, *American Slavery*, 123–24.

69. Mullin, "Biblical Critics and the Battle Over Slavery," 214.

Against Slavery could be applied to this aspect of Caruthers's manuscript and the general impression given by other such antislavery literature: Weld was praised for his assertion that the Bible did not *sanction* slavery, while conversely criticized for his claim that it did not *contain* it.[70]

The close attention given by Caruthers and other antislavery writers to vocabulary and circumstances related to slavery in the Bible, and their conclusions, have been assiduously considered in critical studies. Caroline Shanks' early treatment of antislavery literature describes its "lengthy and recondite examinations" of Hebrew words that bolstered the foregone conclusions of the abolitionist argument.[71] More recently, Albert Harrill has charted the development of the "philological subterfuge" and "semantic obfuscation" of textual studies that preceded the move away from biblical literalism. Similarly, E. Brooks Holifield identifies such studies as "a portentous historical turn in the debate" as they presaged the diminishing of biblical literalism, cultivating a reception for more critical methods of biblical interpretation.[72] Caruthers's arguments against slavery in this section of his manuscript contain such tendencies and portentousness.

Like their antislavery counterparts, proslavery writers also sought to distill the spirit of Christianity from texts far removed from the circumstances of nineteenth-century slavery. Elizabeth Fox-Genovese and Eugene Genovese conclude that "proslavery men had much better of the historical argument."[73] The proslavery argument was certainly presented as the more historically and biblically accurate, even though the racially based slavery of the South and the specific legal relationships created by American slavery had no parallel in the Bible. None of the forms of slavery mentioned in the Old Testament are the same as the race-based slavery of eighteenth and nineteenth-century American history.[74] Nevertheless, antislavery writers "conceded the exegesis" of particular passages to proslavery writers.[75] Within the guarded parameters of interpretation in the antebellum era, the proslavery argument was made formidable by its dependence on the similarities of slavery to the biblical record. It could only be answered by a more

---

70. Ibid., 215.

71. Shanks, "The Biblical AntislaveryArgument of the Decade 1830–1840," 138.

72. Holifield, *Theology in America*, 501.

73. Fox-Genovese and Genovese, *The Mind of the Master Class*, 511; Noll, *America's God*, 391.

74. Meyers, *Exodus*, 35.

75. Noll, *The Mind of the Master Class*, 391.

CH 7: THE SIMILARITY OF CARUTHERS TO OTHER ANTISLAVERY LITERATURE

compelling argument within those same boundaries, a knockout blow that pages 65–136 of Caruthers's manuscript does not deliver.

Divine opposition to American slavery could not be shown from the texts regulating slavery scattered throughout the Bible, but there was, for Caruthers, a text that spoke convincingly. One drawn from a larger story, privileged with authority above all others by virtue of its tradition and its proven power to inspire and transform. The story was Israel's exodus and the text was Exod 10:3. "If the command addressed to Pharaoh was not intended for us and for all others who are in similar circumstances we know not why it was recorded in the volume of inspiration," Caruthers writes of the Exodus text in an earlier preface to his manuscript, "and we can think of no reason why it should not be regarded as an expression of his will for the liberation of the enslaved and oppressed here, now, and everywhere and at all times." Caruthers was not alone in his convictions. There were others who agreed, for whom the Exodus text was supreme.

Chapter 8: The Exodus Text in Nineteenth-Century Discourse

THE APPLICATION OF THE Exodus story to oppressive circumstances previous to the nineteenth century and the countless references or allusions to it throughout Western history support David Lyle Jeffrey's naming of Exodus as "the single most important biblical sourcebook for Jewish and Christian typology as well as hymnody." Exodus "provides plot and theme to countless narratives, a list of which would occupy a volume in itself."[1] Referring to Exodus in his speech to a newly seated parliament in 1654, Oliver Cromwell declares that they had heard from a preacher "today in the Sermon . . . the only parallel of God's dealing with us that I know in this world." The preacher on that occasion was the Puritan and Independent, Thomas Goodwin.[2] Numerous references to Exodus within Goodwin's published works relate Israel's escape and their journey through the wilderness to the life of the individual Christian or the church at large.

Michael Walzer's political exploration of Exodus in our own era reflects on Cromwell's comments and the similar hope of the American Civil Rights movement "for a more sustained parallel" with Israel's ancient deliverance from Egypt.[3] According to Walzer, the Exodus story powerfully "generates a sense of possibility" about our world for those who are oppressed. It carries a message of hope: Not all the world is Egypt! God's promise to lead Israel into a land flowing with milk and honey resonates with those who are struggling against oppressive conditions, inspiring them to envision and pursue a quality of life that is shown by Israel's story to be politically attainable in the present world.[4] In Exodus and Israelite prophecy, writes Jurgen Moltmann, "the God of hope" was made known, a revelation that "confronts us with a promise of something new and with

---

1. Jeffrey, "Exodus," 259.
2. Carlyle, *Oliver Cromwell's Letters and Speeches with Elucidations*, 305–7.
3. Walzer, *Exodus and Revolution*, 3.
4. Ibid., 8.

CHAPTER 8: THE EXODUS TEXT IN NINETEENTH-CENTURY DISCOURSE

the hope of a future given by God."[5] The affinity in Moltmann's thinking to Latin American liberation theology is seen in the shared emphasis on the importance of collaboration to overcome oppression in light of this Exodus hope.[6] Gustavo Gutiérrez, influenced by Moltmann and other early European explorers of political theology, designates the "two fundamental insights" of liberation theology as "its theological method and its perspective of the poor."[7] Yahweh "is the God who liberates slaves" and "who causes empires to fall and raises up the oppressed."[8]

In a sermon, included with his manuscript, Caruthers asserts that the Exodus text is " binding on all who are in similar circumstances, or upon all in every land and every age, from that hour to the present, who are holding their fellow beings in bondage."[9] He writes: "the passage . . . has long appeared to me . . . as one of the most decisive and important in favor of a prompt and universal emancipation that is to be found in the oracles of revealed truth."[10] Others in Caruthers's era thought so, too, but antislavery writing that shares his view of the Exodus text is largely unexamined as a body of literature.

A comprehensive study of the pamphlets, treatises, antislavery society reports, and other documents citing the Exodus text does not exist. A study of such specialized focus would require a survey of the entire body of American antislavery literature, a monumental task, and one beyond the purview of this study. The alternative is the following limited conspectus of American antislavery literature quoting the Exodus text in thirty examples ranging in publication between 1807 and 1865. The importance of Exod 10:3 to the American slavery controversy was not original to Caruthers. The following examples are quoted at length and stand alone in order to convey the widespread use of the Exodus text in nineteenth-century antislavery literature. They also provide a context for appreciating Caruthers's larger and unique development of the text. For the convenience of scanning the examples, each occurrence of the Exodus text is in bold print, however, careful attention to each use of the Exodus text reveals at least three underlying similarities shared in every occurrence. Each example

5. Moltmann, *Theology of Hope*, 16.
6. Paeth, *Exodus Church and Civil Society*, 12–13.
7. Gutiérrez, cited in Tombs, *Latin American Liberation Theology*, xiii.
8. Gutiérrez, *A Theology of Liberation*, 69.
9. Caruthers, "Let My People Go That They May Serve Me: Exodus 10:3."
10. Ibid.

adapts and utilizes the Exodus text to direct attention to the perspective of the oppressed, assert God's providential power, and to identify the oppressor with pharaoh.

Exodus Text Conspectus (1807–1865)

1. James Stephen, 1807.

James Stephen, maritime lawyer, member of Parliament and the author of a comprehensive treatment of West India slavery,[11] despairs in an earlier work of "the singular resolution of a Christian legislature, to prosecute for years to come, a career of acknowledged oppression and bloodshed, upon principles of national convenience." It "seems to amount to a sin, which not only in its degree, but in its kind, is unprecedented and enormous . . . a kind of high treason against the Majesty of Heaven. England is "in open contempt of his laws" because of its dedication to "commerce, our colonial interests, and navigation" Stephen voices a mock supplication on behalf of England, "It is true O God," he prays, that "thy laws are good, but the laws of commercial policy are better" and "we must continue, for a while at least, to violate thy most solemn commandments, and to destroy, as well as oppress, thy rational creatures; because we can no otherwise preserve our commerce, our colonial interests, and navigation."[12] He likens the "perverse and audacious extension" of slavery in the West Indies to "Pharaoh's answer to that demand of God, *Let my people go, that they may serve me*" when "he audaciously straitened those bands of oppression which he was commanded to relax."[13]

2. Letter on British Slavery in the West Indies, 1826.

An anonymous letter on British slavery in the West Indies calls upon "those who have leisure and influence" to "make it their business to diffuse more general information of the horrors of . . . slavery" and "to incite" in the British Parliament, "a deeper and more general sympathy for its wretched victims." The rights of those enslaved can only be restored by the government because "they are themselves too feeble to demand them" and "because they

---

11. Stephen, *The Slavery of the British West India Colonies*.
12. Stephen, *New Reasons for Abolishing the Slave Trade*, 45–46.
13. Ibid.

are so crushed by oppression that they dare not even beg for them." The "procrastinating selfishness" of the slaveholders has induced indifference towards "lacerating whips and galling chains" and towards those who have "been so long the victims of lawless power" and who "have so long been accustomed to the yoke."[14] Those who kidnap the "Negro from his friends and country, and puts him in irons on board a slave-ship; who buys him of the slave merchant" or "stamps brandmarks into his flesh with hot irons" or compels "him to labor all the days of his wretched existence, without wages, under the lash of the cart-whip" or "if he attempt to escape, or make any resistance, hunts him down like a beast of prey, chains and flogs him without mercy" and "shoots and gibbets him at his pleasure; seizes upon his children also, from generation to generation, as his lawful prey" are not " guilty as they are . . . the most guilty parties in these transactions of iniquity." The greater guilt most be born by their employers, "who make it worth their while" and "who bribe them to commit these atrocities."

God's image has, "in these His abused creatures, been . . . long trampled underfoot." The "sacred name" is "mocked" by any "principle of gradual emancipation" which is only another of many "new modifications" which are in fact "more disguised and subtle modes of oppression." *Let my people go* "is the authoritative language of the great Parent of the Universe" for " all who have ears to hear the voice of reason, of conscience, of revelation." The listener must "keep aloof from the confused Babel of sordid interest and political expediency" and " turn a deaf ear to those artful glosses, those self-ish evasions, those 'vain traditions' that render God's command " of none effect." *Let my people go* " is as clearly the Divine command" for American slavery " as it was respecting the oppressed Israelites." With respect to the West Indies "the command is not less intelligible, in a Christians ear, because conveyed by the spirit, instead of the letter." Although "the punishment of disobedience" does not come immediately, it will "fall in heavier inflictions upon Christian, than upon Egyptian slave-holders."[15]

3. George Thompson, 1832.

Abolitionist George Thompson's "Three Lectures on British Colonial Slavery, delivered in the Royal Ampitheatre, Liverpoole, on the 28th and 30th of

---

14. *Letters on the Necessity of a Prompt Extinction*, 92–95.
15. Ibid.

August, and 6th of September," make repeated use of the Exodus text as cited below in Benjamin Lundy's review.

> Ah, it is impious to say that an unoffending being is not fit for liberty; it is a libel upon the government of the great God himself. I repeat it, and I charge my opponent to put it down . . . I repeat it is both cruel and impious to say that men are not fit for freedom. The wretched subterfuges of ancient times. Pharaoh set the example—*Let my people go*"said God by Moses, to the Egyptian tyrant. "I will not let them go," he replied; and he might have added and perhaps did add—"they are not fit for freedom—they cannot cross the Red Sea—they will starve in the wilderness—they are numerous and powerful where they are, it would be unkind to let them go." *Let my people go* was however the imperative command; and when he hardened his heart and refused God sent a fearful plague, and again the Almighty and the command was reiterated *Let my people go*—again he hardened his heart and refused, God sent a fearful plague, and the command was reiterated *Let my people go*—again he hardened his heart, and again the Almighty sent the plague; and it was not until the first-born throughout Egypt were destroyed that he sent them forth to serve God in the wilderness. And what was the consequence? Were they led forth to destruction, or left to perish? No. The same arm which brought them forth out of the house of bondage divided the waters of the Read Sea, so that they went over upon dry land; and the same arm overwhelmed their enemies beneath its surges. Were they left to hunger, to thirst, and to die in the wilderness? No. They were fed with manna from heaven, and refreshed with water from the smitten rock; and the liberated people of the Lord were thus sustained until they entered into the land flowing with milk and honey. *Let my people go,* is the command still given in the sacred canon of our faith. The practical reply is "No," we will not let them go" and the motive is the same as in ancient times—*Pharaoh wanted more bricks, and the West Indians want more sugar.*[16]

4. Captain Charles Stuart's Letter to the Archbishop, 1833.

In his letter to the Archbishop of Canterbury Captain Charles Stuart recounts the dramatic failure of the Society for Propagating the Gospel in its attempt to demonstrate the compatibility of Christianity with slavery. Stuart

---

16. Cited in Lundy, *Genius of Universal Emancipation*, 91.

CHAPTER 8: THE EXODUS TEXT IN NINETEENTH-CENTURY DISCOURSE

was an early and important influence on American abolitionists, especially Theodore Dwight Weld. Before his conversion to antislavery views he had played a central role in the establishment of the fugitive slave community in Canada during the early 1820s. By 1830 he was a formidable antislavery activist.[17] William Lloyd Garrison includes the letter in his publication, *The Abolitionist*, because "though written principally in reference to the course pursued by the Society for Propagating the Gospel, it applies with great force to slaveholders in the United States" and will "be read with interest by all who acknowledge the rights of slaves to freedom."[18]

In 1710 Christopher Codrington had bequeathed two plantations with over three hundred slaves in Barbados to the SPG requesting that the Church of England send missionaries to live there and establish a college and provide for the education of the slaves. Tension between the need for profitability and the intended reforms doomed the experiment from the beginning. England's Slavery Abolition Act of 1833 set into motion the end of the plantation, but not before the publication of Stuart's letter by William Lloyd Garrison.

"That Society," the Captain Stuart writes of the SPG, "is a slaveholder." In deference he calls the archbishop "my Lord" and warns that "it is an easy thing to wear a mitre and a cross; but an awful thing to give account . . . before the Judge of the quick and dead." Warnings against hatred from Lev 19:17 and against riches from James 2:10 are "solemn words" that inform his objections. "The Society has had the said estate with Slaves, for upwards of 100 years. God, no doubt put it into their power, that they might obey Him, and let the 'oppressed go free.'" and "Col. Codrington put it into their power, that they might educate a certain number of white youths, and give religious instruction to the blacks." He reminds the archbishop "how poorly both of these objects have been answered" and asks "what has the Society been doing since 1710, when the bequest was made them?" Only "preparing to obey God, as soon as might be prudent or convenient." Recalling that "three thousand years ago, the Jews were in bondage in Egypt," the writer asks, "Did God sanction Pharaoh's keeping them in bondage, until the Egyptian task masters had prepared them for liberty? No! He commanded Pharaoh to *let His people go*." If someone might argue that the Hebrews were prepared for liberty, Garrison counters: "Their bones scattered in the wilderness, where

---

17. Yacovone, Review of *Black Soldiers in Blue*, 467.
18. Garrison, *The Abolitionist*, 82–84.

they sinned, and the golden calf, molten and graved at the very foot of the Mount, fearfully reply that they were not."

Stuart goes on to review the enslavement of Israel subsequent to Exodus that is recorded in the book of Judges. After their enslavement under king of Mesopotamia and their deliverance by Othniel in Judg 3:7–11 he asks "Did God permit him to keep them in bondage, till he had prepared them for liberty? No! God raised up Othniel, and delivered them, though He knew that they could soon again reduce themselves by their crimes, to bondage." In the case of their oppression under Eglon, the King of Moab and their deliverance by Ehud in Judg 3:14–30 "history supplies a similar evidence: God delivered them from slavery, most unfit as they proved themselves for freedom." Summing up the enslavement of Israel recorded in Judges 4–10 and their deliverance by Deborah, Stuart says, "I venture to affirm . . . without reserve, that we have no instance in the Bible, in which God sanctions one man, in keeping another man, without a crime, in bondage, in order to prepare him for liberty. The process is totally unscriptural." Invoking "the nature of God's holy Providence" Stuart says "it is unalterably a crime, for any power to subject any man to bondage, or to keep him in bondage, except as a righteous punishment for his own crimes; and until the Negroes be fairly tried and found guilty of some crime, which would warrant such a dreadful penalty, there can be no right to keep them in bondage, even for a moment."[19] As seen in the following excerpt, Stuart's appeal to the archbishop presents the Exodus text as a recurring divine demand for the freedom of the slaves from the SPG, creating a dialogue that lends an unmistakable air of Pharaoh-like defiance to the society's hesitation and postponement.

Here are my poor, said God, they have been oppressed. I put them into your hands. *"Let them go, that they may serve me."* We will, replied the Society, as soon as we have fitted them for it. So, thirty years rolled away, a generation passed into eternity, and the next generation was still enslaved, and still not fitted. *Let my people go*, said God, in 1740, '*that they may serve me.*' They are not ready yet, replied the Society. A third generation rose in 1770, and again God said—*Let my people go, that they may serve me."* We are getting them ready, replied the Society, as fast as we can. Do pray give us two generations more, for to tell you the truth, we want them to serve ourselves a little longer, and to make money for us, that we may build a college, and educate the white youths; and besides it would be

19. Ibid.

running so sadly counter, to the generous and cultivated Barbarians! Another generation passed into eternity unredressed; and then another; and still the Society, instead of obeying, is only preparing to obey.... What but a similar procedure, my Lord, awakened the midnight echoes of Egypt, with the howl of the slaughter of the firstborn?... Now, my Lord, the question which I wish to place before you with affectionate boldness, is: What is the real character of measures, which consist in 'preparing to let the oppressed go free,' instead of letting them go?[20]

5. Rhode Island Antislavery Convention, 1836.

The *Proceedings of the Rhode-Island AntislaveryConvention*, held in Providence in 1836 asserts the humanity of the slave in common with all Americans, arguing also for the rights given by the Creator. The Exodus text is cited in a call for the restoration of all privileges and as a warning that Pharaoh's fate would befall slaveowners if they did not listen. They do not plead "for the white man or the colored man" but for all humanity "for Americans,... for the people of the United States,....for our country, our whole country, our undivided country,... for our entire race, for rational, immortal and moral beings, for the children of our common Father, for the purchase of our common Redeemer." On this basis they make their appeal for the freedom of the slaves.

> We ask for them the rights given them by their Creator the rights they never have forfeited, rights identified with their spiritual existence, rights essential to their temporal and eternal welfare... The contest we espouse was commenced simply by a pleading for the poor slave! And this plea we shall never cease to urge. Our voice to the oppressor, in the name of the Lord of Hosts, shall still be *"LET MY PEOPLE GO THAT THEY MAY SERVE ME!"* Restore to them their Bibles, their sanctuaries, their Sabbaths, their firesides their family sanctities, their unshackled consciences, their deathless intellects, their undying souls, their liberty to serve their Creator and enjoy him forever! Today, if ye will hear his voice, harden not your hearts to say with Pharaoh, "tomorrow !"[21]

20. Ibid.
21. *Proceedings of the Rhode-Island AntislaveryConvention*, 37.

6. The Ladies New York City Antislavery Society, 1836.

The story of Stephen from the book of Acts is recalled by *The Ladies' New York City Antislavery Society*. The cause of freedom for slaves is identified with the activities and martyrdom of the primitive Christian church. "Never was there any cause undertaken to benefit suffering humanity," they write, "in which, more than in this, its advocates must lift up its claims, as the first martyr Stephen closed his dying sermon, looking up steadfastly into Heaven, and catching thence the spirit that will make the raging of the angry and mistaken crowd as impotent to disturb the soul, as to deter, in the least degree, from duty." In a further comparison of the abolitionists to ancient Christians, they cite Acts 4:29: "Such a spirit must they have as breathes in the memorable prayer of the Apostles, *And now, Lord, behold their threatenings, and grant unto thy servants, that with all boldness they may speak thy word.* They are "a band of Apostles for this holy cause" of abolitionism " raised up; and amidst such odium and persecution as proved the divine origin, and called out the unyielding energies of the primitive church," and their campaign for immediate emancipation and the resulting persecution is a parallel to the proclamation of the gospel by its early heralds.[22]

> They have gone from one mountain top to another, kindling their beacon light, and from one plain to another, planting their standard, and unfurling to every eye its startling motto, Thus saith the Lord, *Let my people go that they may serve me.* Through their instrumentality the deep slumber of our guilty nation, on the subject of slavery, has at length been broken.[23]

7. La Roy Sunderland, 1836.

La Roy Sunderland withdrew from the Methodist Episcopal Church in 1842 along with two other well-known abolitionists, Orange Scott and Jotham Horton. An antislavery newspaper produced by Scott, *True Wesleyan*, announced their withdrawal and explained that they could no longer tolerate their denomination's policy on slavery.[24] Earlier, in 1836, Sunderland had published a study of slavery that includes "Extracts from the writings

---

22. *First Annual Report of the Ladies' New York City Antislavery Society*, 4.
23. Ibid.
24. Jacob "La Roy Sunderland," 1–17.

of Moses" in which he expresses his belief in the continuing application of the text. Even though "the people of God were held in slavery by the Egyptians," the bondage which they were compelled to endure was certainly not so cruel and severe as that which nearly three millions of American citizen are now doomed to suffer.[25]" He asks,

> And how can a believer in the truth of the Bible suppose, for one moment, that this same unchangeable God is now an indifferent spectator merely, to the accumulated wrongs which thousands of the poor slaves are forced to endure in this Christian land? *Let my people go.* And now, if God uttered his testimony against the slavery which his people endured thousands of years ago, and if he commanded their oppressors to let them go free, how can it be made to appear that he does not do this now?[26]

8. Western Presbyterian Church, 1838.

Members of Western Presbyterian Church in Philadelphia who were "actively engaged in the efforts, now being, put forth in favor of immediate Emancipation" complained to the larger congregation that "the address recently delivered by our Pastor on the subject" was "professedly designed" to "elicit the sympathies of the congregation against those of us who had openly espoused the cause of the slave." What exactly the Reverend John Patton said in an address "at the close of the sermon" on Sunday morning, December 16th, they do not review only "that the drift of the whole was, to hold up the active Antislavery men and women among us, as disturbers of the peace of the Church, as the promoters of strife, and as working against the temporal and spiritual interests of the Church" and as "prosecuting measures of which the Session had unanimously disapproved." For Patton's congregation this was the "unexpected introduction of an exciting subject." According to the author the impression given by the Rev. Patton on this occasion is that certain members of the congregation were "engaged in a fanatical crusade . . . as pledged men . . . like the forty men who conspired against the life of Paul, resolved to carry out their revolutionary plans, even at the hazard of all that is valuable in the institutions of Christianity." "Once more" they complain, " we are told, that the efforts of Northern

---

25. Sunderland, *The Testimony of God Against Slavery*, 14–15.
26. Ibid.

Abolitionists however well meant, have only had the effect to retard the cause of Emancipation." The actions of the abolitionists are blamed for the worsening conditions of the slaves. The "full refutation" of this "oft refuted charge" will not be given, they write, even though they could "adduce evidence to an almost unlimited extent,"

> from the day that Moses and Aaron went in unto Pharaoh, in the name of Israel's God, saying, *Let my people go,* down to the glorious first of August, 1838, when the efforts of English Abolitionists resulted in the immediate Emancipation of nearly one million of Slaves, in the British West Indies. Suffice it to say, further, that those who are willing to examine the testimony which has been collected in relation to this part of the subject, may be fully satisfied, that the prevalence of Abolition sentiment at the North, and especially in the Church, has not only awakened the attention of professing Christians at the South, to their duty in relation to the Emancipation of their Slaves; but also to meliorate, to some extent the condition of the Slaves who are still held in bondage.[27] In view of all that has been said, we now cast ourselves upon your Christian candor, and your enlightened judgment; and ask of you an honest verdict, whether we are guilty, or not guilty, of the charge of stirring up strife, and disturbing the true peace of the Church, and deserving, on account of what we have done in this matter, to be excluded from your Christian fellowship and affections.[28]

9. George Thompson, 1846.

In a letter to his colleague Henry Wright in Edinburgh, Scotland, George Thompson uses the Exodus text to encapsulate his own responsibility and calling as an abolitionist. Overwhelmed by the injustices of slavery, but still resolute, he portrays a "slave on earth" now suffering but who is also a " free man in heaven" and in a state of confusion "running up and down Jacobs ladder, from the plantation on earth to the New Jerusalem in glory from the horrible bondage of the slave below to the glorious liberty of the Son of God above."[29]

Thompson rhetorically frames his moral outrage with a series of biblical texts and allusions that are contradicted by the actions of slaveholders.

27. "Address of the Union AntislaveryAuxiliary, 3.
28. Ibid., 19.
29. Thompson, *The Free Church and Her Accusers,* 5.

CHAPTER 8: THE EXODUS TEXT IN NINETEENTH-CENTURY DISCOURSE

Christ comes knocking on the door of the slaveholder "and if any one opens; I enter and abide there. But never mind me. The house is yours." The slaves "may lay up treasure in heaven" but "all they have and are, are yours, on earth." On the one hand Jesus says, "If any do the will of his Father in heaven, the same are his mother and his sister and his brother" however, "Christ has no objection to his mother his brother or his sister being a slave." Although slaves are in their "origin, their destiny, and their faculties . . . but a little lower than the angels" their owners " may make them a little lower than the beasts." Although "they were redeemed out of spiritual bondage with the precious blood of the Son of God" their owners "may sell them into temporal bondage for such corruptible things as silver and gold."

The coming day of judgment when "Christ shall know his own" and "when the Shepherd shall claim his sheep" will soon arrive Thompson writes. A day when " that temple shall be built in heaven, the stones whereof have been fashioned by the Divine Architect on earth." In this temple Thompson sees " the negro, a living stone" and excluded from the temple in the judgment are the slaveholders "who claimed the child of God as theirs" and who are now arraigned by Christ:

> I was on earth, but ye bought and sold me ye manacled and scourged me ye outlawed and enslaved me ye despised and insulted me; I came to ye in the form of a black man. I was poor, ignorant, friendless, powerless as a black man; and, while ye professed to worship me, seated at the right-hand of my Father, in majesty and glory, ye spurned me from the door ye drove me to the field, and hunted me with dogs: I came to ye as a little child, and in the helplessness of infancy asked ye to succour me, and train me for heaven; ye ranked me with the calves of your stall and fed me only for the flesh market and sold me on the shambles.[30]

"For better, for worse," Thompson concludes, "I link myself with thy suffering poor and glory in the name of Infidel." He believes that "it is not thy will that one of these little ones should perish" and he prays: "Appear for their deliverance; make those strong who lead their cause. Be with thy servants when they go in unto Pharaoh, and cry *let my people go*.[31]

---

30. Ibid.
31. Ibid.

10. Peter Randolph, 1855.

Peter Randolph, ex-slave and pastor of Ebenezer Baptist Church in Boston, Massachusettes arrived in the city in a group of sixty-six former plantation slaves from the estate of Carter Edloe, from Petersburg, Virginia, September 1847. As stipulated by Edloe's will the entire work force of the plantation was given their freedom upon his death and the guarantee of fifty dollars each as well as transportation to a free state. Edloe died in 1844, but the executor of his estate delayed their exodus for three years and of the fifty dollars, each received less than fifteen.[32]

Randolph's chief work, *Sketches of Slave Life*, recounts the details of life on Edloe's plantation, Randolph's family background, conversion to Christianity and the story of the slaves' liberation. It is largely a response to a specific variety of proslavery literature that portrayed a favorable view of plantation life and which is in view when Randolph responds to the "erroneous conclusion" that "the institution of slavery is a benevolent missionary enterprise."[33] Randolph mentions the author of one such portrayal, "Dr. Nehemiah Adams," and "his visit to the South, where became so much in love with the 'peculiar institution'. Randolph gives a very different account of slavery, detailing horrific beatings in the "galling yoke of bondage." He appeals "to the Christian Church to lift up its voice" and "to the men of America . . . to help this cause" and "the women of America, that they plead for their suffering sisters" and "little children" to "remember in their prayers those little colored brothers and sisters who are robbed of their parents" and "have no homes for their weary little frames." Finally, he appeals "to high Heaven to listen to the heart-breaking cries of the captive negro" and to "the great Jehovah to soften the hard hearts of the many Pharaohs, that they may let the people go free!"[34]

Randolph's use of Exodus is found in the poetic conclusion of his autobiography, "The Blood of Slave." The poem achieves its effect through the repetition of the refrain "the blood of the slave cries unto God," moving rapidly through the dialogue between the conscience of the nation and unyielding slaveholder, and ending with a confession of the sin of slavery against God, humanity, and the Declaration of Independence. The refusal of the slaveholder to grant liberty has provoked "the AntiSlavery voice"

---

32. Bassard, "Crossing Over," 113, 117.
33. Ibid., 117.
34. Randolph, *Sketches of Slave Life*, 31, 79.

CHAPTER 8: THE EXODUS TEXT IN NINETEENTH-CENTURY DISCOURSE

which awakens the nation to "cry aloud against this great evil" and to "lift up your voice like a trumpet, and show the people their sins, and the nation its guilt." All citizens are to "pray that God may have mercy upon us" and "forgive this great sin." The "God of justice" is called upon to "give us hearts and consciences to feel the deep sorrow of this great evil" in which "we have so long indulged."[35] A national act of repentance is required for the forgiveness of "this great evil, the evil of selling, whipping, and killing men, women and children." America has "sinned against Heaven"; "against light"; "against the civilized world" and "against that declaration which our fathers put forth to the world" that "all men are created equal."

> The blood of the slave cries unto God from the ground,
>
> and it calls loudly for vengeance on his adversaries.
>
> The blood of the slave cries unto God from the rice swamps.
>
> The blood of the slave cries unto God from the cotton plantations.
>
> The blood of the slave cries unto God from the tobacco farms.
>
> The blood of the slave cries unto God from the sugar fields.
>
> The blood of the slave cries unto God from the cornfields.
>
> The blood of the slave cries unto God from the whipping-post.
>
> The blood of the slave cries unto God from the auction-block.
>
> The blood of the slave cries unto God from the gallows.
>
> The blood of the slave cries unto God from the hunting-dogs that run down the poor fugitive.
>
> The blood of men, women and babes cries unto God from Texas to Maine. Wherever the Fugitive Slave Law reaches, the voice of its victims is heard.
>
> The mighty God, the great Jehovah, speaks to the consciences of men, and says, "*Let my people go, **free**!*"
>
> And the slaveholder answers, "Who is Jehovah, that I should obey him?"[36]

---

35. Ibid., 79–81.
36. Ibid., 80–81.

11. John Dixon Long, 1857.

An "Exhortation by a Colored Preacher" included in *Pictures of Slavery in Church and State* recounts the Rev. John Dixon Long's experience of hearing a sermon in which the Exodus text was used by a preacher opposing the argument that abolitionists had made it worse for slaves than before.

> Now, brethren, *Moses was an abolitionist.* The Master told him to go to Pharaoh and tell him that the Lord says, *Let my people go that they may serve me.* But Pharaoh said; 'Who is the Lord? I will not let his people go.' So Pharaoh oppressed the people more and more; and they went to Moses and told him that he had made things worse than they were before; and they blamed Moses for stirring up Pharaoh. Now, my brethren, we must make the devil made before we can do any good. The abolitionists have done good, because they have called the attention of the people to our brethren, who are under their taskmasters.[37]

12. James Redpath, 1860.

While living in the Kansas Territory and working as a journalist for several newspapers in the late 1850s, nineteenth-century political activist, James Redpath, met the abolitionist John Brown and soon became a leader in the movement to prevent Kansas from becoming a slave state. At Brown's request he moved to Boston in 1858 to recruit assistance and support for a slave insurrection. When Brown's attack on Harpers Ferry in 1859 failed, Redpath helped some of the participants escape and was himself pursued as an accomplice.[38] In his book, *Echoes of Harper's Ferry*, Redpath offers a collection of essays, letters, and prose with sentiment that resonates with Brown's attempt to incite an insurrection. Several of the selections utilize the Exodus text.

A letter from one of Brown's cousins states that God "who made of one blood of all nations of men to dwell on the face of the earth sent his servants Moses and Aaron to Pharaoh, king of Egypt, saying, 'Thus saith the Lord God of the Hebrews *Let my people go, that they may serve me*'" but like Southern slaveholders "Pharaoh said in the pride and stoutness of his heart 'Who is the Lord, that I should obey his voice to let Israel go? I know

---

37. Dixon, *Long Pictures of Slavery in Church and State*, 313.
38. McKivigen, *Forgotten Firebrand*, x, 19.

CHAPTER 8: THE EXODUS TEXT IN NINETEENTH-CENTURY DISCOURSE

not the Lord, neither will I let Israel go.' " The writer warns: "So may the wicked slaveholders of the South say respecting those whom they cruelly hold in bondage; but the same king who delivered the children of Israel from Egyptian bondage will surely deliver those who are oppressed in our own country, and it is not in the united power of earth and hell to prevent their deliverance."[39]

13. Edwin Wheelock, 1860.

Also included in Redpath's work is the work of Reverend Edwin Wheelock who declares the American government, "incarnate in Pharaoh" to whom "these solemn words were slowly thundered: Thus saith the Lord, *let my people go that they may serve me*. God has "surely seen the affliction of my people and have heard their cry" and has "come down to deliver them," knowing "the oppression whereby they are oppressed" and "their sorrow." But when Egypt "had shown itself hardened in inhumanity and sin, and every moral and spiritual appeal had been vainly made, then we read that the 'Lord plagued Egypt.' "This," Wheelock remarks, "is the record of slavery always and everywhere. Never yet in the history of man was a tyrant race known to loosen its grasp of the victim's throat, save by the pressure of force."[40]

14. George Cheever, 1860.

Similarly, the Rev. George Cheever, says that "God's voice thunders *Let my people go!*" but the "Christian Pharaoh in our Egypt" hides behind "theological technicalities" which is tantamount to Pharaoh's question, "Who is the Lord, that I should obey his voice to let the people go?"[41]

15. Osborne Anderson, 1861.

Osborne Perry Anderson, one of John Brown's men, eluded capture and presents John Brown and Harper's Ferry as part of a movement dating "back to a period very far beyond the memory of the oldest inhabitant." In

---

39. Redpath, *Echoes of Harper's Ferry*, 431.
40. Ibid., 178; cf. Wheelock, *Harper's Ferry and its Lesson*, 6.
41. Redpath, *Echoes of Harper's Ferry*, 144.

a comparison of Brown to Moses, Anderson says that the events of Harpers Ferry were to John Brown like "the appointed work . . . of an ancient patriarch spoken of in Exodus . . . who, true to his great commission, failed not to trouble the conscience and to disturb the repose of the Pharaohs of Egypt with that inexorable, 'Thus saith the Lord: *Let my people go!*'" John Brown and Harper's Ferry is one more occurrence of the same message "coming down through the nations." Regardless of national boundaries, it has "been proclaimed and enforced by the patriarch and the warrior of the Old World, by the enfranchised freeman and the humble slave of the New," all forming "an unbroken chain of sentiment and purpose from Moses of the Jews to John Brown of America."[42]

16. Stephen Vail, 1862.

The Reverend Stephen Vail's sermon preached at the Methodist Biblical Institute in Concord, New Hampshire in 1862 is one of the longer treatments of the Exodus text. According to Vail, Moses might be seen as a "poor abolition fanatic" who fears "that he could do nothing with such a great king as Pharaoh and such a mighty people as the Egyptians." He is certain people "will not believe on him." For Vail "this describes the case of many of the Christian churches and the Christian ministers of our day" who "hesitate and are fearful" and consider slavery "a political matter altogether." They only want "simply to preach the gospel and let this negro question alone." Regarding the states protection of slavery they claim "it is wicked to resist the powers that be" because "he that resisteth the power resisteth God." Until recently, Vail's "own branch of the church has been excusing herself" and "even allowed her members to hold men and women in cruel bondage."[43]

Vail's sermon filters the Exodus account through the lens of the nineteenth-century slavery controversy. While Moses is hesitant, Aaron " proved to be a ready abolitionist" and their meeting with the elders of Israel is a " general abolition meeting" and their work is "abolition agitation," or "abolition preaching" or "abolition teaching." The first plague that turns water into blood is a picture of the "bloody nature of the slave power" and the maiming of the slaves "by hard labor, by whips, by shooting, hanging and blood hounds." The stink of the dead fish further demonstrate that the " cruelties of the Slave Power of our own land have made it a stench in the

---

42. Anderson, *A Voice from Harper's Ferry*, 7.
43. Vail, *Overthrow of the Slave Power*, 10–12.

CHAPTER 8: THE EXODUS TEXT IN NINETEENTH-CENTURY DISCOURSE

nostrils of all good men both North and South." The "slave power in our own land" has a "blood thirsty nature" and just as Pharaoh attempted to thwart Moses, God's "chosen vessel" so the "diabolical Slave Power of our own land . . . had plotted the death of our modern Moses, Mr. Lincoln."[44] Just as God published his "proclamation of Freedom to the downtrodden people by his servant Moses" but Pharaoh "harkened not" so "we need not be surprised then if we should witness a similar disregard in respect to the recent Proclamation of our President."

The second plague of dying frogs symbolizes "the Garrisonian abolitionists." Like frogs covering the entire land of Egypt and then dying, Garrison extremists advocated not only "the abolition of slavery, but the abolition of the church of God, the ministry, and the Union and the Constitution." Such radicals "like the frogs of Egypt became a stench over all the land." The lice of the third plague are "the political and ecclessiastical compromisers" of slavery, "a very numerous yet detestable race." The fourth plague's flies represent the members of "the free soil party." They became "very numerous and flew very extensively even over to distant Kansas and California, and bred . . . very fast, and in 1858 came very near electing Mr. Fremont as President." The fifth plague's dying livestock symbolize "the great Democratic party of the North upon which the slave power was accustomed to ride into office" most of which died "but a few still live to influence elections, and so in love are they with their old trade that they beg still to carry the infamous Slave Power on their backs." The accompanying boils represent the "abolition and free soil newspapers" whose ideas, like the dust sprinkled by Moses and Aaron, "cleaves to the sides" of proslavery thinking causing severe itching and inflammation."

The absence of hail from Goshen during the sixth plague is a picture of the American slave's safety from "the iron hail of the contending armies." The "bursting shells flashing along the ground do not touch him" because he is "far away in the rice swamps and the cornfields of the south."[45] The pride of the North says "we will not fight side by side with negroes" and Southern tyranny says "let him dig on the plantations" or "throw up our fortifications for us." Either way "the bondsman escapes God's hail and fire." The complaints of Pharaoh's servants during the locusts of the seventh plague who urge him to release Moses and the people "that they may serve the Lord their God" is "precisely what many persons of the border States are

---

44. Ibid.
45. Ibid., 12–13.

beginning to say: let the slaves go." They are finally yielding to the " locusts of armies both of the North and of the South. With the treatment of each plague visited upon Egypt and its corresponding fulfillment in the American controversy, Vail follows the pattern of the Exodus story repeating the text, *Let my people go that they may serve me.*[46]

17. William Lloyd Garrison, 1862.

A speech made by William Garrison in 1862 uses the Exodus text to underscore the moral urgency of emancipation in the nation. He recounts that of "the forty thousand pulpits" in the Union only "a very small portion advocate instant abolition as a religious duty." Of the more than "three thousand public journals" fewer than "half a dozen oppose" slavery "as inherently iniquitous." The excuses for continuing slavery are well-known: "The victims are an inferior race" or "they are better off in slavery than they would be out of it." The slaves really "do not want to be free" or "they could not take care of themselves because of their laziness." Racial "prejudice against them is natural and unconquerable" and " they can never rise in the scale of being here."[47] Such opinions are expressed "by all classes in every section of the country with as much assurance as though they were eternal verities." But these are all "lies" or "if true, then the Declaration of Independence is indeed 'a rhetorical flourish,' and "the rights of human nature are mockeries, and the Golden Rule no test of moral obligation."

Garrison argues that if it is illegal to enslave " a native on the African coast" then "it is no less so to enslave one of African descent in the United States." If one slave has a right to be free such is the right of every other slave. For Garrison the call for the freedom of slaves is the "same demand . . . made through the prophet Isaiah to Jewish oppressors. They were to "loose the bands of wickedness, undo the heavy burdens, let the oppressed go free, break every yoke." This must include "all yokes and "leaves no one in the house of bondage. It "brings instant and universal deliverance." Those who "profess to believe in the Bible as the inspired word of God, and to be the disciples of Him who came to set the captives free" cannot believe it. "Lord," they answer, " give us time; not today, but in the distant future; not all at once, but very gradually" because "it is a very delicate and complicated matter." Yet "the heavens" still declare: "Break every yoke!" The

---

46. Ibid., 13–17.
47. Garrison, *Our National Visitation*.

proslavery response is to consider "the loss of the cotton crop" and "the blow that would be given to commerce." Garrison labels all such arguments as "atheistical distrust" and "guilty apprehensions." He reminds his listeners of "the most cheering assurances and the richest promises" that accompany obedience. If they will remove "the yoke from your midst" and "satisfy the afflicted soul" then "the Lord will guide you continually and satisfy your soul in drought and strengthen your bones." Such emancipators "shall be like a watered garden, and like a spring of water that does not fail." God's promises "are sure, and human nature is the same in all time, throughout the world." The abolitionist stands before America as Moses did before Pharaoh. Moses' "demand was for immediate, unconditional, universal emancipation; in other words, what in this land is everywhere denounced as fanatical, destructive, pestilent abolitionism." But the call for abolition is nothing less than another visitation of the voice that spoke "in behalf of the oppressed children of Israel" and now speaks to America, "Thus saith the Lord God, *Let my people go*."[48]

18. Charles Sumner, 1862.

Charles Sumner's Boston speech in 1862 appeals to the Exodus text as the grounds and motivation for the prosecution of the ongoing war when all else fails. In the aftermath of President Lincoln's unpopular Emancipation Proclamation, Sumner calls upon his listeners to "uphold the Union against treason" and "uphold freedom, without which bloody treason will flourish over us." They are reminded that "the hour of debate has passed" and that "the hour of duty has sounded." It is through "the arms of our soldiers, that the war will be waged but the "Proclamation" is also "now a war measure" and the "same loyalty which supports the one is now due to the other." Lincoln's decision to free the slaves in the southern states of the rebellion "must be sustained as you sustain an army in the field." But "if the instincts of patriotism did not prompt this support" then the "duty which we all owe to the Supreme Ruler, God Almighty" is demanded by the Exodus text, *Let my people go*. Sumner is hesitant to make himself "the interpreter of his will" but these words capture for him "a venerable maxim of jurisprudence" that anyone who "would have equity must do equity." Regarding slavery, God "plainly requires equity at our hands," and a successful outcome to the war cannot be achieved "while we set at naught this requirement" which is "proclaimed in

48. Ibid., 4–10.

his divine character" and " in the dictates of reason." Using the narrative of Exodus, Sumner declares that "great judgments have fallen upon the country . . . plagues have been let loose; rivers have been turned into blood, and there is a great cry throughout the land, for there is not a house where there is not one dead." With "each judgment we seem to hear that terrible voice which sounded in the ears of Pharaoh . . . *Let my people go*, that they may serve me."[49] Neither the Exodus text nor Lincoln's Emancipation Proclamation have changed the "object" of the war but now "its character is derived from the new force" of its moral mission to free the slaves. A new alliance between "Liberty and Union, now and forever, one and inseparable" has made it more than a war for country, but a war "for all mankind." While "slavery yet lingers in Brazil, and beneath the Spanish flag" in in Cuba and Porto Rico, it cannot "survive its extinction here." And if slavery is defeated in America "we open its gates all over the world, and let the oppressed go free." If America is saved "we shall save civilization."[50]

Sumner uses the familiarity of his listeners with John Bunyan's *Pilgrim's Progress* to illustrate the nation's burden and goal. The war is now against slavery, the "heaviest burden of humanity" and "the only burden our country has been called to bear." As Bunyan's character, Christian, travels to heaven after he is relieved of his burden, so unburdened of slavery "our happy country" unburdened of slavery "with humanity in its train, all changed in raiment and in countenance . . . will hurry upward to the celestial gate." So far in its history, America's "example has failed . . . because of slavery." Even with "unparalleled prosperity, the comfort diffused among a numerous people" and "resources without stint," the nation's example was still "powerless" because of slavery. But now the removal of slavery " will revolutionize the world," and "the battle which we now fight belongs to the grandest events of history." Few world events like this have ever come and "this is one of those epochs from which humanity will date" The war against slavery is "one of the battles of the ages." As the Battle of Tours repulsed the expansion of the Muslims and "Western Europe was saved" for Christianity, so " no effort can be too great" and "no faith can be too determined" in this great fight for all humanity. Those who die in this cause "will be remembered as the heroes through whom the Republic was saved and civilization established forever." *Let my people go* is " that sublime edict" which

---

49. Sumner, "Emancipation!"
50. Ibid., 22.

provides "the soldier both sword and buckler" and "gives to the conflict all the grandeur of a great idea."[51]

19. Henry Clay Fish, 1862.

The pastor of First Baptist Church in Newark, New Jersey, Reverend Henry Clay Fish combines citations from the book of Psalms and Israel's early history along with the Exodus text in his warning against any resolution over slavery less than its complete eradication. America must learn from the example of God's own determination depicted in Ps 9:12 that "when He maketh inquistion for blood . . . He forgetteth not the cry of the humble." Just as "Saul was cursed for not hewing Agag in pieces when he had him in his hands" and "Ahab was cursed for not destroying Benhadad when he could have destroyed him" so the nation will be cursed now if the body of slavery is not dismembered and destroyed. America cannot "afford to give" slavery "a new lease of life, as would some who cry, 'Peace' and 'Compromise.' " What is needed is "deliverance from the agitation and danger of slavery: not a temporary respite." Since slavery " cannot live without owning and controlling the Government" and it has now "attempted to kill the Government," then " let it be killed." It should be "buried in the grave which it dug for the nation." The tombstone of the grave is to be changed from "Here lies the American Republic" to "Here lies American Bondage." Any compromise with slavery would only "adjourn the crisis-laying it over upon our children." The nation must not merely "regulate" or "suppress this terrible conflagration, enkindled in the South" but completely "extinguish it, even to its coals and embers." It is "better that the war last for years" than for it to end without "deliverance from this scourge." In support of President Lincoln's Emancipation Proclamation, Fish concurs that the war must involve the "speedy justice" of emancipating the slaves of the Confederacy or "we may not have years to fight in" because "an offended GOD may have something to say about that."[52] If the nation walks "contrary to God, depend upon it, God will walk contrary to us." If America does not "now rid itself of this foul blot" then " God will not let this nation live and prosper."

Without the destruction of slavery while it is in the nation's capacity to carry it out, it may be "that we are only just now dipping our feet into the shallow edge of the deep river of blood through which God will make

51. Ibid.
52. Fish, *Duty of the Hour*, 16.

us wade." America must "begin . . . to DO RIGHT; to do what God bids us, whether we can see our way clear or not" or he "may yet transfer to our necks the yoke which we have so long left upon the neck of the poor negro, by bringing us, for a time at least, into political subjugation to the Slave power." The "key of success" America's "salvation" lies "in the prompt, courageous, and thorough execution of the most effective emancipation measures." The perspective of the slaves themselves is captured in one of their songs of liberation that marks 1862 as "the year of jubilee" when "My people must go free." For Fish the song is indicative of "what a power is arrayed against our enemies in these prayers of the slaves!" He calls upon his readers to "see to it that we place ourselves as a nation upon the side of these prevailing prayers, and not against them" for "the voice of God . . . plainly is, *Let my people go!*[53]

20. Edward Lounsbery, 1862.

In a sermon to his congregation Reverend Edward Lounsbery uses the Exodus text to justify the increasing severity and casualties of the ongoing war. Just as the Egyptians suffered the loss of every first born for Pharaoh's refusal, so America must now suffer loss of life as the liberation of the slaves is carried out. The rector of St. Judes Church in Philadelphia encourages his congregation to have faith in the midst of the "very darkness that surrounds us, and above the din of the appalling strife which is fast filling our hearts with mourning and our homes with the dead." The Exodus account is "one of many that illumine the pages of the ancient story," the "history of God's covenant people" from which they may draw insight and understanding in their distress. America's treatment of the slaves parallels Egypt's cruel oppression and "the unrequited toil and hard servitude of the helpless millions whom she had first invited to her soil" and then "reduced to bondage." Like Egypt America's "pride and her oppressions grew with her growth; until the cry of these poor captives came up unto God, and his sword was drawn for their deliverance." America, like "Egypt had been desolated—blasted as by the breath of the Almighty" and "fear and despair settled down upon the terror-stricken people." Just as "the heart of Pharaoh refused to bow, and grew but more defiant as the vials of wrath fell more heavily upon his head" so the heart of America was hardened and defiant and now, "one more judgment remains-the heaviest, sternest of them all." A "land that

53. Ibid., 17.

had long groaned with the oppressions of the slave, must now be bathed in the blood of the master." In Egypt "the devouring sword is commissioned to enter every house in the land, until, there was not a house 'where there was not one dead.'"

Lounsbery does "not . . . trace the analogy in full" but "in more points than one, our situation is like that of Egypt." As a prosperous nation, "we have forgotten the God who redeemed us, and spurned the hand that fed us."[54] The fear of God has been replaced with "impiety" and "selfish greed" and "his word despised." Now, "the sword is going through the land, piercing . . . every home, filling our streets with mourners and loading the very air with the wail of agony!" Just as "the iniquity of Egypt was full, and the hour of Israel's release had come" so it is with America. The escalating severity and casualties of the war recall "the message . . . sent to Pharaoh, *Let my people go!*" and the "sorer judgments" provoked by the refusals of "haughty monarch." America "must be redeemed from its sins" and "our iniquities must be purged away" but before that is accomplished the "dire calamity that lacerated the heart of Egypt" must be experienced "and not a house be left without its sacrifice."[55]

21. Lydia Maria Child, 1862.

In her letter to President Lincoln regarding forcing fugitive slaves into labor for the military in the northern states, Lydia Maria Child incorporates the Exodus text as she has heard it in a black spiritual. She identifies Lincoln as a modern Moses who is responsible for their just treatment. It is the nation's "duty, as well as our best policy, to deal justly and kindly by the poor fugitives who toil for us, and to stimulate their energies by making them feel secure of their freedom." But Lincoln himself must personally intervene because "your word, officially spoken, can alone do this."[56] The arbitrary treatment being received in the North by "the poor creatures, whose minds are darkened by ignorance, and perplexed by their masters' falsehoods about the Yankees" is not only wrong but unwise. If the masters of slaves in the South, are promising freedom to those slaves who fight against the Union, the slaves "would doubtless accept the offer as the best bargain they

---

54. Lounsbery, *Safe Refuge in the Day of Calamity*, 4–5.

55. Ibid., 5.

56. Mrs. L. Maria Child to President Lincoln , 1862, Samuel J. May Antislavery Collection, Cornell University.

could make" because "they have been unable to find out what the United States means to do with them."

Lincoln has been placed by God "as a father over these poor oppressed millions." He must "remember their forlorn condition" and "think how they have been for generations deprived of the light of knowledge and the hope of freedom!" Their wives have been "polluted" and "their children sold." As fugitives they have been forced to live in swamps "infested with snakes and alligators." The slave codes have inflicted "cruel laws . . . for trying to learn to read the Word of God." They were "guided toward freedom by the North Star," but then "hurled back into bondage by Northern bloodhounds in the employ of the United States!

Now, even though they do not know "whom to trust" in "their present woeful uncertainty" yet "in the secrecy of their rude little cabins" and "from their bruised hearts" their "uncounted prayers go up" for God's blessing on their president. How can he allow the lashings and mistreatments of fugitive slaves to continue by officers in the military "on the plea that the President has given no orders on the subject? In the military there are a few "noble souls" whose "moral enthusiasm" for justice Lincoln will "stifle" and disappoint along with "the poor helpless wretches who trust in you as the appointed agent of their deliverance" unless he acts. If he does not then "may God forgive you!" Child understands "in some degree, the embarrassments" of Lincoln's position, and " . . . the heavy weight of responsibility that rests upon you shoulders." She realizes that he is "surrounded by devils that have squeezed themselves into the disguise of toads" but pleads with him to stop "counting these toads, and "look upward instead of downward." His "reliance on principles rather than on men" will serve him better. He need only place his "right arm on the buckler of the Almighty, and march fearlessly forward to universal freedom in the name of the Lord." She is "impelled to write this because, night and day, the plaintive song of the bondmen" is resounding in her ears—*Let my people go*. The spiritual she heard will guide him, too: "Go down, Moses" she tells Lincoln, "go down to Egypt's land, and say to Pharaoh: *Let my people go*.[57]

---

57. Mrs. L. Maria Child to the President of the United States, 1862, Samuel J. May Antislavery Collection, Cornell University.

CHAPTER 8: THE EXODUS TEXT IN NINETEENTH-CENTURY DISCOURSE

22. Francis William Bird, 1862.

Francis William Bird, a paper manufacturer and Massachusetts state legislator, argues for the enlistment of slaves, "the strong arms of over a million of loyal men . . . ready to aid our government in its imminent peril." He compares the "lying message" of "Gradual Emancipation" to Moses' first proposal—'*Let my people go* that they may hold a feast unto me in the wilderness. ' Gradual freedom is a compromise. It similarly weakens the demand of God.

> God said: *Let my people go that they may serve Me*. Moses said, Let them go and hold a feast in the wilderness—only "three days' journey into the wilderness"—a respite from the tasks, a holiday, a little "gradual emancipation." God said, These oppressed people are my firstborn, and I will treat their oppressors as their oppressors have treated them. Had Moses at once proclaimed to Pharaoh the whole counsel of God, who can say but he would have obeyed and averted all the plagues and all the blood which followed the temporizing policy of Moses and Aaron?

Bird sees a "parallel between this history and our own." During the debate over slavery "the conscience of the nation has been earnestly addressed, and every willing ear has heard that solemn demand—*Let my people go that they may serve me*; and we have refused, and the plagues have come" in the form of "war in Florida, war with Mexico, war upon every right of freemen." The result has been that "our manliness has been eaten out, and plagues worse than flies and lice and frogs combined have infested pulpit and press and politics and social life." The plagues have so far been endured "so that the full tale of cotton and sugar was delivered." Not unlike Pharaoh "in our pride and power we have said, 'Who is the Lord that I should obey his voice? I know not the Lord, neither will I let his people go.' "[58]

> And now, suddenly as a thief in the night, comes the beginning of the end—the wail for our first-born is heard in the land. Is the heart of the nation still hardened so that the last vial of the wrath of God *must* be poured out? Already the smoke and flame of burning store houses and plantations stir the rapt enthusiasm of the fugitives at Beaufort, as the pillar of cloud by day and of fire by night inspired the fugitives from Egyptian bondage. As one reads the following from Hilton Head, a slight stretch of imagination

---

58. Bird, *Let My People Go*, 3–8.

carries on back to the triumphal procession led by Miriam with timbrels and dances.

Is the parallel to be perfected? Now that the madness of the slaveholders has released us from every possible constitutional obligation to slavery; now that in the providence of God the hour of emancipation *has struck,* shall we ... in a vain attempt to reinslave those God has summoned to freedom, bring down upon ourselves the final judgment, which not only in Egypt, but in all ages and everywhere, He has visited upon the oppressor who turned a deaf ear to his warning? ... dare we follow them into the Red Sea?[59]

23. Marmeduke Miller, 1862.

In an address to representatives of the United Methodist Free Churches meeting at Nottingham, the Rev. Marmeduke Miller employs the Exodus text. Warning England to be wary of the Confederacy, he says, "Let us be in no feverish haste to recognize a government the cornerstone of which is the damning, cursing sin of slavery" and urges his readers to remember "those honest men in the North, who are really and truly struggling with slavery" even though "they are not all of this character." English readers are told that "good men have appealed to the oppressors" and southern slaveholders have been urged "to let the captives go free" but "like the efforts of Moses and Aaron on behalf of the oppressed Israelites, the result has been to increase their hardships."[60] Like "Pharaoh of old, they have turned a deaf ear to the voice," and have said, we will not let them go, we will fasten their chains still more tightly, and any man who comes to us or our slaves with that message, we will shoot him dead." Even still "the voice has been repeated, and still they have refused, until at length the signs, and the wonders, and the war, and the plagues have come upon them in dreadful earnestness." The casualties of the war are "the first-born of many a house" that "now lies dead on the battlefield." The war is a "bloody chapter ... rapidly coming to a bloody end." Although the "South is suffering the most, for their guilt is the deepest" the North also suffers because "their sin too is great" because of their commercial gain from slavery and because "many of them have treated the poor Negro in a most disgraceful way." Also England must "drink of the same bitter cup of suffering, for she in past

---

59. Ibid.
60. Miller, *Slavery and the American War,* 44–46.

times shared in the same guilt." The ending of slavery has instruction for all nations, so "let us all lay the lesson to heart" and "bring forth fruits meet for repentance." Through the events of "Providence" the voice of God can be heard and "has long been saying to the oppressors: "*Let my people go* from the house of bondage, let them go."[61]

24. N. Haycroft, 1863.

In an article for an English publication, *The Baptist Magazine,* the Reverend Haycroft traces "the operation of a retributive Providence" in the American Civil War to its origins in "a selfish policy which has yielded more and more to the demands of the slaveholder, until he could dog the steps of his fugitive bondsman through every State in the Union, and drag him back from the borders of Canada to the rice and cotton-swamps of the South."[62] The fugitive slave laws "prostituted the principles of liberty, State-rights, common humanity, and the laws of the infinite God, to the influence of the dollar" and "could be expected to issue only in disaster and destruction." For the Baptist minister, "slavery is a corroding ulcer in the vitals of a nation" that "emasculates the moral manhood" and "drains away the pith and marrow of a people's virtue. America's ruin has not come from "any external foe" but "the overthrow of the United States has come from elements within herself" because "she has refused to hear the cry of the Holy One, *Let my people go.*" Like Egypt, "she has fallen on the doom of Pharaoh, to perish in a sea of blood." It is "by her close and unholy alliance with slavery" and "by her persistent disobedience to the primary laws of justice and humanity" that "she has drawn upon herself the swift and avenging wrath of Almighty Providence" and "forged the thunderbolt which is dashing the whole fabric of her institutions to atoms."[63]

25. Committee of Merchants for the Relief of Colored People, 1863.

The "Report of the Committee of Merchants for the Relief of Colored People, Suffering from the Late Riots in the City of New York," comments

---

61. Ibid.
62. Haycroft, "Slavery and the Civil War in America," 209.
63. Ibid.

on the distribution of $40,799 by the "Executive Committee appointed for the relief of the colored people of New York and the adjacent places" which "concluded the work assigned to them" and now reports " to the contributors to the fund placed at their disposal."[64] The money was given "by the contributors in prompt response to the simple announcement that it would be needed" after the riots and "no special appeals were necessary to urge subscriptions, and consequently no commissions were paid to collectors." The funds are used "in protecting those who have lost their property in the late riots, in the prosecuting of their claims against the city, in providing for the widows, orphans, and other dependent members of the families of those who were killed, and in such other ways as they may find will do the most good." In the report the "two methods of action" in disbursement of the funds: personal visits to "ascertain the facts of the case" and "immediate aid upon the best information that could be obtained from the persons applying for assistance or through colored pastors we employed."

The hope of the merchants and contributors is that through the aid "the colored people in time to come from the experience of the past few weeks will trust the white man as their friend." The report sounds some of the usual notes found in antislavery literature, observing that "human wisdom is utterly unable" to resolve the issue of slavery and recognizing "God in his providence alone can do it." A hope for the gradual emancipation after preparation for "the enjoyment of liberty and the discharge of the duties and obligations attendant thereon" has gone unfulfilled.

Haunted by "the great question of the age" the anonymous author describes the futility of trying to ignore or escape the specter of slavery and racism. In an ironic twist the writer complains of a nation's troubled conscience that cannot escape the claims of truth, like a slave for whom there is no liberation.[65] And such a conscience, like the slaves, is not to blame for the scourge of war and its casualties. Nineteenth-century America is an ancient and oppressive Egypt, and judgment comes to the oppressors in their pharaonic role. The angel of the slaves' liberation is also an angel of their oppressors' death. The mourning of families over the loss of fathers, husbands, and sons, both North and South, is the mourning of a once haughty empire over the death and destruction that inevitably accompanies the end of the slavery and the beginning of deliverance. Using the

---

64. "Report of the Committee of Merchants for the Relief of Colored People," 5, 36–38.

65. Ibid.

Exodus text, the author identifies the New York riot, its aftermath, and the loss of life in the ongoing war with the throes of a liberation arising from divine intervention.

> Go where we may the black man does not escape us, when we sit at our tables surrounded by our families although you arc not personally present in bodily shape still you are there, when we retire to our chambers you follow us and even in the sanctuary of the most High God the question will come without bidding to every heart, what shall be done with the negro.

The writer believes that "twice in the world's history has He [God] signally interposed in behalf of the enslaved. Once in generations long gone by . . . when his people Israel were under the yoke of the Egyptians, He brought them forth with a mighty hand and an outstretched arm He told that haughty nation these words, *Let my people go* free. This they refused, until finally there was no home among the Egyptians in which on that eventful night there were not cries and lamentations over the dead body of the first born son." The second intervention of God commenced "three years ago" when "we little thought that we should for a like cause learn over again the same lesson." He laments that now "there is hardly a family circle at the North and almost certainly there is not one at the South, where the mother does not mourn over her dead boy or where the wife has not been made a widow." Comparing enslaved Africans to the enslaved Hebrews, he believes that "all this has come to us because your people [the Africans] dwelt among us, the innocent cause of untold woes. We know full well that you and yours are not responsible for these calamities." "It seems to me," he continues, "that disguise it as we may Slavery in these United States is doomed. It may not end this year nor the next, but end it will and that speedily; a voice rings through the air clearer and louder than the loudest thunders, *Let the oppressed go free.*[66]

26. Noel Baptist Wriothesley, 1863.

Australian barrister and judge Noel Baptist Wriothesley argues that "slaveholders are acting in direct opposition to the two great attributes of God—His justice and His goodness." Citing various psalms, selections from the gospels and letters he says, "Our business here is to be loving,

---

66. Ibid.

kind, bountiful, compassionate, like Him" and this is the very opposite of what slaveholders are doing when they "inflict misery upon their labourers by their cruel slave code." It is the "slaveholders, with the name of Christians" who "oppose the law of Christ, the spirit of His gospel, and his own sacred example." He cites the treatment of marriage, the absence of wages, as proof. "These slaveholders rob these children of God, these brothers of Jesus Christ, of their liberty, their time, and their labour, of education, of legal protection, of civil rights, of their wives, of their children, of all their happiness, and then call themselves Christians." American slavery, is a "system is so essentially anti-Christian, that no possible amendment can bring it into harmony with His law or His example."

Wriothesley focuses on the breaking of powerful oppression as the mark of Christ's present reign which he describes by means of Psalm 72—"He shall deliver the needy . . . the poor also, and him that hath no helper. He shall redeem their soul from deceit and violence; and precious shall their blood be in his sight." He uses the Exodus text as the summary:

> At this very time, indeed, God is, by the voice of His providence, calling these slaveholders to emancipate their slaves, as He once called those of Egypt by the voice of Moses. By the emancipation of our West Indian slaves, after a controversy of many years, by the light which has come upon the mind of Europe, by the universal condemnation of the slave system, by the revelations so clearly made of its enormities, by the wastefulness of its cultivation, by the mischief which it does to all who are connected with it, by the growing sense of justice and humanity in the Free States, by the evidence forcing itself upon the minds of all patriotic men that it is incompatible with the safety of the empire, by the war which it has kindled, by the blood which it has shed, by the miseries already suffered in the Southern States, and the worse which are looming in the future, by all the inflictions of His providence, and all the denunciations of His Word, God is saying to Mr. Jefferson Davis and his adherents, what he said to Pharaoh and his servants, *Let my people go, that they may serve me.*[67]

---

67. Wriothesley, *The Rebellion in America*, 92, 278, 311–15, 344.

CHAPTER 8: THE EXODUS TEXT IN NINETEENTH-CENTURY DISCOURSE

27. Giles Pease, 1864.

The pastor of Third Congregational Church in Lowell, Massachusetts, Giles Pease, wrote an antislavery treatise for a church conference in 1854 that was subsequently published in 1864.[68] Many of the arguments normally associated with antislavery literature are found in Pease's work. "The principle of Slavery," he writes, "consists in the chattelizing of humanity, the annihilation of human relationships, the brutalization of men, the adjudging and treating of men, made in the image of God, like brute beasts, as articles of merchandise." "In confirmation of and illustration of this interpretation of Slavery," he cites "brief extracts from the slave codes of several . . . slave states."[69] He goes on to "glance briefly at a few characteristics of the bondage of the Hebrews . . . under the government of Pharaoh."

Pease's intention is to compare the governments of ancient Egypt and nineteenth-century America and contrast Pharaoh's government with the "atrocities and barbarities of American slaveholding legislation, judicial, and executive government action." The Exodus text, *'Let my people go, that they may serve me'* shows that God's demands for the liberty of his people falls upon conditions less harsh than those of American slavery. At least in Egypt, he reasons, the Hebrews built, owned, and dwelt in their own houses and their families lived together. Within the record of the Old Testament "there is not a particle of evidence that any individual of the Hebrews, male or female, lived with, or dwelt in any house that belonged to, an Egyptian. The circumstances of the Bible narrative all go to show that the reverse was true."[70]

28. Joseph Symmes, 1864.

Reverend Joseph Symmes employs the Exodus text to check any hesitation in the process of emancipation. If "God has said to us, *'Let this people go,'* he writes, "our duty is obedience to God" and "he will take care of the consequences." Like others in his era, Symmes discerns "the Providential design in this great war" to be written "in letters of living light; it is to destroy slavery." Slavery is "the great sin of this nation in our relations to men; and we were all guilty, therefore we must all suffer." It is "God's design to destroy

---

68. Pease, *"Who Is on the Lord's Side?"*
69. Ibid., 15.
70. Ibid., 19–20.

slavery . . . not man's." Since it was protected by the Constitution "we could not touch slavery in the States. And certainly there were few who desired to do so." Regardless of "whether it was right or wrong . . . very few of us desired to interfere with the system where it existed." Either slavery or freedom would "control the policy of the government" and slavery could only be removed "by the people of the slave States themselves, or by violence." The slave states would not remove slavery, and the North would never have invaded the South to end slavery, but the latter's rebellion has incidentally or providentially brought about violence required. Just as in the case of Israel's deliverance "God made a way where man could not, and found a place, and took care of his people" in the Exodus story, so now he is making a way to free the slaves of the South. "It behooveth us to listen carefully for the voice of God" because the consequences of Pharaoh's failure to act when "God sent unto him, saying, *Let my people go*," will certainly be the same and "a Red Sea disaster will overtake us."[71]

29. Samuel A. Goddard, 1864.

Merchant and gunsmith, Samuel Aspinwall Goddard of Birmingham, England was a former resident of Brookline, Massachusetts. In addition to the development and manufacturing of ordnance such as the breech loading cannon, he gained a reputation for a number of antislavery tracts. In one of these publications he responds to a speech delivered by S. W. Lindsay, a Member of Parliament from Sunderland, England. Apparently, Lindsay had suggested that Abraham Lincoln strike a conciliatory tone with those seceding from the union as Abraham of the Old Testament did with Lot. He should,

> say to the rebels as his namesake of old said to Lot, Let tbere be no strife between us I pray thee, between thee and me, is not the whole land before thee? Separate thyself I pray thee from me: if thou wilt take the left band, then I will go to the right, or if thou depart to the right hand then I will go to the left.

This text is "inapplicable to the case" of slavery and does not inform an appropriate response according to Goddard. Abraham Lincoln, he argues, has been called by God to "obey my commands." He cannot "permit the oppressor to take either the right or the left in a crusade against the

---

71. Symmes, "National Thanksgiving," 19–20.

CHAPTER 8: THE EXODUS TEXT IN NINETEENTH-CENTURY DISCOURSE

rights of his fellow man." America is to "overcome this heartless, tyrannical slave-holding Oligarchy" and secure "equal rights to all throughout the nation from the highest to the lowest."[72] Specifically, "the black race" must be given "a position to acquire political equality with the white" as well "free schools" and "churches for the worship of God." Instead of Abraham's words to Lot, Lindsay should "seek an example in that remarkable manifestation of Divine interposition, in the appearance to Moses in the burning bush; commanding him to deliver the Israelites from the bondage of the Egyptians." Referring to Exodus he writes:

> We have it on the evidence of Holy Writ, that the holding of fellowmen in slavery, was regarded by the Almighty as a heinous offense against his holy rule. Appearing unto Moses, he declared, I have seen, I have seen, the afflictions of my people, and have come down to deliver them. Depart, and say unto Pharaoh let my people go.

Goddard asks further, "Is God a respecter of persons? Is not the poor negro cared for, as well as the Israelite?" The era of the New Testament has brought about a change in how God is revealed, a "new dispensation," but there is no change in his opinion of slavery. "God does not indeed appear to man face to face, nor, in the burning bush; but in the revelation of Jesus Christ" and "by precept, by example, by the power of conscience; as manifestly, and as authoritatively, as He did to Moses." Through these precepts and "channels" by which a "Christian may be reached" God has spoken to Abraham Lincoln as he did to Moses: "Go forth and strike the fetters from the slave."[73]

30. Horace James, 1865.

The final example is from Caruthers's home state. In his appendix to his North Carolina Report, Reverend Horace James uses the Exodus text to express the ongoing liberation of the freed slaves through literacy and education. The discouragements are significant because "the growth of character is slow . . . if one must unlearn the traditions of a lifetime." The "elevation" of the black race "is a work of patience and time" and "one is

---

72. Goddard, "Reply to Mr. Lindsay's speech at Sunderland," 15–16. Cf. Goddard, *The American Rebellion*, 453–73.

73. Goddard, "Reply to Mr. Lindsay's speech at Sunderland," 15–16.

sorely tempted . . . to throw up the work in disgust." Like unpromising soil, they are so "choked with poisonous weeds, as to defy cultivation." They "are so untrustworthy, so full of all deceitfulness and dishonesty, so enveloped in dirt and rags" that one must wonder if "there is rain enough in the sweet heavens to cleanse them, or grace sufficient to renew them." These misgivings, however, are "but for a moment; for these poor creatures are surely more sinned against than sinning." Recognition of the great evil of slavery changes "the shadow of a passing disgust at the abject negro . . . into the fervor of a holy indignation." "The voice of the Lord" is heard "like muttering thunder, saying, *Let my people go,* demanding "liberty and laws, art and enterprise, learning and pure religion" not only for those in North Carolina but in "every corner of the South."[74]

Evaluation and Implications

The examples above demonstrate the adaptability of the Exodus text to the slavery controversy of the nineteenth century. From a theological perspective, the divine authority of the text gave it a privileged position during the American slavery controversy because it effectively united what David Brion Davis has called the Christianity's "latent egalitarianism" with the fuller development of nineteenth-century America's vision of human rights.[75] It gives a voice to the oppressed and an identity to the oppressor. These characteristics are the key to understanding the adaptability of the text to the American slavery controversy by all who employed it, including Caruthers. By employing the Exodus text, writers shifted the slavery controversy away from the supposed rights of slaveholders to the outlook of the slaves themselves. The Exodus text voices the perspective and hope of the oppressed. Because it is from the perspective of those enslaved, it was adaptable to the efforts of the abolitionists in turning the slavery question away from the present claims of the slaveholders to the hope of the slaves for their own future. The beginning of a political or public theology emphasizing the perspective of the poor and their right to justice can be found in this shift from the perspective of the slaveholders to the outlook of the slaves.

---

74. James, "Annual Report of the Superintendent of Negro Affairs in North Carolina."

75. Davis, *The Problem of Slavery in Western Culture,* 294.

CHAPTER 8: THE EXODUS TEXT IN NINETEENTH-CENTURY DISCOURSE

As mentioned at the outset, the use of the Exodus text in the examples also shows a common commitment to a belief in providence or providentialism. "Providentialists," according to Robert Forbes, are the evangelical category of the abolitionist movement that understood the controversy of American slavery as a religious issue. Forbes observes that beginning with Thomas Clarkson's *History of the Rise, Progress, and Accomplishment of the Abolition of the African Slave Trade*, published in 1808, the first generation to write about abolition was religiously involved in the issue. James Stephen—the first example above and also published in 1808—along with Clarkson, and others like Granville Sharp, were highly committed Evangelicals. They understood abolition primarily as a " religious question, fought and won on religious grounds." Unlike other perspectives that understood abolition "as a step in the inexorable and impersonal march of Progress" it was for them, like all of life, "a manifestation of God's Providence." They all view the abolition of slavery as a result of divine intervention. Forbes categories are intellectual, not chronological, and conflicting or moderated perspectives can be embodied in a writer.[76] The examples above show that it is possible to find Providentialists in practically any era of abolition, from early to late nineteenth century. Because the Exodus is part of the record of God's intervention in the history of the Hebrew people, the text perfectly expressed the Providentialist view: God was intervening and abolishing slavery in the nineteenth century.

Finally, the examples demonstrate how the lack of a specific identity or name for the pharaoh of Exodus is exploited by all of the writers. "Pharaoh" is an oppressor without a proper name in book of Exodus. The writer of Exodus may have used the title of "pharaoh" as representative, not only of a specific ruler in Egypt, but of all such oppression familiar to Israel. The Bible does not usually shy away from identifying foreign kings. Later biblical books name at least two other pharaohs. First Kings 11:40 and 14:25 identify Shishak. In 2 Chron 35:20, 22, and 36:4 the name of Neco appears. In the Bible, kings of Israel and other nations are usually identified by their proper names. In the words of Adele Reinhartz the title, pharaoh, "offends this general pattern." Pharaoh's anonymity "enforces the point of the Exodus story as a conflict between the pharaoh of whom we know little, and Yahweh" whose "nature is named" and clearly identified as they both compete for the Hebrew's loyalty.[77]

---

76. Forbes, "Truth Systematized," 6–7.
77. Reinhartz, *Why Ask My Name?*, 139–40; cf. Friedman, *Commentary on the Torah*,

The lack of a name for the pharaoh in Exodus gives an ahistorical quality to a character in a book that has a definite historical quality. Not only is the name of God disclosed in Exodus, but even the midwives are identified by their particular names. It seems likely that the name of the particular king oppressing the Hebrews and refusing to release them from his service was known but intentionally not disclosed. What might be the reason for a purposeful omission? Carol Meyer believes it was to both expand and slight a lesser character.

> The anonymity of key figures in biblical narratives can serve rhetorical purposes. By not having a specific name, the pharaoh who subjugates the Israelites can represent all such oppressors. At the very least, denying him a name may serve to demean him.[78]

Moses consistently addresses himself, not to Egypt, but to a nameless ruler of Egypt, the pharaoh. The lack of a proper name enhances the character's suitability for personalizing and representing oppression. For this reason, in many of the examples above, the pharaoh of Exodus can personalize and represent oppression in nineteenth-century America. In these examples the impersonal system of slavery becomes an easily recognizable individual who can be confronted. Pharaoh becomes the slaveholding powers of America or the system of slavery in all of its legal power. The response of slave states is characterized throughout the examples as pharaonic. The masters, floggings, overseers, laws, and death for resistance are all part of his nature. The violation of the enslaved's relationship to God is the height of American slavery's numerous violations in their exercise of its despotic power.

Summary

The employment of the Exodus text by such a variety of writers gave unity to abolition's diverse religious character. Members of Parliament, black preachers, English abolitionists, Methodists, Baptists, Congregationalists, Quakers, Presbyterians, congressmen, eastern radicals, and ex-slaves, all employed the text. Although none of the examples examined in this chapter develop the meaning of the Exodus text in the unique and expansive manner of Caruthers's manuscript, their importance for the study of abolition's

---

169–70.

78. Meyers, *Exodus*, 34.

CHAPTER 8: THE EXODUS TEXT IN NINETEENTH-CENTURY DISCOURSE

biblical roots is evident. They demonstrate the role of the Exodus text in the "profound cultural shift in attitudes about the capacity of men and women, acting in accordance with God's will, to change and redeem their society" that culminated in the nineteenth century.[79] The unity underlying this diversity of writers is their shared belief that God was hearing the voice of the oppressed and intervening to abolish slavery. The anonymous figure of the oppressor also made the text highly adaptable to these writers in the circumstances of American slavery. As Walzer has stated, Exodus is " a big story, one that became part of the cultural consciousness of the West."[80] The agents of change envisioned by a democratic society found in the text a divine momentum which, when combined with their escalating standards of benevolence, brought about the end of American slavery.

---

79. *Prophets of Protest*, xvii–xviii.
80. Walzer, *Exodus*, 8.

Chapter 9: Caruthers's Method

THIS CHAPTER COMPARES CARUTHERS'S approach to the issue of slavery with his contemporary, James Henley Thornwell. Caruthers's manuscript exemplifies how the issue of slavery could prompt movement away from the literalism or plain sense interpretation of texts related to slavery to a reading of scripture that focused on thematic elements such as equality, liberty, dignity, and just compensation. Two keys to understanding Caruthers's method are the shifting roles of reason in the interpretation of the Bible and the recognition of certain texts being more instructive than others. Reason was thought to favor the proslavery argument, but only as long as its exercise was restrained to the role of rendering slavery reasonable through a somewhat flat deductive reading of the numerous texts that mentioned it. Caruthers, however, admitted the operation and findings of reason beyond simple deduction, and gave the Exodus text a privileged status that condemned slavery for all time.

The American slavery controversy demonstrated the inadequacy of biblical literalism or the Reformed literal approach to the Bible.[1] During the nineteenth century a literal or plain sense interpretation of a passage, as developed from its grammatical construction and historical context, was thought sufficient for understanding and application. In an era influenced by Baconian principles of investigation, any reader of a passage was thought to have had the ability to "see clearly and without ambiguity what the Bible said," writes Noll, resulting in a "biblicistic knowledge" that could even enable the interpreter to make determinations between moral cause and moral effect, greatly diminishing the ambiguities and complexities of their world and lives. This was "the common person's counterpart to the Enlightenment confidence displayed by intellectual elites who employed learned formal moral philosophy to the same ends," and, in both cases, "a liberated modern self was the starting point for biblical interpretation."[2]

---

1. Holifield, *Theology*, 494–95; Noll, *America's God*, 367–85, 386–87; Snay, *Gospel of Disunion*, 64–65; Noll, *The Civil War*, 32–33.
2. Noll, *America's God*, 381.

CHAPTER 9: CARUTHERS'S METHOD

Even though the texts to which proslavery appealed were written two thousand years earlier in a very different culture, proslavery writers "assumed the horizon of biblical experience and their own to be one."[3] According to one of James Stirling's letters published in 1857, it is a view of the Bible that holds "every direction contained in its pages as applicable at all times to all men."[4] If there was a measure of exaggeration in Stirling's characterization, it was very close to the truth. "We are neither to question or to doubt," James Henley Thornwell wrote, "but simply to interpret and believe."[5] When preaching the dedicatory sermon to the newly opened Zion Church, built by white Presbyterians and Episcopalians for a black congregation in Charleston, South Carolina in 1850, Thornwell selected Colossians 4:1, *Masters give to your servants that which is just and fair*. Here was a text for all times to all masters and their slaves that spoke clearly and was applicable to slavery in America.

Thornwell, of course, is considered the great theologian of Antebellum America, but with regard to the issue of slavery, Caruthers's orientation is more thematic and, arguably, more theological. As his proslavery counterpart, he also believes the Bible's teaching is morally actionable and applicable but the importance of most texts in the proslavery argument were diminished in his thinking by the overarching importance of the Exodus text. George Hutchison has described the nineteenth century's coincidental relationship between the issue of slavery and a more critical reading of Scripture as a "dawning recognition of the complexity of biblical materials."[6] The result was that both sides selected texts and had versions of a 'canon with a canon' in order to adjudicate the diverse points of view they found within the Bible.

For Caruthers, the Exodus text was privileged. In the battle over the Bible's view of slavery all other texts quit the field when confronted by the Exodus text. It was his key to the right conclusions about slavery. As has been shown, Caruthers asserts that the Exodus text is " binding on all who are in similar circumstances, or upon all in every land and every age, from that hour to the present, who are holding their fellow beings in bondage."[7]

---

3. Hutchison, *The Bible and Slavery*, 143.
4. Cited in Noll, *America's God*, 369.
5. Cited in Snay, *Gospel of Disunion*, 65.
6. Hutchison, "The Bible and Slavery," 148; Davis, *The Problem of Slavery in Western Culture*, 316–17.
7. Caruthers, "Let My People Go That They May Serve Me: Exodus 10:3."

He writes: "the passage . . . has long appeared to me . . . as one of the most decisive and important in favor of a prompt and universal emancipation that is to be found in the oracles of revealed truth."[8]

From the outset of his manuscript he complains "that nearly all the passages which were thought to have any bearing on the question have been cited and expounded; but with so much ignorance or willful perversion of their meaning that the controversy served only increase the exacerbation of feeling."[9] He insists that "enquiry into the teachings of inspiration on this important subject" must be " conducted with a right spirit."[10] As he works these ideas out in his manuscript, he moves away from literalism or a plain sense of the text to a more thematic reading of the passages. As shown in chapter 3 above, he constructs ideas on the basis of multiple texts drawn from a large range of Old and New Testament passages where he observes themes of equality, liberty, dignity, or just compensation for labor, themes that corroborated the Exodus text and demonstrated that the "whole tenor of the Bible" is against slavery.[11]

As has been shown in chapter 3 and elsewhere, Caruthers did have other passages besides the Exodus text and between which he sees important thematic connections that were supportive. For example, 1 Cor 7:21, which he understands to be encouraging slaves to take their freedom if it is offered was "the key to the exposition of all of these [proslavery] passages, " including the Col 4:1. This is all that could be said "with prudence and it was just telling them that liberty was vastly desirable."[12] The Corinthians passage is one of his own selections from texts he believes are more indicative of divine will.

Caruthers was a pastor who also appreciated history and published his research. His approach to the Bible was probably influenced by his work as an historian. As the author of historical works he was often engaged in local research that required personal contact, interviews, and reasoned judgment. As George Troxler observes, Caruthers interest in the American Revolution prompted him to collect information and personal accounts of the war. His *Interesting Revolutionary Incidents and Sketches of Character Chiefly in the 'Old North State'* involves a detailed defense of the

---

8. Ibid.
9. Caruthers, *American Slavery*, 1.
10. Ibid., 64.
11. Ibid., 143.
12. Ibid., 119.

CHAPTER 9: CARUTHERS'S METHOD

North Carolina militia in the Battle of Guilford Courthouse. Caruthers relates how General Nathanial Greene purposely placed the militia on the front line and ordered them to fire and then retreat, taking a position behind the Virginia militia on the second line, positioned in a couple of hundred yards to their rear. Greene placed his regular army, the Continentals, on the third line behind both militia. The use of untrained militia in this way was a common one throughout the Revolutionary War. After the battle was over, and Cornwallis defeated, a number of accounts from authoritative sources contended that the North Carolina militia ran before firing or did not hold its ground long enough, fleeing the advance of Lord Cornwallis' advancing army. Caruthers went about vindicating the militia, relying on careful research that included personal interviews with Virginia and North Carolina militiamen, some of them members of his Alamance congregation.[13]

The historical research Caruthers conducted in order to resolve the conflicting accounts of Guildford Courthouse is perhaps analogous to his resolution of various testimony regarding slavery ascribed to the Bible in his era. Like the interviews he conducted, he investigates the passages associated with slavery, attempting to reconstruct and understand the place of each in redemptive history. Through the process he became convinced that certain texts, especially Exodus, were more relevant, and others diminished or increased according to their proximity to the principles he drew from it. Not far from his doorstep a great and bloody war of warring interpretations was taking place. Insights were gathered, words were weighed, connections between previously isolated passages were made, and finally formed into a theologically coherent and persuasive conclusion:

> The Lord did not authorize Moses and Aaron to charge Pharaoh with his cruelty to the Israelites nor to urge upon him the necessity of a mild and humane treatment, but positively and absolutely *to demand their release. Let them go* was reiterated to him with the annunciation of every plague from first to last and as nothing more was required nothing less would exempt him from the terrible inflictions of God's displeasure. This is his demand now upon all slaveholders in this country and nothing else will exempt us from the penalty of this disobedience.[14]

---

13. Troxler, "Caruthers," 104.
14. Caruthers, *American Slavery*, 392.

George Hutchison has more sharply categorized the different approaches to the Bible on the slavery question such as exemplified in Thornwell and Caruthers as "prescriptive simple" and "prescriptive general."[15] This emphasizes the prescriptive approach to scripture shared by both sides of the slavery debate. Both sides were using the Bible for ethical guidance on the slavery issue. A prescriptive approach primarily views the Bible as a revelation of God's moral requirements that are to be obeyed. The emphasis is on the claims of God's morality upon humanity. It focuses on the deontological nature of the Bible, that is, the moral duties it prescribes. The prescriptive approach diverges in the slavery debate. The literal approach can be described as "simple" because it attempts "simple equations between ancient practices and the demands of modern morality."[16] It does not seem aware of the historical problems involved in making specific slavery texts of the Bible authoritative for another era two thousand years later. The thematic or perhaps, more theological, approach is "general" because it looks more broadly at a range of texts for ethical guidance, making inferential judgments that are more complex.

Such distinctions made between writers like Caruthers and Thornwell, or any other writers of the era, whatever the terminology, can seem contrived, artificial, and even self-serving, but they move us closer in understanding important differences in the debate they represent. A fuller account would show that such distinctions are easily contradicted. For example, Caruthers could very much be a literalist, at times, and Thornwell's reading of Scripture was not always literal. While helpful to a point, these categories provoke closer examination of the different mindsets they attempt to describe. In order to better understand, the role of Scottish Common Sense Realism, discussed in chapter 6 above, requires further elaboration.

Biblical interpretation at Princeton, and throughout America during the nineteenth century, was shaped by Scottish Common Sense Realism. Common Sense argued that the perceptions in the mind were largely dependable. It affirmed human ability to clearly perceive the natural order of the world established by God and the creator's moral law.[17] Our experience of the world presupposes implicit judgments about our own existence, cause and effect, and many other facts that are axiomatic and

---

15. Hutchison, *The Bible and Slavery*, 136–50.
16. Ibid., 192.
17. Marsden, *The Evangelical Mind*, 233.

foundational. They cannot be proven but must be assumed as reliable. Mark Noll groups several examples of common sense reasoning and their distinctive emphases under the general umbrella of Theistic Common Sense including "moral philosophy," "commonsense moral reasoning," "theistic mental science" and "evangelical Enlightenment."[18] Shared by all of these manifestations of common sense reasoning was the assumption that God's intentions and expectations for humanity could be discovered through a scientific investigation of human nature, quite apart from the traditional sources of religious authority.

An explanation of how American Protestants and evangelicals, whose theological heritage had serious misgivings about human ability, came to embrace a moral philosophy that appealed to universal human ability, experience, and self-evident truths is a complex task, and beyond the scope of this book. According to Mark Noll, the short explanation might be that evangelicals sought to maintain traditional Christianity without appealing to unpopular religious tradition or its authorities. The emerging intellectual respectability of the common sense method made it a suitable substitute in their search for "alternative modes of justification" for their beliefs.[19] To put it more cynically, they were "hiding their closed minds behind a Baconian façade."[20] Whatever the answer, there is no doubt that evangelicals believed in the ultimate consistency of nature and revelation.[21] That they came quickly to embrace such methodology is evident in a statement Caruthers himself probably heard as a student at Princeton from Archibald Alexander regarding the dependability of the mind: "To prove our faculties are not so constituted to misguide us, some have had recourse to the *goodness* and *truth of God*, our creator, but this argument is unnecessary. We are as certain of these intuitive truths as we can be . . . Besides, we must be sure that we exist, and that the world exists, before we can be certain that there is a God, for it is from these *data* that we prove his existence."[22] "Truth and Reason," he contends elsewhere, "are so intimately connected that they can never with propriety be separated."[23]

---

18. Fiering, *Jonathan Edward's Moral Thought and Its British Context*, 6–7.
19. Fiering, cited in Noll, *America's God*, 103.
20. Hovencamp, cited in *The Metaphysical Confederacy*, 149.
21. Farmer, *The Metaphysical Confederacy*, 149.
22. Noll, *America's God*, 236.
23. Cited in Marsden, *The Evangelical Mind and the New School Experience*, 232.

Reason, however, was limited in evangelical Enlightenment. With Baconian methods of scientific investigation, Common Sense was able bring the Enlightenment's emphasis on human reason under control. Like a dog placed on a leash, it could not wander or run away into the wilds of Rationalism. Doubt cast on biblical authority by the Enlightenment's emphasis on reason rather than revelation and the threat of Rationalism was countered in Common Sense by the employment of scientific principles associated with Francis Bacon. Bacon's scientific method acted as a means of establishing the limitations of reason, and the method was a critical element in Scottish Common Sense Realism as promulgated by John Witherspoon at Princeton.[24] Samuel Miller, another of Caruthers's professors at Princeton, told his own readers that science had confirmed "Lord Bacon's plan of pursuing knowledge by observation, experiment, analysis, and induction."[25]

Reason, in the scheme of the evangelical Enlightenment, could not transcend the empirical realm in which it operated. It could only operate upon those things visible or discoverable to the human senses. These "things" included even the human conscience, opening the way for the multiple sciences of morality published in the era. The impact of this approach to the acquisition of knowledge, issues of ethics, and methodology in every discipline including science and theology cannot be overstated. Knowledge acquired through reason would always be relative to the capacities of the finite mind. Because of these insuperable barriers, reason could not preclude or rule out the role of faith and special revelation. For Protestant America, "Christianized common sense was a godsend."[26] In the words of Sir William Hamilton, "A learned ignorance is the end of philosophy, as it is the beginning of theology."[27]

Reason, however, slipped off its leash with the antislavery movement. Caruthers speaks for many others when he writes, " I find nothing in the Bible, in reason, or in common sense and the nature of the case that gives any kind of sanction to slavery."[28] For Thornwell, this statement demonstrates the precise problem. Reason is alongside the Bible instead of in submission to it. "How much of the declamation against Slavery, in which

---

24. Farmer, *The Metaphysical Confederacy*, 95; For limits on inductive reasoning, see Farmer, *The Metaphysical Confederacy*, 143; Holifield, *Theology*, 175.

25. Cited in Holifield, *Theology*, 174.

26. Noll, *America's God*, 233–38; Holifield, *Theology*, 175.

27. Cited in Holifield, *Theology*, 178.

28. Caruthers, *American Slavery*, 28.

CHAPTER 9: CARUTHERS'S METHOD

Christian people are prone to indulge, is founded upon principles utterly unsupported by the Scriptures! One man very complacently tells us that every man is entitled to the fruit of his own labor; and that the master, in appropriating that of the slave, defrauds him of his right." Slavery is "denounced as one of robbery and plunder, which every good man should strive to banish from the earth. But where is the maxim, in the sense in which it is interpreted, to be found in the Scriptures?" And especially, he asks, "Where, even in any respectable system of Moral Philosophy?"[29] A "respectable" philosophy kept reason in its place.

His early biographer, Benjamin Morgan Palmer, remembers Thornwell's "first effort" in a class "was to mark the boundaries of reason within whose limits he thought with all the vigor and self-reliance of a mind conscious of its own powers, but beyond which he never permitted himself to pass."[30] The "office of reason," according to Thornwell, "was to study the facts of revelation as they are given, and not to indulge in . . . speculations . . . The attitude of reason here is simply that of recipient. It listens and accepts the Word."[31] Reason was to be exercised but must be kept within the boundaries of its proper domain and be in submission to the Bible. The problem with the "opposition to slavery," was that it "has never been the offspring of the Bible" but was instead " sprung from visionary theories of human nature and society" and " from the misguide reason of man."[32] As misguided as reason could become, however, Thornwell recognized its role in the slavery question. In a telling remark he both complains and concedes: "We have tried our cause by the Word of God; and though protesting against the authority of Reason to judge in a question concerning the duty of Church we have not refused to appear as its tribunal."[33]

For Caruthers, the authority of the Bible could not be used to justify or minimize the awfulness of American slavery. His manuscript is filled with his investigation of scripture, ancient and modern history, and state laws, all of which were part of his thinking. There was also personal experience that influenced him as shown in the numerous accounts to which he alludes in his manuscript. One incident in particular had a lasting impact.

---

29. Thornwell, *Ecclesiastical*, 389.

30. Palmer, *The Life and Letters of James Henley Thornwell*, 538; Farmer, *Metaphysical Confederacy*, 146.

31. Thornwell, *Theological*, 51.

32. Thornwell, *Ecclesiastical*, 393.

33. Ibid., 462.

> I have seen gang after gang driven through the streets of the village where I live, apparently about middle age, or near it, and ten or a dozen in a gang, every one of whom was hand cuffed to a long heavy chain like a log chain which was just the length of their line, carried by them day after day, while the "speculator" and one or two others rode along armed with whips and pistols. These men, I was told, had been torn from their wives and children and could not be trusted. As one of these gangs were driven by the courthouse one autumn evening, they were singing "Hail Columbia, happy land." The severest irony on this boasted land of freedom that I have ever read or heard. Most of the Spectators felt it keenly and some of them even dropped a tear of pity.[34]

We can imagine the irony in the scene Caruthers describes. A dusty road, late in the day, filled with men torn from their families in heavy chains passing the courthouse, an emblem of justice, strangely singing the praises of America as a crowd watches, and a local minister taking it all in. Scenes like this caused Caruthers's reasoning on slavery to became more than an exercise of deducing the meaning of slavery passages in the Bible presumed to support the practice of American slavery. Hutchison thinks "the way abolitionists employed reason in the interpretation of the Bible . . . opened up a kind of hermeneutical circulation between biblical truth and everyday experience which had direct implications for what they understood the Bible to say about slavery. . . . a kind of dialogical style of encounter with the biblical text."[35] "Abolitionists," he writes, "saw the role of reason operating not only deductively, to draw moral conclusions from specific biblical mandates" but "also saw it operating inductively, to make sense of the particulars of human experience . . . and relate them to the witness of biblical teaching," thus, "a less circumscribed role for reason."[36] Caruthers might not have realized it but reason was pushed in his thinking beyond its understood boundaries in the evangelical Enlightenment, not only by his instincts and studies but by what he saw and experienced in the everyday life of a slave state. He was driven by these experiences to "want an answer which will satisfy enlightened reason and unbiased conscience."[37]

Certainly, Thornwell had witnessed such scenes, too, but he did not admit the observations as evidence against his arguments. Antislavery

34. Caruthers, *American Slavery*, 305–6.
35. Hutchison, *The Bible and Slavery*, 68.
36. Ibid., 69.
37. Caruthers, *American Slavery*, 16.

writers, according to him, were "blinded to scriptural truth by theories of human rights and humanitarian schemes, conceived in the womb of rationalistic philosophy."[38] Thornwell laments the unleashing of reason that condemns slavery, the "expansion of benevolence" and "fury of philanthropy" and the "prevalence of sentiment."[39] For him, reason must be kept on its leash, restrained to operate within the parameters of tradition. Slavery is reasonable if reason looks "more narrowly into the nature and organization of society" and " at the origin and extent of the rights of man."[40]

Thornwell, however, put no limits on his reason when defending slavery. He lets go all the powers of his mind to convince his listeners that slavery is not as it seems to those who oppose it. Ridiculing antislavery rhetoric, he asks how slavery can actually be considered as the "property of man in man—as the destruction of all human and persona rights, the absorption of the humanity of one individual into the will and power of another"? Such slavery is "a fiction to which even the imagination cannot give consistency." The slaves are still individuals with "moral and responsible agency" and unique personalities. How can slavery "divest its victims of humanity" if they remain moral agents and if their soul is still free? The idea of such is inconceivable, a "palpable impossibility"! Slavery does not change, possess, or alter the individual's soul or moral agency. What is slavery? Only the "obligation to labor for another, determined by the Providence of God, independently of the provisions of a contract."[41] Elsewhere, he asks, "Where are we taught that the labor which a man puts forth in his own person is always his, or belongs to him of right, and cannot belong to another? How does it appear that what is his must be legally his? . . . where do the Scriptures teach that an essential quality as men implies a corresponding equality of state?"[42] Thornwell could have easily answered himself: "According to the spirit of the Gospel of Jesus Christ," but he did not.

In a different frame of mind, Thornwell all but concedes that in the future "Slavery must cease to exist" when the "perfection of the race" is accomplished through "the design of Christianity." It is not clear when Thornwell imagines this happening but if he is envisioning an end to slavery on earth in the near future, he is coming to a conclusion that is not plainly

38. Thornwell, *Ecclesiastical*, 380.
39. Ibid., 400, 401.
40. Ibid., 402.
41. Ibid., 408–14.
42. Ibid., 389.

found in the Bible. To the contrary, in the Bible—understood plainly as Thornwell advocated—the loss of the slave trade in Rev 18:13 and 19:18 is mourned and a role for human bondage in humanity's most distant future is implied. But Thornwell reasons better than this, sounding much more like Caruthers and other antislavery writers: "Slavery is inconsistent with the spirit of the Gospel" because slavery is "a state of things, an existing economy which it is the design of the Gospel to remove." But if he believed that the design of the Gospel was to remove slavery, why could it not happen sooner rather than later? The answer for Thornwell is that slavery "is part of the curse which sin has introduced into the world, and stands in the same general relations to Christianity as poverty, sickness, disease, or death."[43] On this point he should be faulted for not reasoning further that, regardless of sin's curse, slavery should be treated as if it were, indeed, like poverty, sickness, disease, or even death—all of which ought to be remedied, cured, or postponed in the world whenever humanly possible.

Summary

The role of reason on both sides of the slavery debate should not be underestimated. Robert Calhoon's observation on the use and explanation of biblical citations in early proslavery petitions arguments from Halifax County, Virginia could be applied to the entirety of the proslavery defense: "What is interesting about those citations is the vast historical argument required to bring them to bear on the issue of slavery."[44] Vast amounts of Baconian scientific reasoning were also required. The participants in the dispute over the Bible and slavery all "shared the basic epistemological assumptions" of the Enlightenment's moderate element.[45] Perhaps the "*disembodied* rationality" of Beverly Harrison captures the means by which a proslavery argument kept experience and feeling out of its way.[46] The acquisition of knowledge was based on a body/mind dualism in which objective knowledge resulted from a process of observation and comparison carried out by the mind "in a kind of value free state quite apart from the body." Both sides, in Hutchison's view were disposed to "value mind over matter, spirit over flesh, and to regard reason as something completely

---

43. Thornwell, *Ecclesiastical*, 419–20.
44. Calhoon, *Evangelicals and Conservatives*, 126.
45. Hutchison, *The Bible and Slavery*, 62.
46. Harrison, *Making Connections*, 13–14.

CHAPTER 9: CARUTHERS'S METHOD

separate from bodily experience."[47] According to Hutchison, the revelation of the Bible was directed towards to the mind as thus conceived but with different results:

> Proslavery interpreters summoned reason and drew on scripture to *reaffirm tradition and order.* Yet they could not in the nineteenth century simply reassert traditional wisdom. The had to show that it was *reasonable,* and they attempted to do so by reference both to passages specifically mentioning slavery and to the history of interpretation. Abolitionists on the other hand used rational argument to push the limits of what had been the prevailing interpretation of the Bible with respect to social reality, by emphasizing the *prophetic traditions* of scripture and the *teachings of Jesus.* . . . Ironically, then, even though both sides at some level sought to absolutize particular biblical teachings, their rationalizing methods served operationally to relativize the authority of the Bible.[48]

The key to understanding the approach to the Bible on both sides can be found in the adjective, "operationally." Consideration of the Bible's teaching for Caruthers required a critical adjudication of different frames of perspective within the Old and New Testament in which some texts, and especially the Exodus text, emerged as more important, more instructive, than others. Passages of scripture had to be considered alongside of human experience rather than over it. The text would somehow have to be brought alongside of the world outside of it. Belief in the authority of the Bible was not abandoned, but commitment to such authority was not sufficient for the resolution of the question. In the slavery controversy, the divine authority of the Bible had to be made a little lower than the angels, subject to the powers of human reason.

In Caruthers's thinking "the fact that learned and good men generally in the south, or those who are respected to be such, have advocated slavery and been blind to the evils of the institution—its injustice, oppression and inhumanity is no proof that it is right." Theirs was a "desperate depravity which stills belongs to the best of men." Such blindness did not "release others from their personal responsibility in this matter, or from their moral obligations to make an honest and thorough investigation for themselves." Caruthers shows no readiness to acknowledge the diligent efforts of churchmen like Thornwell to reform slavery. It is slavery, in

---

47. Hutchison, *The Bible and Slavery,* 63.
48. Ibid., 345–46.

Caruthers thinking, that is wrong. It should not be reformed but discarded. The early judgment passed on the militia at the Battle of Guildford Courthouse had been wrong, and proslavery judgment was wrong, too. People needed to look again and think more carefully about the scriptures they treasured, honestly and thoroughly, as Caruthers believed he had done. The proslavery argument would "do an immense injury to the present and coming generations." Summing up its argument and literature, he writes, "they shame reason, trample on humanity, undervalue truth and bring a reproach upon religion."[49] For Caruthers, the morality of the Bible and the unleashed reasoning of humanity were plainly ashamed of American slavery, and no one could rightly think otherwise.

---

49. Caruthers, *American Slavery*, 128.

Chapter 10: Caruthers and Recent Studies

WHILE MODERN COMMENTARIES' TREATMENT of New Testament slavery texts bear many resemblances to the typical nineteenth-century antislavery argument, what truly sets Caruthers apart from his contemporaries and their modern counterparts is his atypical emphasis upon Exodus. This final chapter demonstrates that the privileged status Caruthers gives to the Exodus text in his manuscript is prescient, a foreshadowing of the importance of Exodus in more recent scholarship. The recurring allusion to Exodus in a variety of studies, including its role in Paul's thought and its overall centrality for biblical interpretation, is examined and submitted as confirmation of the importance given to it by Caruthers.

Modern Commentaries and Slavery Texts

Caruthers's modern day counterparts believe that slavery is wrong. They reach this conclusion by following the trail left by nineteenth-century evangelicals, who adjusted the method of interpretation formally enshrined in their tradition. Echoes of typical antislavery reasoning are heard in modern day commentators' assertions of a "sufficiently radical change of attitude" in the New Testament that "paved the way"[1] to end slavery or prepared "for the withering away of slavery as a social institution in later Christian civilization"[2] or "the lesson of Paul's reticence about slavery" that recognizes the necessity of the church to first grow in influence before it effects radical change.[3] Like the image of the embedded growing seed, these constructions allow for the Bible to be against slavery even if certain texts seem supportive.

Christianity's change of heart in the nineteenth century over slavery, however, does not really resemble an organic or growing development.

---

1. Wood, "Ephesians," 11:83.
2. Hays, *First Corinthians*, 125.
3. Lovelace, *Dynamics of Spiritual Life*, 388.

Instead, the widespread rejection of slavery appears sudden after centuries of acceptance, erupting almost volcanically when evangelical conscience combined with Enlightenment reason to create explosive pressure beneath already rising standards of benevolence in the nineteenth century. Nevertheless, as the three following examples show in the treatment of Eph 6:5–9, modern commentators mirror the antislavery literature of the antebellum era, asserting that the seeds of the institution's demise were, knowingly or unknowingly, embedded by the writers of the New Testament.

John Stott has said that the "indolence or cowardice" of the early post-apostolic church should not be defended for their failure to eradicate slavery even though it was a social evil. Stott's censure of the early church probably assumes too much about the sensibility of the early Christianity to slavery as a social evil. While there may have been exceptions, it is doubtful that the early church thought slavery wrong. For the most part, arguably until as late as the seventeenth century, slavery was generally accepted throughout culture, as N. T. Wright says, "like electricity, cars, and gas. You couldn't imagine society without it."[4] Stott goes on to say that "we can at the same time rejoice that the gospel immediately began even in the first century to undermine the institution" and "lit a fuse which at long last led to the explosion that destroyed it."[5] Over time, the church and society grew to understand that slavery was wrong.

F. F. Bruce argues that Christianity's "mission was spiritual in essence and only collaterally social. Had it assailed the established system of serfdom point-blank, it would have ruined that primary object by inflaming political antagonisms to an incandescent furnace heat." The wars of Rome had "shaken society to its base and helped to precipitate imperial dictatorship as the sole effectual preservative against social insecurity" and "the institution of slavery was in fact bound up inextricably with the legislation of the ancient world and could only dissolved with its dissolution." If the church had attacked "that deep-rooted curse directly" Christianity would have come into "deadly conflict with the 'powers that be' and merged itself in a gigantic extrinsic upheaval fatal to its intrinsic purpose. "Divine wisdom is not so shortsighted as to be thus side-tracked." It was enough that "truths of the gospel laid the axe at the roots of the evil; for they proclaimed spiritual liberty, equality, and fraternity *in excelsis.*" Christianity "is

---

4. Wright, *Paul for Everyone*, 199.
5. Stott, *The Message of Ephesians*, 257.

eminently economic; it never does too much," and slavery was "like a tree notched, that it might be felled in due season."[6]

Ben Witherington describes "Paul's approach" of putting "the leaven of the gospel into the structure of the Christian community, not into the larger society directly" thereby allowing "it do its work over the course of time." As in the case of women and their place in the church, similarly with respect to slavery "Paul believes in living a true Christian life and letting natural implications of that bring transformation to the patriarchal and slave society." The church is "to live out its new freedom, thus bearing witness to the larger community about their values." Attempts at revolution to "change the fabric of ancient society were not made by the early Christians, rather " it was by means of witness and change *within* the Christian community that a new worldview was promulgated.[7]

Awareness of the Bible's complexity on the issue of slavery underlies the thinking exhibited in the examples above and demonstrates the similarities between modern day biblical commentators like Stott, Bruce, or Witherington with nineteenth-century Evangelicals like Albert Barnes or Theodore Dwight Weld. They accommodate and yet condemn slavery. The presence of slavery in the Bible is accepted but slavery is condemned as a social evil. Rather than simply observe the presence of slavery in the early church, all sense the need to explain its presence and account for Christianity's changing attitude towards it. There are no references to a specific text or texts but to general principles against slavery believed embedded, knowingly or not, by New Testament writers.

Though commentaries can seem reluctant to acknowledge early Christianity's less than decisive posture toward slavery, biblical scholars generally recognize that slavery was not an issue for the early church. Kathy Ehrensperger has put it plainly: "Although unacceptable from a contemporary perspective, it was obviously beyond even their power of conception to envisage a society other than one in which slavery was a given."[8] It is, in fact, highly unlikely that the New Testament can be legitimately enrolled in the lists against slavery. As Ehrensperger has remarked on the letters of Paul, it was "beyond the scope of what was seen to be the changing effect of the gospel." As for the disregard of difference between slave and free announced in Gal 3:28, it certainly does not mean that slaveholders were

6. Bruce, *The Epistles to the Colossians, to Philemon, and to the Ephesians*, 140, 141.
7. Witherington III, *Conflict and Community in Corinth*, 186.
8. Ehrensperger, *Paul and the Dynamics of Power*, 194.

put out of the movement, but it does mean that slaves were considered fully human and fully members of the primitive church. This was a marked sociological improvement over and against Graeco-Roman society and a critical change in the perception of slaves.[9]

Complementary Studies to Caruthers

Caruthers's own reliance on a typical antislavery reading of the New Testament during his era as examined in chapter 7 or exemplified in modern equivalents such as the examples above, should not detract from his singular contribution. The unique nature of his manuscript resides in its treatment of the slavery question on the basis of the Exodus experience of Israel. For Caruthers, the Gospel rang out with antislavery ideas, but in the final analysis these were only sympathetic overtones to principles deduced from the Genesis account of creation and the most significant Old Testament passage on slavery, the demand from the book of Exodus that the Hebrews be released from Egypt.

The remainder of this final chapter demonstrates that the preeminence assigned to Exod 10:3 by Caruthers is complemented today by a number of studies. The following is by no means complete but only a sample of a growing body of theological literature going back to the political hermeneutics of early liberation theologians and moving forward to more complex treatments explaining Exodus as definitive deliverance or a pattern of deliverance and service, or as having a determinative role in Israel's theology or the theology of Paul.

Exodus is the model in liberation theology's foundational works by Gustavo Gutiérrez, Jose Miranda, and Leonardo Boff. Their prophetic attention to the poor and oppressed made Exodus "the influential paradigm in the 1970's" in Latin America and other parts of the world.[10] If the idea of liberation resists becoming a "conceptual abstract, because it points resolutely to social and economic realities," it is due, in part, to the adaptation of the Exodus story.[11] The oppression and escape of Israel seems tailored for liberation theology's unity of theory and practice—not simply perceiving

---

9. Ibid., 195.
10. Tombs, *Latin American Liberation Theology*, 226.
11. Hays, *Moral Vision of the New Testament*, 203.

CHAPTER 10: CARUTHERS AND RECENT STUDIES

truth, but doing truth in the midst of organized struggles against various kinds of oppressions.[12]

Miranda and Gutiérrez, are representative of liberation theology's dependence on Exodus as the certain means of illuminating the nature of God as the liberator of the oppressed. In Miranda's adaptation of Marxism, Exodus is definitive of God's justice in action. The "salvation of the oppressed is . . . effected against the unjust. Among a people in which injustice reigns, it is always Yahweh-justice who reveals himself by intervening." In other words, only in Exodus is the true meaning of the name of Yahweh revealed. God "who reveals himself by intervening in our history is always Yahweh as savior of the oppressed and punisher of the oppressors."[13] Gutierrez describes the centrality of the Exodus to biblical theology as a theological norm for a liberating hermeneutics. Yahweh "is the God who liberates slaves" and "who causes empires to fall and raises up the oppressed."[14] For Boff, Exodus "recounts the epic of the politicoreligious liberation of a mass of slaves who, through the power of the covenant with God, became the people of God."[15]

The difference between liberation theology and the traditional Reformed theology of Caruthers seems extreme, but less so if the uncritical adoption of Marxist analysis as a means of fully accounting for the experience of oppression, advocacy of socialism, and tendency to veer towards violent confrontation, all of which are often associated with liberation theology, are not integral to its core as has been argued by David Tombs.[16] Caruthers's articulation of Exodus's meaning for the oppressed and their oppressors in his own time shares liberation theology's prophetic concern for the oppressed and warning for their oppressors, as well as its recurrent allusions to the book of Exodus from which it chiefly draws its understanding of God as Liberator. Regarding the book of Exodus Caruthers would have endorsed Gutierrez's appreciation: "The memory of Exodus pervades the pages of the Bible and inspires one to reread often the Old as well as the New Testament."[17]

---

12. McCann, "Liberation Theology" 350.
13. Miranda, *Marx and the Bible*, 80–81.
14. Gutiérrez, *A Theology of Liberation*, 69.
15. Boff and Boff, *Introducing Liberation Theology*, 35.
16. Tombs, *Latin American Theology*, 294.
17. Gutiérrez, *A Theology of Liberation*, 90.

Northrop Frye describes Exodus as the "definitive deliverance" of literature, in which a series of misfortunes turns the story down to its lowest point, after which a plot development turns it upward to a satisfying conclusion.[18] Humanity begins in possession of paradise in Genesis, loses it in the form of the tree and water of life, but gets it all back at Revelation's conclusion. The story falls when Adam and Eve fall and are exiled from Eden, but the first rise comes with the establishment of cities by Cain. The story falls again with the flood, but begins a second rise when Noah and his family are finally able to disembark and reaches another height with the introduction and calling of Abraham. The book of Genesis ends with Israel in Egypt but soon plummets downward into four hundred years of slavery.

Frye's third rise begins under the leadership of Moses, as Israel escapes and passes through a sea and a wilderness. Joshua, the successor of Moses, leads the people to the high point as they enter into the promise land. As the book of Judges show their fortunes fall as various enemies, oppress them, especially the Philistines. With the anointing of Saul and then David, the Philistine hold is broken, and the city of Jerusalem becomes the center of Israel's worship. After David's successor, Solomon, dies, the kingdom is divided and spirals downward yet again. The northern kingdom is destroyed by Assyria in 722 BC. Jerusalem, in the southern kingdom, is captured by Nebuchadnezzar in 586 BC and the exile to Babylon begins.

The fourth rise begins with the return of the exiles to their land and the rebuilding of the temple under the leadership of Zerubbabel, a descendant of David. History falls again as the Selucid ruler, Antiochus Epiphanes, oppresses the Jews. The Maccabean revolt brings the fifth rise and deliverance, as Judea gains it independence but falls again when the Roman domination of Judea begins. A divergence takes place in Christian and Jewish perspective over the sixth rise. For Christianity, Jesus inaugurates the sixth upward turn and his resurrection achieves a definitive deliverance that will never end. For Judaism, it adherents continue to endure a kind of exile as they still wait for promised Messiah.[19]

Elements of Frye's analysis are supportive of Caruthers's belief in the continuing relevance of Exod 10:3. When the entirety of the Old and New Testament is viewed from this perspective, the Exodus is really the only thing that happens in the Bible, since the entirety of biblical literature is a series of falls and rises, structured like it and interpreted by it, Frye's

---

18. Frye, "Exodus: The Definitive Experience."
19. Frye, *Exodus*, 73–75.

"U-narrative."[20] For example, if, as Frye illustrates, a continuum can be drawn like a straight long across and through the repetitions of the U-narrative, and on that continuum all oppression can be plotted, that line begins with Pharaoh and runs straight through all subsequent oppressors. Whether it is the Philistines, Nebuchadnezzar, Antiochus Epiphanes, Rome, or the slaveholding states of the nineteenth century, they are all Pharaoh. Similarly, all slavery, regardless of location or time, is Egypt, and all deliverances are from Egypt.

Frye's graphic analysis complements Caruthers's assertion that the Exod 10:3 is "binding on all who are in similar circumstances, or upon all in every land and every age, from that hour to the present, who are holding their fellow beings in bondage" or that "if the command addressed to Pharaoh was not intended for us and for all others who are in similar circumstances we know not why it was recorded." For him, it is "the divine will for the instantaneous emancipation of an enslaved, oppressed and degraded people and we can think of no reason why it should not be regarded as an expression of his will for the liberation of the enslaved and oppressed here, now, everywhere and at all times."[21] The "demand which was first made on Pharaoh, king of Egypt by Moses and Aaron . . . is now made by the lively oracles of God on all, here in America and every where else, who are holding their fellow men in bondage."[22]

Caruthers's emphasis on the purpose or reason of Exod 10:3—*. . . that they may serve me*—and the state of liberty as a precondition for service to God, is complemented by research emphasizing Israel's service to God as the result of their freedom from Pharaoh. David Daube observes the importance of Israel's description as God's firstborn son (Exod 4:22). "Here," he writes, "is a very close relationship where the highest degree of loyalty may be expected of the protector, and where his opponent is grievously in the wrong." When he finally capitulates to the demand, Pharaoh is "consenting to the change of ruler, the transfer of the Israelites from his service to that of God." Therefore, "as a result of God's intervention the children of Israel, from being slaves to the Egyptians, became slaves to God."

Most significantly, " the social protection given by the law is rested on that change of master, on the Israelites having passed under divine

---

20. Ibid.
21. Caruthers, "Let My People Go That They May Serve Me Exodus 10:3."
22. Caruthers, *American Slavery*, 156.

rule which, essentially, precludes any other."²³ The change of allegiance is brought out in the Passover eve liturgy's opening section: "Originally our fathers were servants of strange service . . . but now God hath drawn us close to his service."²⁴ Midrash comments on Psalm 113, traditionally sung on Passover eve, make a similar point, remembering that God "recovered us and brought us out to freedom, for we were slaves unto Pharaoh and thou recovered us and made us into slaves unto thee."²⁵

John Byron has similarly argued that "Israel was not removed from Egypt simply to be free, but so that they might serve God instead of Pharaoh."²⁶ Byron has detected the scheme of Humiliation-Obedience-Exaltation in the "ongoing attempt" of Jewish literature "to reconcile the Jewish identification of slaves of God with slavery that was forced upon them by foreign oppressors."²⁷ This scheme stands in contrast to the Sin-Exile-Return pattern of Israel's justified enslavement such as their disobedience and subsequent exile to Babylon and their later return. When they were obedient and faithful to God but enslaved by another power they were humiliated. Their course, however, was to remain obedient in the hope of being rescued and thus brought into a state of exaltation.

The story of Joseph with his enslavement, faithfulness, and subsequent elevation is the paradigm for the scheme of Humiliation-Obedience-Exaltation. The book of Exodus is a continuation of the story of Joseph's family in Egypt, and the conflict between God and Pharaoh in Exodus centers on whom Israel will serve. As slaves of the Egyptian state, the Hebrews were never assimilated in Egyptian society as domestic slaves under masters of households. They served only Pharaoh, and it is their enslavement to him that is challenged by Yahweh through Moses. Service to God is "the ultimate intention" of Exodus, which "represented a historical event that formed the basis on which Israel understood itself as the slaves of God."²⁸

Caruthers would have agreed. The Israelites are slaves of God and therefore cannot be enslaved by anyone else without violation of their relationship to God, and the same is true for all believers. The findings of

23. Daube, *The Exodus Pattern in the Bible*, 42–43.
24. Cited in ibid., 45.
25. Ibid., 46.
26. Byron, *Slavery Metaphors in Early Judaism and Pauline Christianity*, 49.
27. Byron, *Recent Research on Paul and Slavery*, 86; cf. Byron, *Slavery Metaphors*, 72–75.
28. Byron, *Slavery Metaphors*, 50.

CHAPTER 10: CARUTHERS AND RECENT STUDIES

Daube and Byron confirm his own views. Citing Rom 12:1–2, Caruthers understands the reference to Jewish sacrifices and the presentation of those sacrifices to God, and he writes, "So all believers are required to give themselves up to the Lord, in the spirit of sacrifice, to be as wholly devoted to Him as the whole burnt offering, no part of which was allowed to be reserved or put to any other use; but while the sacrifices required by the law were slain at the altar, the Christian sacrifice or offering of himself must be a *living sacrifice*."[29] Similarly, First Corinthians 6:20, emphasizes "both *body and spirit*" and the "two include the whole man so that since Christ redeemed the body as well as the soul and both constitute but one accountable being he claims the entire services of the whole man, soul, and body."[30]

The high rank Caruthers confers upon Exod 10:3 is given by Carol Meyers to the entire book. Exodus is arguably, "the most important book in the Bible," and of all the books in the Hebrew Bible, "perhaps has the greatest impact beyond the ancient community in which it took shape." Israel's escape from oppression eventually becomes "a great narrative of hope for peoples all over the world."[31] The structure of the story is easy enough to grasp and remember. The first words of the book, literally translated "and these," connects the book with Genesis and presents its material as a continuation of the story of Joseph. Previously, in Gen 46:31–34, his family had come to Egypt and settled. On the occasion of his death he tells his brothers that they will someday leave Egypt and finally inherit the promised land (Gen 50:24). Joseph begins as slave but rises in prominence obtaining for his family "the best of the land (Gen 47:11)." Eventually a new Pharaoh comes to power "who knew not Joseph" (Exod 1:8). Threatened by the increasing population Pharaoh uses forced labor which he ruthlessly escalates making the lives of Joseph's descendants "bitter with hard service" (Exod 1:14). Under instruction from God, Moses, along with his brother Aaron, demands the release of Israel, performing a series a miracles, executing successive plagues, and eventually leading the Israelites out of Egypt at the conclusion of the first Passover ceremony. Examples from the Old Testament and Jewish literature demonstrate the power of the narrative as the language or elements of the exodus are employed in their history.

Regarding Israel's emphasis upon the Exodus, Horst Dietrich Preuss has commented that a people who described the earliest stage of their

---

29. Caruthers, *American Slavery*, 313.
30. Ibid., 318.
31. Meyers, introduction to *Exodus*, xv.

history "as one of bondage . . . in order to emphasize the redemptive act and salvific nature of its God . . . deserves to be closely noted."[32] The importance of remembering their slavery, their escape and journey, is repeatedly mentioned throughout the Torah beginning in Exodus 12. A seven-day festival of unleavened bread commemorates Israel's perilous escape and the Passover offering becomes a ceremony "for all time (Ex. 12:24)." The event is celebrated in Miriam's song at Exod 15:21—"Sing to the Lord for he has triumphed gloriously! The horse and rider he has thrown into the sea!" Deuteronomy 4:34–37 asks, "Did God ever try to go and take for himself a nation from the midst of another nation, by trials, by signs, by wonders, by war, by a mighty hand and outstretched arm, and by great terrors, according to all that the Lord your God did for you in Egypt before your eyes? . . . And because he loved your fathers, therefore he chose their descendants after them; and he brought you out of Egypt with his presence, with his mighty power."

Both occurrences of the preamble of the Decalogue in Exod 20:2 and Deut 5:6 characterize Israel's escape from Egypt and the crossing at the sea as the establishment of a community between Yahweh and Israel. Psalm 114:1–2 similarly reflects on the event, presenting God's selection of Israel as taking place in exodus event: "When Israel went out of Egypt, the house of Jacob from a people of strange language, Judah became His sanctuary and Israel his dominion." Of all the events in the history of the nation, Israel is especially charged to remember their deliverance from Egypt. In Exod 13:3 Moses commands them to "commemorate this day, the day you came out of Egypt, out of the land of slavery, because the Lord brought you out of it with a mighty hand," a phrase repeated, and often in what Preuss calls a "formal compressed style," throughout the Pentateuch and beyond.[33]

Subsequent eras of Israel's history are revisited by the reminder of the Exodus, further witness to the lasting power and adaptability of Israel's experience within multiple and varying contexts. The prophet Jeremiah condemns the enslavement of previously freed slaves reminding the people of their own deliverance from slavery in Egypt (Jer 34:13). When the prophet Micah voices Yahweh's accusations against Israel the people are similarly

---

32. Preuss, *Old Testament Theology*, 43.

33. Exod 13:9; 16:1; 18:1; 20:2, 20; 29:46; Deut 4:20; 5:6, 15; 6:12, 21; 7:8; 8:14; 13:6, 10; 15:15; 24:22; 29;24; Lev 11:45; 19:36; 22:33; 25:38, 42; 26:13, 45; Josh 24:6, 17; Judg 2:12; 6:8, 1 Sam 8:8; 10:18; 12:6, 8; 1 Kgs 8:16, 21, 51, 53; 9:9; 12:28; 2 Kgs 17:7, 36; Jer 2:6; 16:14; 32:20–21; Dan 9:15; Amos 2:10; Neh 9:18; Ps 81:10.

reminded of their deliverance from slavery (Mic 6:4, 5:9). According to the prophet, Hosea, the nation of Israel's relationship to Yahweh not only originates in their exodus experience but also disintegrates in its aftermath: "I am the Lord your God ever since the land of Egypt, And you shall know no God but me; for there is no Savior besides me. I knew you in the wilderness, in the land of the great drought." But after Israel came into the land, "when they had pasture, they were filled; they were filled and their heart was exalted; therefore they forgot me (Hos 13:4–5)."

Within the prophetic literature of the Old Testament, a second and better Exodus builds on the first Exodus going beyond it (Isa 43:1; 44:22f.; 48:20; 51:10; 52:9, Jer 23:7).[34] According to Jurgen Moltmann, this new exodus is by virtue of hope.[35] Unlike the first Exodus, those that go out will neither hunger nor thirst (Isa 48:21). Their path is easy because all hindrances will be cleared away (Isa 49:11). The people leave in haste but they do not travel as if in flight, but as part of a festive procession in which they are led by God (Isa 52:12). Nature also participates in the joy of the final liberation of God's people which all the nations witness (Isa 35:6, 49:13, 55:12).

The *Book of Jubilees,* also known as *The Little Genesis,* is a second-century BCE consolidation of material from Genesis and Exodus, recounting Israel's history according to "their jubilees throughout all the years of the world."[36] *The Book of Jubilees* exercises certain liberties with the Old Testament account in its consolidation, especially its designation of the Israelites' suffering as the justification for their deliverance. "The Egyptians honored the children of Israel all the days of the life of Joseph" the reader is told. After Joseph's death, however, the writer amplifies the precise intentions of the king of Egypt towards Joseph's descendants: "let us afflict them with slavery."[37] The amplification indicates that the retelling of the Exodus within the context of their continuing suffering in the struggle to maintain national independence during the second century was an important interpretive exercise that identified the nation's struggles in the author's own era with his ancestors' escape from Egypt.

Catherine Hezser has also shown that ancient Jewish writing is replete with evidence that Israel's story of liberation from Egypt became the most

---

34. Cf. Ezek 20:33–44 and its description of Israel's restoration and dependence upon the language of Exodus.

35. Moltmann, *Theology of Hope,* 93, 130.

36. Introduction to the Book of Jubilees.

37. Book of Jubilees 46:2; 46:13.

significant feature of Judaism's religious memory and practice.[38] Imaginative allusions and adaptations throughout Jewish literature demonstrate that the Exodus account was the paradigm for freedom of every kind—physical, political, and, even spiritual. Philo fashions Egypt as a symbol for lust and desire in *The Posterity and Exile of Cain* and describes the escape as deliverance "out of our bodily passions."[39] This is similar to the practice that would develop later in patristic literature, as observed by Ruth Sandburg, of viewing Egypt as a "symbol of negative desires and vices," such as Ambrose's interpretation of the Red Sea crossing as "passing over from vices to virtues, from the desires of the flesh to grace and sobriety of mind."[40]

During the period following the destruction of the Temple in 70 CE, the book of Exodus captures the attention of rabbis seeking explanations for the Roman oppression and subsequent hardships of foreign rule. Was their present subjection to Rome somehow justified by their behavior, and did the book of Exodus hold any clues for what they needed to do now in order to gain their redemption and freedom?[41] They examined the text in the search for answers. The loss of the Temple created a rare cultural opening as worship shifted away from the priesthood and the Temple to families and homes, some of whom had slaves. In her detailed study of the Passover, Hezser notes its transformation during this time from a temple ritual into more familial settings, carrying the potential for a "socially transformative function" in which even the servants of wealthy Jewish families experienced a rare equality with their masters.[42] Long after the events described in the Exodus, the story exerted the power of a living document, informing and shaping the response of Israel's religious leaders to the nation's struggles, as well as influencing their own social customs.

Keesmaat and Exodus in the Writings of Paul

An examination of research that complements Caruthers's own view of the importance of Exod 10:3 is not complete without notice of Sylvia Keesmaat's examination of Romans 8 and the Exodus tradition. Building on Richard Hays' understanding of Paul as "as a Christian interpreter whose Bible

38. Hezser, *Jewish Slavery in Antiquity*, 363–77.
39. Cited in ibid., 366.
40. Cited in ibid.
41. Ibid., 370.
42. Ibid., 363.

was Israel's Scripture,"[43] and who extended "meaning in new directions,"[44] Keesmaat views the Exodus as a particular tradition that undergoes interpretation and transformation throughout Israel's scriptures and finally in the writings of Paul. The particular traditions of Israel, primarily accessed through biblical texts, functioned as traditions do for all people, helping "to organize reality and to characterize the nature of the world in which they live."[45] For Keesmaat the "fundamental narrative which provides the framework for reflecting on salvation is one that is rooted in the exodus, where God redeemed Israel from slavery and set Israel free."[46] Permeations of Matthew's gospel and other parts of the New Testament with allusions to Exodus have long been recognized and discussed.[47] The presentation of Jesus's own life "in terms of Exodus motifs" as well as the "importance of the narrative for other New Testament authors" indicates "Paul's evocation of the exodus occurred in a context receptive to such allusions and echoes."[48] Exodus "informed the imagination of those who awaited Exodus "was not only central in the textual tradition but also informed the imagination of those groups who expected God's new in-breaking activity in the present"[49] or "God's new act of salvation."[50] Within the writings of Paul, the Exodus narrative is "evoked in such a way that the contours of the exodus story itself become the means for describing the story of the Galatians and Romans communities." As interpreted by Paul, it is "central to the believers' experience."[51]

Keesmaat's method of intertextuality examines the structure of relations between one or more biblical texts, and while they are several categories of intertexuality, her work is especially concerned with the "dynamic occurring between texts which is not dependent on or limited by intentionality or lack thereof." Unlike the focus of inner-biblical exegesis on the explication of a specific text that Paul uses intentionally within his own text, intertextuality makes allowance in Paul's writings for "echoes and meanings"

---

43. Hays, *Echoes*, 5.
44. Ibid., 4.
45. Keesmaat, *Paul and His Story*, 15.
46. Ibid., 67–68.
47. E.g., Danielou, *From Shadows to Reality*, 153–65.
48. Keesmaat, *Paul and His Story*, 219.
49. Ibid., 221.
50. Ibid., 218.
51. Ibid., 219.

which may have been intentional or may have been hidden from Paul himself, and which belong to "a larger matrix of ideas than those confined to a particular text or texts."[52] Paul, according to Keesmaat, "is not merely echoing and alluding to certain texts related to the exodus but is evoking a whole intertextual matrix, a larger narrative world made up of the whole exodus story, from bondage and suffering in Egypt, to the wanderings and rebellion in the wilderness, to the inheritance of the promised land."

With respect to Romans, Keesmaat argues that if Romans 8 is understood in light of echoes and allusions to Exodus, it is more coherent with the question of God's faithfulness to Israel and the "explicit discussions" of this question in Romans 9–11, and with the argument of the entire letter.[53] After the expulsion of the Jews by Claudius in 49 CE, the church mostly consisted of Gentiles. When Jewish Christians returned later to Rome, tension would have developed if Gentile Christians were "reticent in welcoming" their Jewish fellow believers. The tension would have been compounded if the Gentile Christians were unwilling to be identified with any persecution Jewish Christians might have experienced. The question of God's faithfulness to Israel would have been raised by believers, Gentile and Jewish.

Paul's letter is directed towards the accomplishment of reconciliation between Gentile and Jewish believers, and the answering of the question of God's faithfulness. He calls the Roman Christians, both Gentile and Jew, to "an ethic of suffering love." He characterizes their experience of salvation "in terms of the climatic new exodus." Jewish and Gentile believers "are part of Israel's story, and indeed the fulfillment of that story."[54] The Gentiles therefore cannot reject the Jews for theirs is a shared experience in this new Exodus, they are joined to them in this redemptive story. For Jewish believers undergoing persecution it would also be a message of hope to hear their redemption in terms of the Exodus because this would mean God's promises to Israel were being kept. The use of the Exodus tradition in Romans 8 thus sets the stage for the more detailed discussion of God's faithfulness in Romans 9–11 and the all important relationship between Jewish and Gentile believers in Romans 12–15. Six points below are drawn from Keesmaat's extensive and detailed examination of the echoes and allusions to the Exodus throughout Romans 8. They sufficiently demonstrate its centrality in the theology of Paul.

52. Ibid., 49.
53. Ibid., 64, 151, 221.
54. Ibid., 154.

Romans 8, according to Keesmaat, should not be interpreted "piecemeal in the light of later Christian concerns" such as the questions of free will, election, or adoption, but in light of "one sustained conceit," a "central Israelite tradition: the exodus event, especially as it is interpreted and reinterpreted in the Septuagint and intertestamental literature." Exodus is "the major formative event in Israelite history," shaping not only Israel's understanding of God's "past and present interaction" with Israel but also their "conception of how God would related to them in the future." Paul's phrase at 8:14, "those led by the Spirit of God" [ὅσοι γὰρ πνεύματι θεοῦ ἄγονται] has little to do with free will or "the manner in which the Christian life is influenced by the Spirit." Instead he is alluding to a "matrix of ideas common in first-century Judaism" that form "an exodus context" in which the entire passage should be interpreted. The verb translated "led" is based on αγεῖν. An examination of the Septuagint reveals that this verb as well as its compounds, εξαγεῖν and εισαγεῖν, and its related synonym, οδηαγεῖν, "occur most prominently in an exodus context." Exodus 15:13 is particularly suggestive: "You have led [ωδηγησας] in righteousness this your people, whom you redeemed." According to Keesmaat, whether or not Paul consciously echoes this verse, its centrality in the exodus tradition, when considered along with the emphasis on God's righteousness in the text and the prominence of the same theme throughout Romans indicates that such themes were known by Paul.

God's leading of Israel out of Egypt as recalled in a number of Psalms in the Septuagint also suggests a background for Romans. Psalm 104 in which the Israelites are led out (vv. 37, 42, 43) remembers that God is faithful to his everlasting covenant with Israel and has an inheritance for Israel (vv. 7–11) and ends with the Israelites gaining their inheritance (vv. 44–45). This is echoed in Rom 8:17 which also speaks of an inheritance, one that "is linked to the experience of suffering with Christ." Psalm 77 recalls how God led Israel (vv. 14, 52) and, strikingly, in v.53, led them "in hope," also found in the Romans passage. The progression of being led not into fear in Rom 8:15 echoes Psalm 23 as God "leads me in paths of righteousness." Even though the paths go through the valley of the shadow of death, "I will fear no evil." These and other passages in the Psalms and prophetic literature of Israel recall the leading of Israel as described in the exodus and frequently utilize themes, vocabulary, and images that occur in Rom 8:14–17. Especially significant is the use of the image in pleas for current and future deliverance such as Ps 31:3 (LXX 30:4), and the Septuagint's compelling rendering of Ps 142:10: "your good spirit will lead me on level ground" [τὸ πνεῦμά σου τὸ ἀγαθὸν ὁδηγήσει με ἐν γῇ εὐθείᾳ], a close approximation of Paul's own thoughts on the leading of the Spirit in Romans 8, depicting a new Exodus on better ground, a journey without the obstacles of wilderness terrain.

The title "sons of God" [υἱοὶ θεοῦ], also echoes its origin from the exodus. Israel is God's "firstborn son" (Exod 4:22), and the image is repeated throughout Old Testament and intertestamental literature recalling the Exodus.[55] The prophet Hosea recalls that "Israel was a child, and I loved him, out of Egypt I called my children" (Hos 11:1). In the declaration of a new Exodus found in Jeremiah 31, God declares "I am a father to Israel and Ephraim is my firstborn" (31:9). The book of Wisdom states explicitly that Israel is "son of God" (Wis 18:13).

Deuteronomy 32 and Isaiah 63 both recall the Exodus in familial terms. The Deuteronomy passage characterizes the people of Israel as God's children and sons and daughters (32:5, 19–20). God is their father who created them (32:6), and Israel is a people led by God in the Exodus (32:12). Incidentally, Keesmaat also highlights Paul's explicit use of Deut 32:21 in Rom 10:19 to describe the jealousy of Israel and Deut 32:43 in Rom 15:10 as a call to rejoice. Beyond Romans, his use of Deuteronomy 32 at several places in 1 Corinthians 10 corroborates Keesmaat's view that Paul's ideas about the exodus "moved within the framework of Deuteronomy 32."

Isaiah 63 recalls God's punishment of the people for their rebellion and their own memory of how God once led them in the Exodus and their desire that he lead them again. Cognizant of their own disobedience, Israel recounts God's constancy and faithfulness. They plead for his return: "Look down from heaven and see from your habitation, holy and glorious. Where are your zeal and your strength, the yearning of your heart and your mercies toward me? Are they restrained? For you are our father, though Abraham does not know us, and Israel does not acknowledge us but you, Lord, are our father" (63:15–16). The cry to God as father in Isa 63:15–16 is echoed in the cry and appeal of Rom 8:15 to God as "Abba, Father." Fulfillment has come. The new exodus is underway, and God is leading his sons and daughters once again.

---

55. E.g., Deut 32:6, 7, 20, 43; Deut 14:1; Hos 2:2 (LXX); 11:1; Isa 1:2, 4; 43:5–7; 45:11; Jer 31:9 (LXX 38:9); 31:20 (LXX 38:20); Sir 36:4; Wis 9:7; 12:6, 21; 14:3; 16:10, 26; 18:4, 13; 19:6.

The phrase "spirit of slavery" [πνεῦμα δουλείας] is a rhetorical foil to "a spirit of sonship." Paul's employment of "slavery" [δουλείας], placed in contrast to "sonship" [υἱοθεσίας], suggests an understanding of sin that is reminiscent of Israel's slavery in Egypt. Moreover, if we are to catch the "overtones" of Rom 8:14-15, the context of "slavery" [δουλείας] must be recognized in conjunction with the character of God. In over half of its occurrences, "slavery" is used in the confessional refrain that characterizes God. "I am the Lord your God who brought out of the land of Egypt, out of the house of slavery" (Exod 20:2, Deut 5:6). The phrase, termed by Martin Noth as "a primary confession of Israel," occurs throughout the Old Testament for God's deliverance of his people from Egypt. Romans 8:14-15 then is more than "isolated phrases which appeal to the past exodus event to characterize God's new saving act in Jesus." The assertion, "you did not receive a spirit of bondage" [οὐ γὰρ ἐλάβετε πνεῦμα δουλείας], echoes God's "self-designation in the scriptures of Israel." The same God who acted then is acting now. His actions now are "fully consistent" with what he has done in the past.[56]

Romans 8:15 speaks of not being led "again into fear" [πάλιν εἰς φόβον]. The Israelites were afraid after they left Egypt, and they wanted to return (Exod 14:10-12). Fear also seized them later when they were on the outskirts of the promised land (Num 14:9, Deut 1:19-46). In Walter Brueggemann's phrase, the wilderness was not "the route of promise" but "unbearable abandonment."[57] Their tendency to pull back in fear suggested more a spirit of slavery than sonship. The Spirit of Christ enables Paul's readers to respond differently. In contrast to the Israelites who wanted to return to slavery in the midst of their trials in the wilderness, the Christian does not have a spirit of slavery leading to fear but a spirit of adoption or sonship which sets them free.

The adoption envisioned by Paul in Rom 8:14-17 also recalls the exodus. Although Paul's use of "sonship" [υἱοθεσίας] has been viewed by many as a use of Graeco-Roman law for purposes of clarifying his views on the believer's relationship to God, Keesmaat argues for its "conceptual background in the exodus event in which Israel finds its birth as a nation as well as its sonship."

---

56. Cited in Keesmaat, *Paul and His Story*, 66n37; cf. Judg 6:8; 1 Kgs 9:9; Neh 9:17; Mic 6:4; Jer 34:13.

57. Cited in Keesmaat, *Paul and His Story*, 69.

To the many citations listed by Keesmaat in support of this view, the subsequent support of John Byron should be added. Whatever Paul knew about Graeco-Roman practices and viewed as applicable to his readers, it should not obscure that his notion of slavery to God and Christ is a natural development from his Jewish heritage. He "interprets the Christ event through the language and imagery of the Exodus."[58] For Byron, the Old Testament background of Israel's Exodus experience is the critical key that unlocks the proper understanding of slavery language describing followers of Christ in the New Testament. Israel is God's firstborn son, "released from the control of Pharaoh to serve God" just as "the believer was released from the control of sin to serve God. Both are declared by God to be sons and heirs of the promise of Abraham."[59] The Exodus "provided Israel with a status as adopted son and the opportunity to voluntarily choose to whom they would be enslaved (Josh 24:14–18)." It provides "the believer kinship with God and the opportunity to choose between enslavement to sin and enslavement to God."[60]

Allusions and echoes of Exodus as it is recalled in Jeremiah 31 (38, LXX) as well as Deuteronomy 32 and Isaiah 63 occur throughout Romans 8. Jeremiah 31, for example, begins with "a description of a new exodus," progressing to the description of the new covenant, and proclaims that only if the natural order of things were to cease would God's faithfulness to Israel end. According to Keesmaat, these promises of God to Israel in Jeremiah 31 "for Paul are now in the process of fulfillment."[61] The created order is not going to cease because, as Romans 8 makes clear, creation itself will be redeemed. Hence, God's faithfulness to Israel will not cease either."[62] Keesmaat thus views the freeing of a cursed creation in Rom 8:18–22 as "affirming God's faithfulness to Israel" and thus in anticipation of the discussion of the same question in Romans 9–11.

Summary

Caruthers belief in the centrality of Exod 10:3 in the slavery controversy is complemented by the consistent role of the exodus in biblical studies, the

58. Byron, *Paul and Slavery*, 86.
59. Byron, *Slavery Metaphors*, 228.
60. Ibid.
61. Keesmaat, *Paul and His Story*, 221.
62. Ibid., 151.

literature and life of Israel, and in the theology of Paul in the New Testament as well. The exodus story serves as a template for understanding deliverance from oppression and service to God that is recycled throughout the Old and New Testaments with powerful results. The multiple evolutions of the theme over the span of biblical history demonstrate that the Hebrews' escape from Egypt became a resource for their understanding of themselves, one they frequently revisited throughout their dilemma filled history, the foundation of the new and better exodus described in prophetic literature of the Old Testament. No other biblical material exerts such consistent influence on Israel's interpretation and understanding of its changing fortunes and circumstances or on early Christians' understanding of themselves.

Securely set within the larger exodus event, Caruthers's central text against American slavery, Exod 10:3, enjoys a privileged status, and, as part of the exodus story, it participates in the theologically determinative position of the exodus, a place of prominence held by no other story throughout the Old or New Testaments. " You may say and no doubt many will say that you never received the passage in this light and you don't see how a demand made upon Pharaoh, King of Egypt more than four thousand years ago can have any bearing upon slaveholders at the present day," he writes, but "the passage which we have placed at the head of this discussion is explicit and positive. It has no condition or limitation."[63]

---

63. Caruthers, *American Slavery,* 139–40.

Chapter 11: Review and Conclusion

Eli Washington Caruthers's manuscript *American Slavery and the Immediate Duty of Southern Slaveholders* is an important primary source in antebellum studies, worth greater attention in the assessment of the American slavery controversy. My transcription and analysis of the manuscript is hopefully a contribution towards an improved understanding of the American slavery controversy's roots in a biblical debate. Caruthers's development of the claim, demand, and reason of Exod 10:3, does not conform to the assessment of American nineteenth-century antislavery arguments as biblically weak in comparison to proslavery arguments.[1] God's *claim* upon all humanity is based upon the Genesis account of creation and the Reformed covenant of redemption. God's *demand* for their liberty is based upon a persuasive typological reading of biblical texts that envision spiritual freedom from sin but without diminishing tangible political liberty. God's *reason* or purpose is based upon his worldwide right to the service of those he has redeemed. One cannot serve two masters. The analysis presented here of the biblical and theological content of Caruthers argument as examined in chapters 2–4, and the significant corollary issues raised by my reading of the manuscript examined in chapters 5–10, demonstrate that his understanding of the Exodus text as an antislavery argument was scripturally and theologically driven, as well as persuasive and prescient.

In chapter 2, it was shown that Caruthers's presentation of the claim of Exod 10:3—"My people . . . "—is dependent upon Gen 1:28–30 and 9:2–3 and the implications of those texts for slavery. There is no allowance at creation or in the aftermath of the flood for humanity to possess its own species. Humanity belongs to God alone. Caruthers also supports his belief in the covenant and its application to the situation of slavery by explicitly citing and correlating the decree of the Lord in Ps 2:7–8 with the promise to Abraham in Gen 22:18. In this part of his argument Caruthers reflects the teaching of the *Westminster Confession of Faith*, a Reformed confession to which he and other Presbyterian ministers subscribed. Its two-fold concept

---

1. Fox-Genovese and Genovese, *The Mind of the Master Class*, 7, 490.

CHAPTER 11: REVIEW AND CONCLUSION

of providence as "preserving and governing," a biblically derived construction defended by an armada of texts, underlies Caruthers's challenge of the use of inequalities in physical strength or mental capacities or any other disadvantages as a justification for slavery. Exploitation of such differences usurps not only the principles of creation but God's ongoing care and preservation of his creation as expressed in the confession.

In chapter 3 my examination of Caruthers's belief in the continuing relevance of God's demand—"Let My people go," has shown the importance he attaches to ideas based on Rom 15:4 and 1 Cor 10:11. The continuing correspondence between the church and ancient Israel implies that God's demand in Exodus for the release of the Hebrews has implications for nineteenth-century slavery and all time. The Exodus text provides a typological origin for God's demand upon American slaveholders, and so God's demand for the release of the Hebrews by Pharaoh must guide the evaluation of slavery for all time. Underneath Caruthers comprehension of the demand of the Exodus text for American slavery there is a conviction about the coherence of Jewish and Gentile experience. The use of Isa 60:1–2 in Luke 4:20 demonstrates that for Caruthers, in distinction from many of his nineteenth-century contemporaries and present day writers, the spiritual freedom from sin typologically derived should not diminish the real social consequences of the Old Testament Jubilee. In his explanation of the demand of Exod 10:3, Caruthers also makes use of other corroborative texts—Ezek 18:4, Rom 6:1, 12:1, Jer 34:8–22, Neh 5:1–12, Isa 58:6, Ps 72:4–14, and Ps 68:31.

In chapter 4 the examination of the purpose of the Exodus text—"that they may serve me"—demonstrates that Caruthers's critique of the legislation of slave states, and especially their enactments limiting the implications of baptism for larger society, is founded upon his Presbyterian theology of baptism as well as specific biblical texts. Baptism not only signifies a recipient's new relationship to God but also a new relationship among equals for the baptized person in the local community. State laws hindering education, family life, and most importantly, human volition, defy the Bible. The offering of a "living sacrifice" in Rom 12:1 envisions the same volition and freedom found in the selection of the sacrifice to God in the Old Testament. First Corinthians 6:20 is also appealed to as evidence that redemption cannot be limited to the realm of the spiritual but must include both body and spirit as one accountable human creature whose service is entirely claimed by Christ and so can be given to no other. According to Caruthers's understanding of these passages the responsibilities of the Christian to God cannot be fulfilled in the system of American slavery.

In chapter 5, I have shown that Caruthers resolves the impression of the New Testament's endorsement of societal forms of slavery by the universal application of the Exodus text. Universally applied, the clear and unambiguous expression of the Exodus text corroborated the principles of creation and Caruthers's own instincts in a way that the supposed endorsement of slavery in the New Testament or anywhere else could not. Within the history of Presbyterianism debate over slavery, he is unlike his Southern or Northern contemporaries, and his manuscript is an example of biblical interpretation arguably unlike anything produced in the slavery literature of the nineteenth century.

In chapter 6 the influence of political ideals that complemented Caruthers's thinking was explored. His admiration and use of the Declaration of Independence was not for lack of a biblical argument. To the contrary, I have shown that he was convinced, as many others in the Reformed tradition, that the political truths of the era were biblically derived. Reliance upon the language of political documents or use of the documents should not mislead. Caruthers's thinking was like many others in the Reformed faith who believed that the idea of human equality embodied in the Declaration of Independence was a political application of the teaching of the Bible regarding the value and dignity of the individual. Like others prior to and during his era, Caruthers underscores the validity of his claims with the popular language and concepts of the Enlightenment. The assertion of human rights as a political truth was, first and foremost, the assertion of God's rights as creator.

In chapter 7 the typical aspects of nineteenth-century antislavery arguments, easily recognized in Caruthers's manuscript, were shown to demonstrate that he was a writer of his era. The familiar and conventional antislavery elements of his manuscript, especially pages 65–136, typify, not only the antislavery argument, but also the confusion surrounding any attempt to resolve the slavery issue within the narrow parameters that controlled biblical interpretation and the admissibility of evidence against the proslavery argument during the nineteenth century. Caruthers's participation within these parameters and the contradictions that sometimes arise provide a glimpse into the interpretive frustration of his era, and stands in contrast to the extended and atypical appeal to the Exodus text that distinguishes him from all other participants in the slavery debate.

CHAPTER 11: REVIEW AND CONCLUSION

Chapter 8 demonstrates that Caruthers was not the only writer to make use of the Exodus text in the nineteenth century. Because it gives both a voice to the oppressed and provides an identity to their oppressor, the text is a critical component in the development of the American vision of human rights in the nineteenth century. As the view of the slave, the Exodus text molded easily to abolitionist's arguments that sought to change the perspective from property rights of the slave owners to the circumstances and hopes of the slaves themselves. As for the slave owners themselves, the text makes their identity easily recognizable. They are all the pharaoh of Exodus, oppressors systematically using their legal and political power to oppress others being held against their will. Among the examples examined in chapter 8 there are none that approach Caruthers's extensive development and application of the text. The examples, however, demonstrate conclusively that the use of the text gave divine impetus to the vision of democracy and the rising standards of benevolence in the nineteenth century.

Chapter 9 contrasted Caruthers's own method of argument with James Henley Thornwell to demonstrate that while both held the Bible in the highest regard, they differed on the role of reason in the slavery debate. Both lived during an era when Baconian methods of scientific investigation and Scottish Common Sense subdued the Enlightenment's emphasis on human reason. Under such control proslavery argument limited reason to a purely deductive task focused on selected texts traditionally supportive of slavery. The example of Caruthers, however, demonstrates the use of reason with less restraint, functioning not only in the role of deduction but also inductively drawing from his own experience and instincts. In his method reason is exercised in all possible venues—induction, deduction, personal experience, and even instinct—which combine to adjudicate between the different perspectives on slavery found in the Bible, judging the Exodus text to be a privileged text, one to which all opinion on slavery must conform.

Chapter 10 examined current research to demonstrate that the privileged status given to the Exodus text by Caruthers has been repeatedly confirmed in an entire range of biblical studies. Throughout the prophetic literature of Israel its significance was recognized in its vision of a future New Exodus. Its value for understanding deliverance from oppression and service to God is proven by the practically countless allusions to it throughout the Old and New Testaments. The repetition and development of the theme throughout biblical literature is a phenomenon of striking singular importance for which there is no equal. Whether it is recycled throughout the Old Testament and Jewish literature or found at the center of Gustavo Gutierrez' liberation theology or the pattern of Northrup Frye's definitive deliverance or echoing in the teaching of Paul in the New Testament, Exodus occupies a determinative role for biblical studies.

Conclusion

All of these chapters demonstrate the significance of Caruthers's manuscript for understanding the biblical roots of the slavery debate in nineteenth-century America. Unfortunately, it was not published during his era but its relevance for the current assessment of the controversy over the biblical sanction for slavery in America has been made clear. In the course of this analysis I have sometimes expressed disagreement with the assessment of Elizabeth Fox-Genovese and Eugene Genovese. "To this day," they have argued, "the southern theologians' scriptural defense of slavery as a system of social relations—not black slavery but slavery per se—has gone unanswered."[2] Caruthers's understanding of Exodus and his argument against slavery as an acceptable system of social relations is an answer that can now be heard. The Genoveses have passed along the proslavery argument as it was received and embraced during its era, as an argument based simply upon scripture, and the antislavery argument as more dependent on the spirit of the Gospel or the ideals of the Enlightenment. In their view the defender of Scripture in Antebellum America was the defender of slavery and antislavery writers were the defenders of the Enlightenment or Declaration of Independence.[3] While this way of framing the controversy may highlight some features of the debate, it appears superficial in light of Caruthers's manuscript.

In answering the question of whether or not evangelical Christianity sanctioned or condemned slavery, Robert Forbes cautions that perhaps it "cannot be answered and may indeed be considered a more appropriate subject for theologians than for historians."[4] His acknowledgment has not kept him or his colleagues away from these questions. The research of Mark Noll, Brooks Holifield, Robert Calhoon, Jack Maddex, Elizabeth Fox-Genovese and Eugene Genovese and the several other historians cited in this book is a body of impressive interdisciplinary scholarship, a remarkable intertwining

2. Ibid., 526.
3. Ibid., 7, 490.
4. Forbes, "Slavery and the Evangelical Enlightenment," 71.

CHAPTER 11: REVIEW AND CONCLUSION

of history, theology, and biblical interpretation in Antebellum America. All of these historians have participated in a largely successful intellectual enterprise that attempts the reconstruction of the development and reception of biblical arguments over slavery within the antebellum era.

Within this particular enterprise sensitivity to particular theological themes or influences within evangelicalism should determine the answer to Forbes' question. Repeated appeals to the Exodus text within antislavery literature produced by evangelicals show that their use of it was more than a literary maneuver. It was theological. Caruthers and all those who appealed to the Exodus text were Providentialists who believed God to be acting in history to end slavery, and the text succinctly and powerfully brought their understanding of God to bear upon the slavery question. As such it served as a theological corrective to preoccupation with the rights of slave owners. It was a catalyst in what Robert Calhoon has described as nineteenth-century America's "grudging acknowledgment of slavery's moral defects."[5] As a developed argument from the Exodus text, Caruthers's expansive manuscript demonstrates that evangelical Christianity theologically influenced by Exodus was decidedly antislavery. David Brion Davis' belief that certain aspects of Judaism, including the deliverance from bondage in Egypt "gave a temporal and social dimension to man's struggle with sin" and that the incorporation of such tradition in the early Christian Church, "profoundly altered the meaning of slavery," means that Christian theology permeated with the Exodus tradition would always and everywhere enlist its adherents in a struggle against their own slavery or on behalf of others.[6] The Exodus text gave a genuine social dimension to the Christian faith, inspiring Caruthers and others to see clearly that "all tyranny, injustice, and oppression of the weak by the strong are the outgrowth of depravity and are, of course, contrary to the gospel of the grace of God, the great design of which is to deliver us from this inherent depravity and from all its physical, social, and moral results."[7]

Sacvan Bercovitch's awareness in Early American studies of the "formidable demands inherent in any interdisciplinary undertaking, especially perhaps where they entail unfamiliar patterns of theology," is also instructive to scholars exploring the biblical and theological roots of

---

5. Calhoon, Introduction to Crowther, *Southern Protestants Slavery and Secession*.
6. Davis, *Problem of Slavery*, 293.
7. Caruthers, *American Slavery*, 110.

the American slavery controversy.[8] I hope my transcription and study of Caruthers will assist in the formidable and further understanding of the unfamiliar. Eli W. Caruthers offers historians and theologians interested in the American slavery controversy a new voice to consider in their interdisciplinary enterprise. His manuscript has a rightful place in a new assessment of the American slavery debate, one no longer held captive by its typical representation.

---

8. Bercovitch, introduction to *Typology and Early American Literature*.

Appendix: Evaluating Former Slave Testimony

SLAVE NARRATIVES, INTERVIEWS WITH ex-slaves conducted during the 1930's,[1] are an invaluable primary source for the study of American slavery. Two evangelical ministers, well-known in conservative Reformed and Presbyterian communities, Douglas Wilson and Steve Wilkins, have argued in a booklet that ex-slaves' descriptions of their former masters as "good" or "kind" in the narratives demonstrate that American slavery has been misunderstood, and that the frequency or severity of whipping has been misrepresented. They claim the existence of "facts which are seldom addressed in public, though they are not altogether unknown."[2] Ex-slave testimony and citations from Robert Fogel and Stanley Engerman's *Time on the Cross*[3] are marshaled by these ministers to challenge and correct those who have been "carefully schooled in the abolitionist propaganda."[4]

The ex-slave testimony cited by Wilson and Wilkins is from interviews conducted throughout the 1930's under the Works Progress Administration of President Franklin D. Roosevelt's administration. According to Wilson and Wilkins, the testimony of ex-slaves "did not fit with the established and reigning orthodoxy, and consequently the narratives have been largely ignored ever since."[5] To the contrary, since their appearance, historians have thought the slave narratives to be "the most authentic and colorful source of our knowledge of the lives and thoughts of thousands of slaves, of their attitudes toward one another, toward there masters, mistresses, and overseers, toward poor whites, North and South, the Civil War, Emancipation, Reconstruction, religion, education, and virtually every

---

1. Rawick, ed., *The American Slave*.
2. Wilkins and Wilson, *Southern Slavery as It Was*, 8.
3. Fogel and Engerman, *Time on the Cross*.
4. Wilkins and Wilson, *Southern Slavery as It Was*, 22.
5. Ibid., 24.

APPENDIX: EVALUATING FORMER SLAVE TESTIMONY

phase of Negro life in the South."[6] An examination of recent works shows that a new historiography of slavery has been well under way for some time with many contemporary historical studies showing the influence of the narratives. George Rawick lists several in his general introduction to their reprint, commenting that "these are just some of the works that reflect the impact of the narratives." Rawick observes that "dozens of other works are in progress or have been published which show the impact of the narratives on the historiography of slavery and demonstrate their potential uses."[7]

Good and Kind Masters

Are the interviews of ex-slaves evidence of "an amazingly benign picture of Southern plantation life" as Wilson and Wilkins contend?[8] They report ex-slaves' "affection for former masters and mistresses . . . expressed in terms of unmistakable devotion,"[9] and " . . . a wistful desire to be back at the plantation."[10] They assert that "in the *Narratives*, out of 331 references to master, 86% refer to their masters as "good" or "kind." These assertions are not footnoted and therefore cannot be examined but it is unlikely that references to "good" and "kind" observed by Wilkins and Wilson are any different the following four examples taken from the narratives.

Example 1

Ex-slave Ank Bishop says "Dey was good to us 'caze Lady Liza's son, Mr. Willie Larkin, was de overseer for his ma, but cose sometime dey git among 'em an' thrashed 'em out."[11] Bishop says that the master was "good," but in the same sentence he says there were group thrashing or whippings. He then elaborates about plantation life. "One time on de niggers runned away, old Caesar Townsy, and ' dey sarnt for Dick Peters to come an' bring his

---

6. Rawick, *From Sundown to Sunup*, 171.
7. Rawick, Introduction to *The American Slave*, ed. Rawick, 1:xxxix.
8. Wilkins and Wilson, *Southern Slavery as It Was*, 24.
9. *The American Slave*, ed. Rawick, 6:24.
10. Ibid., 25.
11. Ibid., 35.

nigger dogs. Dem dogs was trained to ketch a nigger same as rabbit dogs is trained to ketch a rabit."[12]

Example 2

Aunt Tildy Collins recalls that "Ole Marster was good to all he niggers . . ." but "sometime a no 'count nigger tek an' runned erway; but de oberseer, he put de houn's on he track, an' dey run him up a tree . . ."[13]

Example 3

Jennie Bowen remembers, "We use ta have a mean oberseer, white folks, an' all de time dere slaves on our place a runnin' away."[14] The overseer is mean and slaves are running away, nevertheless, Bowen later on concludes, "We-alls had a good time an' us was happy an' secure."[15]

Example 4

Oliver Bell, tells his interviewer, "Us all b'longed t Mr. Tresvan De Graffenreid an' Mistu Rebecca; an' dey was all good to us. Ol' Mistus read de Bible to us an' got us baptized in de river at Horn's bridge . . ."[16] Bell makes it clear that " . . . it warn't so bad wid us. De white folks was good to us niggers."[17] Bell goes on, "One day my mammy done sumpin' an' ol' marster made her pull her dress down 'roun' her waist an' made her lay down 'crost de door. Den he taken a leather strop an' wopped her. I 'members dat I started crying an' Misus Beckie said, "Go git dat boy a biskit."[18]

These examples demonstrate that "good master" is a widely used term in the narratives, a type of moniker, the relative meaning of which must be determined casuistically. Ex-slaves who refer to masters as "good" or "kind" have different things in mind. "Good master" could be applied to

12. Ibid.
13. Ibid., 84.
14. Ibid., 42.
15. Ibid., 43.
16. Ibid., 27.
17. Ibid., 28.
18. Ibid.

someone who allowed no whipping or a master who unleashes dogs or offers a cookie to a child while simultaneously humiliating and whipping his mother in front of him. Bell, himself, understood this as noticed in his comment that " . . . ev'ybody thought dey marster was de bes' in de lan'. Us didn't know better."[19]

Most masters were probably called "good." The threshold of benevolence was simply adjusted to whatever conditions the slaves were forced to endure. The fact of masters being called "good" is not so much a tribute to the master, but to the slaves determination to find some goodness in their bleak world. The attitude of the ex-slaves toward their former masters as recorded in the narratives resonates with the comments of Frederick Douglass on this same topic. He wrote that "slaves, when inquired of as to their condition and the character of their masters, almost universally say they are contented, and that their master are kind."[20] He also writes,

> I have been frequently asked, when a slave, if I had a kind master, and do not remember ever to have given a negative answer; nor did I in pursuing this course, consider myself as uttering what is absolutely false; for I always measured the kindness of my master by the standard of kindness set up among slaveholders around us.[21]

Discussion of the complex reasons which might explain a slave's evaluation of his or her master is beyond the scope of this book, but an example of the same mentality may be seen in abused spouses. Whatever she experiences, an abused wife will describe her husband to most people as a "good" man until she is free from the threat of violence. Even then fear has a way of holding on. Douglass, even after he was free, feared retaliation because he felt there was always "the penalty of telling the truth, of telling the simple truth, in answer to a series of plain questions."[22]

Wilkins and Wilson would have their readers believe that the master and slave relationship was for the most part one of "remarkable affection"[23] on the basis of the ex-slave's evaluation. The testimony of former slaves is important, but the value assigned must involve consideration of other factors. As the examples given above show, and as Douglass makes clear, the testimony of ex-slaves to the goodness of their master must not be un-

19. Ibid.
20. Douglass, *Narrative of the Life of Frederick Douglass*, 21.
21. Ibid., 22.
22. Ibid., 21.
23. Wilkins and Wilson, *Southern Slavery as It Was*, 23.

critically received. Such testimony should be attenuated by contexts and circumstances or it results in a superficial and generally false picture of slavery in the South.

Utilizing the slave narratives Wilson and Wilkins paint their "amazingly benign picture of Southern plantation life," and of ex-slaves' "affection for former masters and mistresses . . . expressed in terms of unmistakable devotion," as well as a " wistful desire to be back at the plantation." The true meaning of the Civil War and the "various biblical and constitutional arguments that swirled around that controversy" [24] can be grasped only when their reader is delivered from the "lie" of our assumptions about Southern slavery. The rejection of slavery by the church is cast as a development of "humanistic and democratic culture," an inflammatory issue which obscured the true meaning of the wa[25] through a campaign of "abolitionist propaganda,"[26] giving "an issue to radical revolutionaries by which they could provoke animosity against the South."[27] The injustice of slavery was a fiction, manufactured by "radical and Unitarian"[28] forces "driven by a zealous hatred of the Word of God."[29]

Contrary to Wilson and Wilkins, the rise of abolitionism in America was facilitated by a national conscience riddled with conflict over slavery and its systemic oppression and abuse. As early as 1820 luminaries of the Republic such as John Quincy Adams believed slavery "the great and foul stain upon the North American Union."[30] Adams envisioned the "dissolution of the Union for the cause of slavery and a war between the two severed portions of the Union" resulting in the "extirpation of slavery from this whole continent."[31] The abolition of slavery was, in his mind, "contemplation worthy of the most exalted soul."[32] Adams' burden for America reflects a national conscience deeply agitated by the slavery issue, hoping for a gradual end of the institution and attempting interim compromises, but ultimately drawn into the war he prophesied.

24. Ibid., 6.
25. Ibid., 11,12.
26. Ibid., 23.
27. Ibid., 36.
28. Ibid., 12.
29. Ibid., 13.
30. Cited in Miller, *Arguing about Slavery*, 187.
31. Ibid., 193.
32. Ibid., 187.

Punishment of Slaves

Wilkins and Wilson urge that whatever "sin and evil" occurred in punishing slaves, it is wrong to "magnify it as though it were representative of the whole" but important links are missing in their chain of argument.[33] We are assured by them that brutal whippings were rare. The basis for this is presented as factual, but it is an assertion without proof. Regarding the interviews of former slave, they claim that "out of 331 references to master, 86% refer to their masters as "good" or "kind" but they do not explain the relationship between this observation and their claims about the severity of whipping. That 86% of the masters are called "good" or "kind" does not support the generalization that "quite a few would not allow whipping at all, and many only allowed it in their presence." What is the proof for this generalization or for their claim that "in other instances, whipping was as mildly applied as the corporal punishment normally practiced within families today'?[34] Is the reader to assume that the 86% did not allow whipping and that only 14% did? Or does it mean that 86% practiced discipline like families today? These questions cannot be answered because the authors offer no quantitative correlation between the narratives and their conclusions. Their argument begins statistically, but abruptly shifts without connection to vague generalizations such as "some" or "quite a few" or "many" or "in other instances."

Evidence for Wilkins and Wilsons' revision of slavery is not found in Fogel and Engermans' *Time on the Cross*, the single source they cite for the statistical proof of their assertions. Upon closer examination and to the contrary, Fogel and Engerman caution that "reliable data on the frequency of whipping is extremely sparse,"[35] and their source is "the only systematic record of whipping now available for an extended period . . . from the diary of Bennet Barrow, a Louisiana planter who believed that to spare the rod was to spoil the slave."[36] Wilkins and Wilson concede some masters were "brutal, even sadistic,"[37] but presumably in Fogel and Engerman's research they have found evidence of someone more "representative of the whole," meting out punishment not unlike the way one might discipline

---

33. Wilkins and Wilson, *Southern Slavery as It Was*, 28.
34. Ibid., 29.
35. Fogel and Engerman, *Time on the Cross*, 145.
36. Ibid.
37. Wilkins and Wilson, *Southern Slavery as It Was*, 29.

misbehaving children. Close examination of Bennet Barrow's diary, however, does not support this impression.

According to the editor of Barrow's diary, Edwin A. Davis, Bennet Barrow was a well-to-to Louisiana planter who "bought and sold land, raised cotton, experimented with sugar cane, and grew or produced most the supplies required on a large plantation."[38] He was, in fact, "typical of his time and section."[39] Barrow's whipping is considered by Davis to be "of the mild variety."[40] Fogel and Engerman write,

> His plantation numbered about 200 slaves, of whom about 120 were in the labor force. The record shows that over the course of two years a total of 160 whippings were administered, and average of 0.7 whippings per hand per year. About half the hands were not whipped and all during the period.[41]

According to other research, Fogel and Engerman's average is off by 69%.[42] A close examination of Barrow's diary reveals that "two years" is really a period of 23 months. The number of whippings is not 160 but 175. The number of slaves is not 200 but 129. The labor force of 120 is really somewhere between 59 and 71. Utilizing all available records, including manuscript returns contained in the National Archives from 1840 Census, Herbert Gutman and Richard Sutch conclude,

> Using their inaccurate count of the number of whippings, their *greatly exaggerated* estimate of the number of hands, and their *erroneous* measurement of the length of time covered, Fogel and Engerman estimated that Barrow's slaves received "an average of 0.7 whippings per hand per year." This statistic is also wrong. Each of their errors contributed to the substantial underestimate of the correct average of 1.19 whippings per hand per year, a figure 69% larger than that reported by Fogel and Engerman.[43]

It should also be kept in mind that 1.19 whippings per hand per year does not include other forms of punishment employed by Barrow besides the whip. Edwin Davis, the editor of Barrow's diary writes that he was

38. Davis, ed., *Plantation Life*, 11.
39. Davis, ed., *Plantation Life*, 38.
40. Ibid., 50.
41. Fogel and Engerman, *Time on the Cross*, 145.
42. David et al., *Reckoning With Slavery*, 63.
43. Ibid., 60, 61, 62, 63.

"constantly devising ingenious punishments, for he realized the uncertainty was an important aid in keeping his gangs well in hand."[44] Examining Barrow's diary, Gutman and Sutch note that "during the two year period under consideration, Barrow jailed, chained, beat with a stick, threatened with death, shot with a gun, raked the heads of, and humiliated his slaves,"[45] forcing some men to "wear women's clothing."[46]

Davis notes that Barrow's punishment was "only severe enough to be conducive to good discipline,"[47] but "brutal whippings ... were administered on occasion," and "some runaways were severely beaten upon being caught." The degree of severity is revealed in an episode from Barrow's diary. Runaways in Louisiana and other slave states were hunted with trained dogs. Davis cites Barrow's diary recording the pursuit of such a slave – "ran and trailed about a mile, *treed* him, made the dogs pull him out of the tree, Bit him badly, think he will stay home a while." An even more brutal example comes later. A runaway is chased and caught. Barrow writes, the "dogs soon tore him naked." Apparently, Barrow did not think that being bitten by dogs was enough punishment or he wanted the individual's fate to be an example to the other slaves, so he arranged a horrifying instant replay. He continues the entry, " . . . took him home before the negro[es] at dark & made the dogs give him another over hauling [sic]."[48] Regardless of his reasons, it seems that someone like Barrow, cited as being representative of plantation owners in general, occasionally committed acts of extreme brutality.

Wilkins and Wilson maintain that whipping was not excessive because "it was far more in the master's interest to motivate his slaves by positive means." For a master to have "devoted, hard-working, responsible men who identified their fortunes with the fortunes of their masters" masters didn't utilize the whip, but "a wide-ranging system of rewards."[49] The record kept by Barrow, however, shows his slaves never quite "identified" with him in this way. If the list of whippings recorded by Barrow is accurate, the 66 slaves listed as cotton pickers in Davis edition of his diary[50] were

44. Ibid., 49.
45. Ibid., 63.
46. Davis, ed., *Plantation Life*, 50.
47. Ibid., 49.
48. Ibid., 48, 49, 50.
49. Wilkins and Wilson, *Southern Slavery as It Was*, 29.
50. Davis, ed., *Plantation Life*, 419–21.

whipped regularly. Gutman and Sutch have observed that 50 of these men and women experienced the whip a total of 130 times in a 23 month period. It is further determined by comparing the list of cotton pickers in Davis' appendix with the list of those female slaves who gave birth that seven of the women whipped by Barrow during this period were mothers, one of them no fewer than four times.[51]

Barrow's conduct is representative of the perplexing and disturbing behavior of many slaveowners. They took care of their slaves, materially speaking. According to Davis Barrow's slaves "were well-fed and housed; and "they received gifts of money at Christmas time." Barrow also "provided medical attention on every necessary occasion."[52] Surely this was due, in large part, to running a successful plantation with a reasonably contented work force. There was also a form of friendship existing between some slaves and masters. Admiration, albeit racist, is displayed in Barrow's comment on the death of one of his slaves recorded in his diary—"a very great loss, one of the best negroes I ever saw or [k]new, to his family as [good as] a white person."[53] Yet, as seen above, he would brutally punish or hunt people with savage dogs, and diligently record it on the same pages without reflection. If Wilkins and Wilson want to demonstrate punishment on the typical plantation was different than what is demonstrated above from Barrow's diary, they will need to look for the proof elsewhere. It is not found in the work of Fogel and Engerman.

Wilkins and Wilson further assert that the slave narratives offer support for their opinions about punishment and abuse: "There was mistreatment, there were atrocities, there was a great deal of wickedness on the part of *some*—but, as the *Narratives* make plain, these abuses came from a distinct and very small minority."[54] To the contrary George Rawick observes that "the narratives almost uniformly render accounts of whippings. One can almost conclude that whippings were daily affairs on most plantations by simply counting the number of interviews that mention whippings..."[55] Rawick's observation is confirmed by the most cursory examination of the narratives. The following examples of ex-slaves interviewed during the

---

51. David et al., *Reckoning with Slavery*, 65.
52. Davis, ed., *Plantation Life*, 41, 42.
53. Ibid., 38.
54. Wilkins and Wilson, *Southern Slavery as It Was*, 26.
55. Rawick, Introduction to *The American Slave*, ed. Rawick, 1:xxxii.

APPENDIX: EVALUATING FORMER SLAVE TESTIMONY

1930's report whipping with great frequency and numerous acts of torture, including murder.

Example 1

Walter Calloway recounts the life long side-effects of a single whipping on a young girl.

> Marse John hab a big plantation an' lots of slaves. Day treated us purty good, but we hab to wuk hard. . . . Oh, yassuh, Marsh John good 'nough to us an' we git plenty to eat, but he had an oberseer name Green Bush what sho' whup us iffen we don't do to suit him. Yassuh, he might rough wid us but he didn' do de whuppin' hisse'f. He had a big black boy name Mose, mean as de debil an' strong as an ox, and de oberseer let him do all de whuppin.' An', man, he could sho' lay on dat rawhide lash. He whupped a nigger gal 'bout thirteen years ole so hard she nearly die, an' allus atterwa'ds she hab spells of fits or somp'n. Dat make Marsh John pow'ful man, so he run dat oberseer off de plantation an' Mose didn' do no mo' whuppin.[56]

Example 2

Aunt Amy, recalls the torture and humiliation of her brother and her own experience of being beaten with a cat-of-nine tails.

> He was de meanes' oberseer us ever had. He tuk my ol'dest brother an' had him stretched out jus' lak you see Christ on de cross; had him chained, an' I set down on de groun' by him an' cried all night lak Mary an' dem done. Dat oberseer was de fus' one dat over putt me in de fiel', an' he whupped me wid de cat er nine tails when I was stark naked. Den dere was anudder mean man . . . who was always a-bettin' nigger women case dey wouldn't mind him.[57]

---

56. *The American Slave*, ed. Rawick, 1:51.
57. Ibid., 59.

Example 3

She goes on in her interview to describe the technique of whipping slaves until they were bloody, then "anointing" their flesh with a mixture of red pepper and turpentine.

> One day I seed ole Unker Tip Toe all bent over a-comin' down de road an' I ax him whut ail him an'he say: 'I's been in de stocks an' been beat till blood come, Den ole Massa 'ninted my flesh wid red pepper an' turpentine an' I's been most dead but I is somewhat better now.' Unker Tiptoe belonged to the meanes' ol' marster around here.[58]

Example 4

Overseers or masters accomodated pregnancy during whipping by digging a hole in the ground. The expectant mother would then lie face down so that her stomach was in the hole. Henry Cheatam recalls how, as a young boy, he watched his pregnant aunt beaten until she miscarried.

> ... old Miss had a nigger oberseer an' dat was de meanest debil dat eber libbed on de Lawd's green yearth. I promise myself when I growed up dat I was agoin' to kill dat nigger iffen it was de las'thing I eber done. Lots of times I'se seen him beat my mammy, an' one day I seen him beat my Auntie who was big wid a chile, an' dat man dug a roun' hole in de groun' an' put her toummick in it, an' beat an' beat her for a half hour straight till de baby come out right dere in de hole.[59]

Example 5

Cheatam is not the only one to witness such unspeakable brutality against expectant mothers. Mandy McCullough recalls, "One woman on a plantation not so far from us, was expectin', an' they tied her up under a hack-a-berry tree, an' whipped her until she died."[60]

---

58. Ibid., 60.
59. Ibid., 66.
60. Ibid., 90, 91.

APPENDIX: EVALUATING FORMER SLAVE TESTIMONY

Example 6

Laura Clark, another ex-slave, recalls how people were stripped, beaten, and then "annointed" with a mixture. The overseer, she recalls,

> had a whuppin' log what he strip 'em buck naked and lay 'em on de log. He whup 'em wid a wide strop, wider'n my han'd, den he pop de blister what he raised and 'nint 'em wid red pepper, salt, and vinegar. Den he put 'em in de house dey call de pest house and have a 'oman stary dere to keep de flys offen 'em 'twell dey got able to move.

She reports people being beaten to death with the handle of a whip and then buried immediately in the field.

> ... dey had reg'lar men in de fields wid spades, and iffen you didn't do what you git tole, de overseer would srop dat strap 'roun' his han' and hit you in de haid wid de wooden handle 'till he kilt you. Den de mens would dig a hole wid de spades and throw 'em in hit right dere in de fiel' jes lack dey was cows— didn't have no funeral nor nothin.'[61]

Example 7

When traveling off the plantation, slaves were expected to carry a pass issued by their master, stating the date and times they could travel. William Colbert describes the whipping of his brother for being an hour late arriving home.

> de massa keep a beatin' til little streams of blood started flowin' down January's chest, but he neber holler. His lips wuz a quiverin' and his body waz a shakin', but his mouf it neber ioen; and al de while I sat on my mammy's and pappy's steps a cryin.' De niggers wuz all gathered about and some uv 'em couldn't stand it; dey hadda inside dere cabins. Atter while, January, he couldn't stand it no longer hsself, and he say in a hoarse, loud wisper: "Massa! Massa! Have mercy on dis poor nigger.[62]

These are only a few examples from the narratives, presented at length to convey the magnitude of material available. There are many

---

61. Ibid., 72.
62. Ibid., 81, 82.

other examples of punishment throughout the sixteen volumes of narratives available. Slaves remember overseers or masters who would "... whup you in a minute,"[63] or "whipped until the blood run down,"[64] or who "had regular days to whup all de slaves wid strops. De strops had holes in 'em so dat dey raised big blisters. Den dey took a hand saw, cut de blisters and whased 'em in salt water."[65]

The above examination of Fogel and Engerman's primary source on the whipping of slaves and consideration of testimony from the narratives which Wilkins and Wilson cite as proof of their assertions offers no support for their proposals. The narratives show that whippings, even severe and brutal whippings, were routine. There were masters who did not commit acts of brutality, even some who did not practice whipping, but there is certainly no proof offered by Wilkins and Wilson for believing such masters were the rule rather than the exception. And from the narratives it can be seen that there were many masters described as "good" who committed acts of brutality. Wilson and Wilkins may believe that "abuses came from a distinct and very small minority" but the certainty with which they argue does not come from the evidence they cite. Rather, the basis of such faith is created by recasting the entire situation of slavery into a mold of their own making. They present no quantitative study of the narratives sufficient for constructing their sweeping generalizations. That one can make such an assertion after reading the narratives is remarkable. It can only be concluded that other lines of reason, left unexplained to their readers by the authors, provide the basis for these opinions.

Revising Slavery for Post Millennialism

An explanation for the views of these two ministers on American slavery is suggested by the larger ministries, activities, and militant post millennialism. Douglas Wilson is one of the principle founders of a small but significant conservative and evangelical community, the Confederation of Reformed Evangelicals. In addition to being the pastor of Christ's Community in Moscow, Idaho, and founder of the Association of Classical Schools as well as New Saint Andrews, a liberal arts college in Moscow, Wilson is a noted author and speaker whose understanding of theology, history,

63. Ibid., 88.
64. Ibid., 90–91.
65. Ibid., 105.

and education is appreciated in a number of conservative Reformed congregations. *The New York Times* has described Wilson's influence and New Saint Andrews as a "new philosophy of evangelical education – one that has inspired a national movement." [66]

Wilson views the outcome of the Civil War as the triumph of Northern based Enlightenment ideology over Southern based biblical fidelity.[67] *American Slavery as It Was* was published as a positive assessment of Southern slavery in 1996 by Wilson and Steve Wilkins, another high profile leader in their denomination. In addition to being a noted speaker and pastor of Auburn Avenue Presbyterian Church in Monroe, Louisiana, Wilkins is also the founder of The Southern Heritage Society, and has been a member of The League of the South Board of Directors. *American Slavery As It Was* circulated throughout a significant number of churches and private schools in the United States until 2004 with little critical review or response.

Unstated in the booklet, but expressed in other publications authored by Wilson, they believe the application of "biblical law," will eventually transform culture in a worldwide fashion, establishing a temporal millennial kingdom which culminates in the return of Christ.[68] According to this view, the temporal realization of a Christianized world is predicted by biblical prophecy, and only such a world fulfills the requirements of prophecy surrounding the millennium.[69] The process of fulfillment began "as the gospel spread throughout the Gentile world"[70] culminating in the establishment of Christendom under Constantine. The South and other "nations which together, with varying degrees of success, acknowledged the Lordship of Jesus Christ over them," also known as "once-converted nations" are early imperfect versions of a steadily emerging and monolithic Christianized world. [71]

The American South is an especially important preview of the millennial kingdom in their outlook. The Confederate South was "the last nation of the first Christendom" and "the Confederate Army was the largest body

---

66. Molly Worthen, "Onward Christian Soldiers," *New York Times*, 30 September 2007.

67. Cf., Wilson, *Black and Tan*, 37–60, endorsed by Eugene Genovese.

68. Jones and Wilson, *Angels in the Architecture*, 145–60.

69. E.g., Ps 2:12; 22:27–28; 110:1.

70. Jones and Wilson, *Angels in the Architecture*, 203.

71. Ibid.

APPENDIX: EVALUATING FORMER SLAVE TESTIMONY

of evangelicals under arms in the history of the world."[72] This is not simply evidence of Christianity's influence on Southern culture, but of Christ's kingdom emerging on earth, growing in worldwide approval. The surrender of the Army of Virginia at Appomattox is cast as the death of the "first Christendom," but a glorious era will come and "the South will rise again."[73] If the existence of slavery is an obstacle, making it difficult for most readers to receive the Antebellum South as a preview of Christ's millennial kingdom, then Wilkins and Wilsons' revision of American slavery is meant to help. Like press secretaries with a public relations nightmare on their hands, they shift between anecdotes, fragments of statistical data, and ex-slave testimony attempting to put a positive spin on antebellum slavery.

They concede that some inhumane treatment must be acknowledged, but "these abuses came from a distinct and very small minority."[74] To the contrary, the narratives betray a widespread culture of whipping and abuse. When an ex-slave testifies to the kindness of their master, they speak as if whipping were part of their milieu. Molly Almond recalls that "[w]e had a mean oberseer dat always wanted to whup us, but massa would't 'llow no whuppin."[75] Charity Anderson remembers that her "[m]assa was a good man . . . But, honey all de whit folks wan't good to dere slaves. I's seen po' niggers 'mos' tore up by dogs and whupped 'tell dey bled w'en dey did'n' do lak white folks say."[76] Emma Chapman, reports that,

> There was no whipping allowed on the curry [sic] plantation . . . [t]he patrollers had no jurisdiction over the Curry slaves. They were given permits by the Currys to go and come, and Emma said if one of the patrollers whipped of "ole Miss's slaves, she would have sure sue'd them." Emma laughingly said the slaves on other plantations always said the Curry slaves were "free niggers," as they could always get permits, and had plenty to eat and milk to drink.[77]

Chapman's account makes it clear that the exceptional feature of the Curry plantation was that no whipping was allowed. The assertion that brutality was rare mistakes the exceptional situation as the rule. Wilson and Wilkins are not the first to make this mistake. Southern statesman

72. Ibid.; Wilkins and Wilson, *Southern Slavery as It Was*, 13.
73. Jones and Wilson, *Angels in the Architecture*, 205.
74. Wilkins and Wilson, *Southern Slavery as It Was*, 26.
75. *The American Slave*, ed. Rawick, 1:10.
76. Ibid., 12.
77. Ibid., 64.

and President of the Confederacy, Jefferson Davis, was against whipping on his Louisiana plantation.[78] He was known for caring, educating and befriending his slaves. As a defender of slavery, no one spoke more passionately about the wonderful quality of life enjoyed by his slaves. Davis' error, however, was that he assumed all slaveholders had his same attitude. He knew little or ignored attitudes and conditions elsewhere. As a recent biographer of Davis points out,

> The fact is that by 1848, the rising spokesman for Southern interests had traveled far more extensively in the North than in the slave states. He had seen only a little of Louisiana and nothing at all of Alabama, Georgia, Florida, the Carolinas, or Virginia. He had seen with his own eyes very little of slavery other than on the banks of the Mississippi from Vicksburg to New Orleans.[79]

Just as Davis needed to travel more in the South, Wilkins and Wilson need more extensive travel through the body of evidence and narratives they have cited.

That one can read the slave narratives or related materials filled with accounts of systematic brutality and assert "there has never been a multiracial society which has existed with such mutual intimacy and harmony in the history of the world"[80] or maintain an "overwhelmingly positive view of slavery"[81] provokes incredulity and suggests they have chosen to suppress the obvious in favor of their broader intellectual and theological convictions.

---

78. Davis, *Jefferson Davis*, 180–81.
79. Davis, *Jefferson Davis*, 180.
80. Wilkins and Wilson, *Southern Slavery as It Was*, 24.
81. Ibid., 25.

Bibliography

Aborgunrin, Samuel O. "Jesus's Sevenfold Programmatic Declaration at Nazareth: An Exegesis of Luke 4.15–30 from an African Perspective." *Black Theology* 1 (2003) 225–49.

Abrahamsen, Valerie. "Episcopal Church." In *The Historical Encyclopedia of World Slavery*, edited by Junius P. Rodrigeuz, 258–59. Santa Barbara: ABC-CLIO, 1997.

Albright, James W. *Greensboro 1808–1904 Facts, Figures, Traditions, and Reminiscences.* Greensboro, NC: Stone, 1904.

Ahlstrom, Sidney. *A Religious History of the American People.* New Haven: Yale University Press, 1972.

Anderson, Charles A. "Presbyterians Meet the Slavery Problem." *Journal of Presbyterian History* 29, no. 1 (1951) 9–39.

Anderson, Osborne P. *A Voice from Harper's Ferry: a narrative of events at Harper's Ferry, with incidents prior and subsequent to its capture by Captain Brown and his men.* Boston: 1861.

Armstrong, George D. *The Christian Doctrine of Slavery.* 1857. Repr., Detroit: Negro History, 1969.

Baker, David L. "Typology and the Christian Use of the Old Testament." *Scottish Journal of Theology* 29 (1976) 137–57.

Barker, William S. "The Social Views of Charles Hodge: A Study in Nineteenth Century Calvinism and Conservatism." *Presbyterion* 1 (1975) 1–22.

Barnes, Albert. *An Inquiry into the Scriptural View of Slavery.* 1855. Repr., Detroit: Negro History, 1969.

Barrow, David. *Involuntary, Unmerited, Perpetual, Absolute, Hereditary Slavery Examined; On the Principles of Nature, Reason, Justice, Policy, and Scripture.* Lexington, KY: Bradford, 1808.

Barth, Karl. *The Doctrine of Reconciliation.* Vol. 4/1 of *Church Dogmatics.* Edited and translated by Geoffrey W. Bromiley. Study ed. 1961. Repr., London: T. & T. Clark, 2010.

Bassard, Katherine Clay. "Crossing Over: Free Space, Sacred Place and Intertextual Geographies in Peter Randolph's 'Sketches of Slave Life.'" *Religion and Literature* 35, nos. 2–3 (2003) 113–41.

Bassett, John Spencer. *Antislavery Leaders of North Carolina.* Baltimore: Johns Hopkins, 1898.

Baxter, Richard. *A Christian Directory.* Vol. 1 of *The Practical Works of Richard Baxter.* 1664. Repr., Ligonier, PA: Soli Deo Gloria, 1990.

Bender, Thomas, ed. *The Antislavery Debate: Capitalism and Abolitionism as a Problem in Historical Interpretation.* Berkeley: University of California Press, 1992.

Berkeley, David. "Typology." In *A Dictionary of Biblical Tradition in English Literature*, edited by David L. Jeffrey, 792. Grand Rapids: Eerdmans, 2008.

BIBLIOGRAPHY

Berkhof, Louis. *Systematic Theology*. Grand Rapids: Eerdmans, 1938.
Berrigan, Daniel. *Exodus: Let My People Go*. Eugene, OR: Cascade, 2008.
Bercovitch, Sacvan, ed. *Typology and Early American Literature*. Amherst: University of Massachusetts Press, 1972.
Bird, Francis W. *Let My People Go*. Boston: Commercial, 1862.
Bock, Darrell. *Luke 1:1—9:50*. Grand Rapids: Baker, 1994.
Boff, Leonardo, and Clodovis Boff. *Introducing Liberation Theology*. Maryknoll, NY: Orbis, 1987.
Bozeman, Theodore Dwight. *Protestants in an Age of Science: The Baconian Ideal and Antebellum American Religious Thought*. Chapel Hill: University of North Carolina Press, 1977.
Broadie, Alexander, ed. *The Cambridge Companion to the Scottish Enlightenment*. Cambridge: Cambridge University Press, 2003.
Brockman, Charles Raven. *Adams, Caruthers, Clancy, Neely . . . and Other Twentieth Century Families of the Carolinas*. Charlotte: Private Publisher, 1950.
Brog, David. *In Defense of Faith: The Judeo-Christian Idea and the Struggle for Humanity*. New York: Encounter, 2010.
Brown, Christopher. *Moral Capital: Foundations of British Abolitionism*. Chapel Hill: University of North Carolina Press, 2006.
Brown, David. *Southern Outcast: Hinton Rowan Helper and the Impending Crisis of the South*. Baton Rouge: Louisiana State University Press, 2006.
Brown, Jerry Wayne. *The Rise of Biblical Criticism in America 1800–1870: The New England Scholars*. Middletown, CT: Wesleyan University Press, 1969.
Bruce, F. F. *The Epistles to the Colossians, to Philemon, and to the Ephesians*. 1957. Repr., Grand Rapids: Eerdmans, 1984.
Burgess, Thomas. *Considerations on the Abolition of Slavery and the Slave Trade upon Grounds of Natural, Religious and Political Duty*. Oxford: Prince and Cooke, 1789.
Byron, John. *Slavery Metaphors in Early Judaism and Pauline Christianity: A Traditio-Historical and Exegetical Examination*. Tubingen: Mohr/Siebeck, 2003.
———. *Recent Research on Paul and Slavery*. Sheffield: Sheffield Phoenix, 2008.
Calhoon, Robert M. *Evangelicals and Conservatives in the Early South 1740–1861*. Columbia: University of South Carolina Press, 1988.
Calhoun, David. *Princeton Seminary: Faith and Learning 1812–1868*. Carlisle: Banner of Truth Trust, 1994.
Calvin, John. *Institutes of the Christian Religion*, 2 vols. Edited by John McNeill. Philadelphia: Westminster, 1975.
———. *Harmony of the Evangelists: Mark, Matthew, and Luke*. Vol. 17, *Calvin's Commentaries*. 1847. Repr., Grand Rapids: Baker, 1989.
Campbell, Duncan. *English Public Opinion and the American Civil War*. London: Royal Historical Society, 2003.
Carlyle, Thomas ed. *Oliver Cromwell's Letters and Speeches with Elucidations*. Vol. 22 of *A Library of Universal Literature*. New York: Collier and Son, 1901.
Caruthers, Eli W. *A Sketch of the Life and Character of the Reverend David Caldwell, D.D.* Greensborough: Swaim and Sherwood, 1842.
———. *American Slavery and the Immediate Duty of Southern Slaveholders*. Durham, NC: Special Collections Library of Duke University, 1862. Microfilm.
———. *Eli Caruthers to Reverend Joseph Merriam*, Randolph, Ohio, 30 December 1824.

BIBLIOGRAPHY

———. *Eli Caruthers to C.H. Wiley*, Greensboro, NC: Session Minutes of Alamance Presbyterian Church, 30 July 1861.

———. *Interesting Revolutionary Incidents and Sketches of Character Chiefly in The "Old North State," Second Series*. Philadelphia: Hayes and Zell, 1856.

———. Oversize MSS Box Run A:5, items 1–252 c. 1. Eli W Caruthers Papers 1821–1862, David M. Rubenstein Rare Book and Manuscript Library, Duke University Libraries.

———. *Revolutionary Incidents and Sketches of Character Chiefly in The "Old North State."* Philadelphia: Hayes and Zell, 1854.

Carwardine, Richard. "The Politics of Charles Hodge." In *Charles Hodge Revisited: A Critical Appraisal of His Life and Work*, edited by John W. Steward and James H. Moorhead, 247–97. Grand Rapids: Eerdmans, 2002.

Cashdollar, Charles D. "The Social Implications of the Doctrine of Divine Providence: A Nineteenth-Century Debate in American Theology." *Harvard Theological Review* 71 3–4 (1978) 265–84.

Chalmers, Thomas. *The Works of Thomas Chalmers*. New York: Carter, 1841.

Charles, Robert H. *The Book of Jubilees*. Translated and edited by R. H. Charles. London: A. and C. Black, 1902.

Chesebrough, David. *Clergy Dissent in the Old South 1830–1865*. Carbondale: Southern Illinois University Press, 1996

———. *God Ordained This War: Sermons on the Sectional Crisis, 1830–1865*. Columbia: University of South Carolina Press, 1991.

Child, L. Maria. *Mrs. L. Maria Child to President Lincoln*. Samuel J. May Antislavery Collection, Cornell University, 1862.

Coogan, Michael, ed. *The New Oxford Annotated Bible*. Oxford: Oxford University Press, 2001.

Cowell, Stephen. *The Five Cotton States and New York: Remarks upon the Social and Economic Aspects of the Southern Political Crisis*. 1861.

Cowherd, Raymond. *The Politics of English Dissent: The Religious Aspects of Liberal and Humanitarian Reform Movements from 1815 to 1848*. New York: New York University Press, 1956.

Craddock, Fred. *Luke*. Louisville: John Knox, 1990.

Crowther, Edward. *Southern Protestants Slavery and Secession*. Auburn: Auburn University Press, 1986.

Dabney, Robert L. *Defense of Virginia*. New York: Hale and Son, 1867.

———. *Discussions of Robert L. Dabney*. 3 vols. 1881. Repr., Edinburgh: Banner of Truth Trust, 1967.

Dain, Bruce. *A Hideous Monster of the Mind: American Race Theory in the Early Republic*. Cambridge, MA: Harvard University Press, 2002.

Daniel, W. Harrison. "The Reaction of British Methodism to the Civil War and Reconstruction in America." *Methodist History* 16 (1977) 3–20.

———. "The Response of the Church of England to the Civil War and Reconstruction in America." *Historical Magazine Magazine of the Protestant Episcopal Church* 47 (1978) 57–72.

———. "English Presbyterians, Slavery, and the American Crisis of the 1860s." *Journal of Presbyterian History* 58 (1980) 52–65.

Danielou, Jean. *From Shadows to Reality: Studies in the Biblical Typology of the Fathers*. Westminster, MD: Newman, 1960.

Daube, David. *The Exodus Pattern in the Bible*. London: Faber and Faber, 1963.

BIBLIOGRAPHY

David, Paul, et al. *Reckoning with Slavery: A Critical Study in the Quantitative History of American Negro Slavery*. New York: Oxford University, 1976.

Davis, David Brion. *The Problem of Slavery in Western Culture*. Ithaca: Cornell University Press, 1966.

———. *The Problem of Slavery in the Age of Revolution*. Ithaca: Cornell University Press, 1975.

———. *Slavery and Human Progress*. New York: Oxford University Press, 1984.

———. *In the Image of God: Religion, Moral Values, and Our Heritage of Slavery*. New Haven: Yale University Press, 2001.

Davis, Edwin Adams, ed. *Plantation Life in the Florida Parishes of Louisiana 1836-1844, as Reflected in the Diary of Bennet H. Barrow*. 1943. Repr., New York: Columbia University Press, 1967.

Davis, William C. *Jefferson Davis: The Man and His Hour*. New York: HarperCollins. 1991.

Degler, Carl. *The Other South: Southern Dissenters in the Nineteenth Century*. New York: Harper & Row, 1974.

Dick, John. *Lectures on Theology*. 2 vols. New York: Dodd, 1864.

Dixon, John, *Long Pictures of Slavery in Church and State*. Philadelphia: n.p., 1857.

Douglass, Frederick. *Narrative of the Life of Frederick Douglass, an American Slave Written By Himself*. Edited by W. L. Andrews and W. S. McFeely. New York: Norton, 1997.

Ehrensperger, Kathy. *Paul and the Dynamics of Power: Communication and Interaction in the Early Christ-Movement*. London: T. & T. Clark, 2007.

Extracts from the Minutes of the General Assembly of the Presbyterian Church in the United States of America: A.D. 1818. Philadelphia: Bradford, 1818.

Fairbairn, Patrick. *The Typology of Scripture*. 2 vols. 1865. Repr., Grand Rapids: Zondervan, 1967.

Farmer, James Oscar. *The Metaphysical Confederacy: James Henley Thornwell and the Synthesis of Southern Values*. Macon, GA: Mercer University Press, 1999.

Fiering, Norman. *Jonathan Edward's Moral Thought and Its British Context*. Eugene, OR: Wipf and Stock, 2006.

Fish, Henry Clay. *Duty of the Hour, or, Lessons from our Reverses: A Discourse*. New York: Sheldon, 1862.

First Annual Report of the Ladies' New York City Antislavery Society. New York: Dorr, 1836.

Fitzmyer, Joseph. *The Gospel According to Luke I-IX: Introduction, Translation, and Notes*. New York: Dell, 1981.

Fogel, Robert, and Stanley Engerman, *Time on the Cross: The Economics of American Negro Slavery*. Lanham, MD: University Press of America, 1974.

Forbes, Robert. "Slavery and the Evangelical Enlightenment." In *Religion and Antebellum Debate Over Slavery*, edited by John McKivigan and Mitchell Snay, 68–106. Athens: University of Georgia Press, 1998.

———. "Truth Systematized." In *Prophets of Protest: Reconsidering the History of American Abolitionism*, edited by Timothy McCarthy and John Stauffer, 3–22. New York: New, 2006.

Foulkes, Francis. *Ephesians: An Introduction and Commentary*. Grand Rapids: Eerdmans, 1989.

BIBLIOGRAPHY

Fox-Genovese, Elizabeth, and Eugene Genovese. "The Divine Sanction of Social Order: Religious Foundations of the Southern Slaveholders' View." *World Journal of the American Academy of Religion* 55, no. 2 (1987) 211–23.

———. *The Mind of the Master Class: History and Faith in the Southern Slaveholders' Worldview.* Cambridge: Cambridge University Press, 2005.

Fretheim, Terence E. *Exodus.* Louisville: John Knox, 1991.

Friedman, Richard. *Commentary on the Torah: With a New English Translation and the Hebrew Text.* San Franisco: HarperSanFrancisco, 2001.

Frye, Northrop. "Exodus: The Definitive Experience." In *Exodus, Modern Critical Interpretations,* edited by Harold Bloom, 73–81. New York: Chelsea House, 1987.

Fuller, Richard, and Francis Wayland. *Domestic Slavery Considered as a Scriptural Institution: In a Correspondence between the Rev. Richard Fuller and the Rev. Francis Wayland.* New York: Colby, 1845.

Garrison, William Lloyd, ed. *The Abolitionist.* Boston: New England Antislavery Society, 1833.

———. *Our National Visitation: An Oration Delivered Before the Adelphia Union Society of Williams College, Monday afternoon, August 4.* Samuel J. May Antislavery Collection, Cornell University.

Gay, Peter, ed. *The Enlightenment: A Comprehensive Anthology.* New York: Simon and Schuster, 1973.

Geldenhuys, Norval. *Commentary on the Gospel of Luke: The English Text with Introduction Exposition and Notes.* Grand Rapids: Eerdmans, 1979.

Genovese, Eugene. *A Consuming Fire: The Fall of the Confederacy in the Mind of the White Christian South.* Athens: University of Georgia Press, 1998.

Gilkey, Langdon. "The Concept of Providence in Contemporary Theology." *Journal of Religion* 43 (1963) 171–92.

Giltner, John H. "Moses Stuart and the Slavery Controversy: A Study in the Failure of Moderation." In *Journal of Religious Thought* 18, no. 1 (1961) 27–39.

Glaude, Eddie S. *Exodus!: Religion, Race, and Nation in Early Nineteenth Century Black America.* Chicago: University of Chicago Press, 2000.

Goen, C. C. *Broken Churches Broken Nations: Denominational Schisms and the Coming of the American Civil War.* Macon, GA: Mercer University Press, 1985.

Goddard, Samuel A. *Reply to Mr. Lindsay's Speech at Sunderland, August, 1864, on the American Question.* Birmingham, UK: Osborn, 1864.

———. *The American Rebellion: Letters on the American Rebellion.* London: Simpkin, Marshall, 1870.

Goppelt, Leonard. *Typos: The Typological Interpretation of the Old Testament in the New.* Grand Rapids: Eerdmans, 1982.

Graham, Preston. *A Kingdom Not of this World: Stuart Robinson's Struggle to Distinguish the Sacred from the Secular During the Civil War.* Macon, GA: Mercer University Press, 2002.

Grant, Daniel. *Alumni History of the University of North Carolina.* Chapel Hill: General Alumni Association of the University of North Carolina, 1924.

Green, Michael. *The Gospel of Luke.* Grand Rapids: Eerdmans, 1997.

Guelzo, Allen C. "Charles Hodge's Antislavery Movement." In *Charles Hodge Revisited: A Critical Appraisal of His Life and Work,* edited by John W. Steward and James H. Moorhead, 299–325. Grand Rapids: Eerdmans, 2002.

BIBLIOGRAPHY

Gutiérrez, Gustavo. *A Theology of Liberation: History, Politics, and Salvation*. Translated by Sister Caridad Inda and John Eagleson. Maryknoll, NY: Orbis, 1988.

Guyatt, Nicholas. *Providence and the Invention of the United States, 1607–1876*. Cambridge: Cambridge University Press, 2007.

Hanley, Mark. *Beyond a Christian Commonwealth: The Protestant Quarrel with the American Republic, 1830–1860*. Chapel Hill: University of North Carolina Press, 1994.

Harrill, J. Albert. "Use of the New Testament in the American Slave Controversy." In *Religion and American Culture* 10, no. 2 (2000) 149–86.

Harrison, Beverly Wildung. *Making Connections: Essays in Feminist Social Ethics*. Boston: Beacon, 1985.

Haycroft, N. "Slavery and the Civil War in America." In *The Baptist Magazine for 1863*, edited by Revs. D. Katterns and W. Lewis, 205–11. London: Pewtress Bros., 1863.

Haynes, Stephen R. *Noah's Curse: The Biblical Justification of American Slavery*. Oxford: Oxford University Press, 2002.

Hays, Richard. *Echoes of Scripture in the Letters of Paul*. New Haven: Yale University Press, 1989.

———. *Moral Vision of the New Testament: Community, Cross, New Creation, A Contemporary Introduction to New Testament Ethics*. New York: HarperCollins, 1996.

———. *First Corinthians: a Bible Commentary for Preaching and Teaching*. Louisville, Kentucky: Westminster John Knox, 1997.

Hertig, Paul. "The Jubilee Mission of Jesus in the Gospel of Luke: Reversals of Fortunes." *Missiology* 26, no. 2 (1998) 167–79.

Heyrman, Christine. *Southern Cross: The Beginnings of the Bible Belt*. Chapel Hill: University of North Carolina Press, 1997.

Hezser, Catherine. *Jewish Slavery in Antiquity*. New York: Oxford University Press, 2005.

"Historical View of the State of Reformed Presbyterian Church in America, Until the Ratification of Their Testimony in May, 1806." In Book 2, Chapter 3, *Reformation Principles Exhibited by the Reformed Presbyterian Church in the United States of America*, 102–40. New York: Hopkins and Seymour, 1806.

Hodge, Charles. *Systematic Theology*. 3 vols. 1873. Repr., Grand Rapids: Eerdmans, 1995.

Holifield, E. Brooks. *The Gentlemen Theologians*. Durham, NC: Duke University Press, 1978.

———. *Theology in America: Christian Thought from the Age of the Puritans to the Civil War*. New Haven: Yale University Press, 2003.

Hood, Fred. *Reformed America: The Middle and Southern States, 1783–1837*. Tuscaloosa: University of Alabama Press, 1980.

Hughes, William. *Answer to the Rev. Mr. Harris's "Scriptural Researches on the Licitness of the Slave Trade."* 1788. Repr., Farmington Hills, MI: Thomson Gale, 2005.

Hutchison, George Whit. *The Bible and Slavery, a Test of Ethical Method: Biblical Interpretation, Social Ethics, and the Hermeneutics of Race in America, 1830–1861*. PhD diss., Union Theological Seminary. New York: 1996.

Jacob, J. R. "La Roy Sunderland: The Alienation of an Abolitionist." *Journal of American Studies* 6 (1972) 1–17.

James, Reverend Horace. *Annual Report of the Superintendent of Negro Affairs in North Carolina, 1864, With an Appendix Containing the History and Management of the Freedmen in this Department up to June 1st, 1865*. Boston: Brown, 1865.

BIBLIOGRAPHY

Jeon, Jeong Koo. *Covenant Theology: John Murry's and Meredith G. Kline's Response to the Historical Development of Federal Theology in Reformed Thought*. Lanham, MD: University Press of America, 1999.

Johnson, Guion Griffis. *Ante-Bellum North Carolina*. Chapel Hill: University of North Carolina Press, 1937.

Johnson, William C. "A Delusive Clothing: Christian Conversion in the Antebellum Slave Community." *The Journal of Negro History* 82, no. 3 (1997) 295–311.

Jones, Douglas, and Douglas Wilson. *Angels in the Architecture*. Moscow: Canon, 1998.

Kaiser, Walter. "Exodus." In *The Expositor's Bible Commentary*, edited by Frank Gabelein, 2:287–497. Grand Rapids: Zondervan, 1990.

Keesmaat, Sylvia. *Paul and His Story: (Re)Interpreting the Exodus Tradition*. Sheffield: Sheffield Academic, 1999.

Klempa, William. "The Concept of Covenant in Sixteenth and Seventeenth Century Continental and British Reformed Theology." In *Major Themes in the Reformed Tradition*, edited by Donald McKim, 94–106. Grand Rapids: Eerdmans, 1992.

Kuenning, Paul. *The Rise and Fall of American Lutheran Pietism*. Macon, GA: Mercer University Press, 1988.

Letters on the necessity of a prompt extinction of British colonial slavery: chiefly addressed to the more influential classes . . . to which are added, thoughts on compensation. London: Hatchard and Son, 1826.

Liefield, Walter. "Luke." In *The Expositor's Bible Commentary*, edited by Frank Gabelein, 8:797–1059. Grand Rapids: Zondervan, 1990.

Lingle, W. L. *Thyatira Presbyterian Church, Rowan County*. N.p., n.d.

Loetscher, Lefferts. *Facing the Enlightenment and Pietism: Archibald Alexander and the Founding of Princeton Theological Seminary*. Westport, CT: Greenwood, 1983.

Longenecker, Ricard N. *New Testament Social Ethics for Today*. Grand Rapids: Eerdmans, 1984.

Lounsbery, Edward. *Safe refuge in the day of calamity: a sermon preached in St. Jude's Church, Philadelphia on Sunday morning, Sept. 7, 1862*. Philadelphia: Ringwalt and Brown, 1862.

Lovelace, Richard. *Dynamics of Spiritual Life: An Evangelical Theology of Renewal*. Downers Grove, IL: InterVarsity, 1979.

Lundy, Benjamin ed. *Genius of Universal Emancipation, A Monthly Periodical Work, containing Original Essays, Documents and Facts, Relative to the Subject of African Slavery* 3 (1862).

Luther, Martin. *Lectures on Isaiah Chapters 40–66*. Vol. 17 of *Luther's Works*. Edited by Hilton C. Oswald. Translated by Herbert J. A. Bouman. St. Louis: Concordia, 1972.

Maddex, Jack. "An Illusory Official Consensus: The Slavery Question in the Old School Presbyterian Church." Paper presented at the annual meeting of the Southern Historical Society. New Orleans, LA: 1977.

MacCullough, Diarmaid. *The Reformation: A History*. New York: Viking Penguin, 2003.

MacGrath, Alister. *Christian Theology: An Introduction*. Oxford: Blackwell, 1993.

MacCleod, Donald. "Covenant Theology." In *Dictionary of Scottish Church History and Theology*, edited by Nigel Cameron, 214–18. Downers Grove, IL: InterVarsity, 1993.

Marsden, George. *The Evangelical Mind and the New School Presbyterian Experience: A Case Study of Thought and Theology in Nineteenth-Century American*. New Haven: Yale University Press, 1970.

BIBLIOGRAPHY

———. "Everyone One's Own Interpreter? The Bible, Science, and Authority in Mid Nineteenth Century America." In *The Bible in America: Essays in Cultural History*, edited by Nathan O. Hatch and Mark Noll, 59–100. Oxford University Press, 1982.

———. *Understanding Fundamentalism and Evangelicalism*. Grand Rapids: Eerdmans, 1991.

Marshall, I. Howard. *Gospel of Luke: A Commentary on the Greek Text*. Carlisle: Paternoster, 1978.

Mathews, Donald. "Charles Colcock Jones and the Southern Evangelical Crusade to Form a Biracial Community." *Journal of Southern History* 41, no. 3 (1975) 299–320.

———. *Religion in the Old South*. Chicago: University of Chicago Press, 1977.

Matthews, John. *The Divine Purpose Displayed in the Works of Providence and Grace*. Philadelphia: Presbyterian Board of Publication, 1840.

McCann, Dennis P. "Liberation Theology." In *Westminster Dictionary of Christian Ethics*, edited by James Childress and John Macquarrie, 349–50. Philadelphia: Westminster, 1986.

McKivigen, James. *Forgotten Firebrand: James Redpath and the Making of Nineteenth Century America*. Ithaca: Cornell University Press, 2009.

McKivigan, John. *The War against Proslavery Religion: Abolitionism and the Northern Churches 1830–1865*. Ithaca: Cornell University Press, 1984.

McLeod, Alexander. *Negro Slavery Unjustifiable, A Discourse*. New York: McLeod, 1802.

McMaster, Erasmus D. "Appendix to General Assembly Speech, May 30, 1859." N.p., n.d.

Meeks, Wayne A. "The 'Haustafeln' and American Slavery: A Hermeneutical Challenge." In *Theology and Ethics in Paul and His Interpreters: Essays in Honor of Victor Paul Furnish*, edited by Eugene H. Lovering Jr. and Jerry L. Sumney, 232–53. Nashville: Abingdon, 1996.

Mendenhall, George. "Covenant." In *The Interpreters Dictionary of the Bible*, edited by George Buttrick, 1:714–23. Nashville: Abingdon, 1962.

Meyers, Carol. *Exodus*. Cambridge: Cambridge University Press, 2005.

Miller, Marmaduke. *Slavery and the American War: A Lecture*. Manchester, UK: Union and Emancipation Society, 1862.

Miller, William Lee. *Arguing about Slavery: The Great Battle in the United States Congress*. New York: Knopf, 1996.

Miranda, Jose Porifirio. *Marx and the Bible: A Critique of the Philosophy of Oppression*. Cantebury: SCM Canterbury, 1977.

Mitchell, Alex, and John Struthers. *Minutes of the Sessions of the Westminster Assembly of Divines While Engaged in Preparing Their Directory for Church Government, Confession of Faith, and Catechisms*. Edinburgh: Blackwood and Sons, 1874.

Moltmann, Jurgen. *The Spirit of Life: A Universal Affirmation*. Translated by Margaret Kohl. Minneapolis: Fortress, 2001.

Moltmann, Jurgen. *Theology of Hope: On the Ground and the Implications of a Christian Theology*. 1967. Repr., Minneapolis: Fortress, 1993.

Moorhead, James H. *American Apocalypse: Yankee Protestants and the Civil War 1860–1869*. New Haven: Yale University Press, 1978.

Morrow, Nancy. "The Problem of Slavery in the Polemic Literature of the American Enlightenment." *Early American Literature* 20 (1985–1986) 236–55.

Mullin, Robert Bruce. "Biblical Critics and the Battle over Slavery." *Journal of Presbyterian History* 61, no. 2 (1983) 210–26.

Murray, Ephraim C. *A History of Alamance Church 1762–1918*. Greensboro: Alamance Presbyterian Church, 1918.

Nash, Ronald. *The Word of God and the Mind of Man: The Crisis of Revealed Truth in Contemporary Theology*. Grand Rapids: Zondervan, 1982.

Nitzan, Bilhah. "The Concept of Covenant in Qumran Literature." In *Historical Perspectives: From the Hasmoneans to Bar Kokhba in Light of the Dead Sea Scrolls*, edited by David Goodblatt et al., 85–104 Leiden: Brill, 2001.

Noll, Mark. *America's God: From Jonathan Edwards to Abraham Lincoln*. Oxford: Oxford University Press, 2002.

———. *Princeton and the Republic 1768–1822*. Vancouver: Regent College, 1989.

———. *The Civil War as a Theological Crisis*. Chapel Hill: University of North Carolina Press, 2006.

Nolland, John. *Luke 1–9*. Colombia: Word, 1989.

Paeth, Scott R. *Exodus Church and Civil Society: Public Theology and Social Theory in the Work of Jurgen Moltmann*. Hampshire, UK: Ashgate, 2008.

Palmer, Benjamin Morgan. *The Life and Letters of James Henley Thornwell: Ex President of the South Carolina College*. Richmond, VA: Whittet and Shepperson, 1875.

Pao, David, and Eckhard Shnabel. "Luke." In *Commentary on the New Testament Use of the Old Testament*, edited by G. Beale and D. Carson, 251–414. Grand Rapids: Baker, 2007.

Patterson, Orlando. *Slavery and Social Death: A Comparative Study*. Cambridge, MA: Harvard University Press, 1982.

Pease, Giles. *"Who Is on the Lord's side?" or, Does the Bible Sanction Slavery? Being an Examination into the Egyptian, Mosaic, and American Systems of Service and Labor*. Boston: Hoyt, 1864.

Pelikan, Jaroslav. *Reformation of the Church and Dogma*. Vol. 4 of *The Christian Tradition: A History of the Development of Doctrine*. Chicago: University of Chicago Press, 1983.

Peterson, Thomas V. *Ham and Jepheth: The Mythic World of Whites in the Antebellum South*. Metuchen, NJ: Scarecrow, 1978.

Polanyi, Michael. *Personal Knowledge: Towards a Post-Critical Philosophy*. Chicago: University of Chicago Press, 1958.

Preuss, Horst Dietrich. *Old Testament Theology*. Vol.1. Translated by Leo G. Perdue. Louisville: Westminster John Knox, 1995.

Priest, Josiah. *Bible Defence of Slavery*. 1853. Repr., Detroit: Negro History, 1969.

Proceedings of the Rhode-Island AntislaveryConvention : held in Providence, on the 2d, 3d, and 4th of February, 1836. Providence, RI: Brown, 1836.

Princeton Seminary Catalogue. Princeton: Princeton Seminary, 1818.

Raboteau, Albert J. *Slave Religion: The "Invisible Institution" in the Antebellum South*. Oxford: Oxford University Press, 1978.

Rael, Patrick. "A Common Nature, A United Destiny." In *Prophets of Protest: Reconsidering the History of American Abolitionism*, edited by Timothy McCarthy and John Stauffer, 183–99. New York: New, 2006.

Ramsay, James. *Examination of the Rev. Mr. Harris's "Scriptural Researches."* London: Phillips, 1788.

Randolph, Peter. *Sketches of Slave Life: or, Illustrations of the "Peculiar Institution."* Boston: n.p., 1855.

Raper, Charles Lee. *The Church and Private Schools of North Carolina: A Historical Study*. Greensboro, NC: Stone, 1898.

BIBLIOGRAPHY

Rawick, George. *From Sundown to Sunup: The Making of the Black Community.* Vol 1. of *The American Slave: A Composite Autobiography.* Westport, CT: Greenwood, 1972.

Rawick, George, ed. *The American Slave: A Composite Autobiography.* 19 vols. 1941. Repr., Westport, CT: Greenwood, 1972.

Ray, Stephen. "Review of *The Myth of Ham in Nineteenth-Century American Christianity: Race, Heathens, and the People of God* by Sylvester A. Johnson." *Conversations in Religion & Theology* 4, no. 1 (2006) 36–43.

Redding, Graham. *Prayer and Priesthood of Christ.* Edinburgh: T. & T. Clark, 2003.

Redpath, James. *Echoes of Harper's Ferry.* Boston: Thayer and Eldridge, 1860.

Reinhartz, Adele. *Why Ask My Name? Anonymity and Identity in the Biblical Narrative.* New York: Oxford University Press, 1998.

Report of the Committee of Merchants for the Relief of Colored People, Suffering from the Late Riots in the City of New York. New York: Whitehorn, 1863.

Rice, C. Duncan. *The Scots Abolitionists, 1833–1861.* Baton Rouge: Louisiana State University Press, 1981.

Ringe, Sharon. *Jesus, Liberation, and the Biblical Jubilee.* Eugene, OR: Wipf and Stock, 2004.

Robinson, Robert. *Slavery Inconsistent with the Spirit of Christianity: A Sermon Preached at Cambridge, Sunday, Feb. 10, 1788.* Cambridge: Archdeacon, 1788.

Ryle, J. C. *Expository Thoughts on Luke.* Vol. 1. 1858. Repr., Edinburgh: Banner of Truth Trust, 1997.

Sailhamer, John. "Genesis." In *The Expositor's Bible Commentary,* edited by Frank Gaebelein, 2:3–284. Grand Rapids: Zondervan, 1990.

Saneh, Lamin. *Abolitionists Abroad: American Blacks and the Making of Modern West Africa.* Cambridge, MA: Harvard University Press, 1999.

Schaff, Philip. *Modern Christianity: The Swiss Reformation.* Vol. 8 of *History of the Christian Church.* Grand Rapids: Eerdmans, 1988.

Schenck, David. *A Short Sketch of the Life of Eli W. Caruthers.* Greensboro, NC: Reece and Elam, 1901.

Scherer, Lester. *Slavery and the Churches in Early America 1619–1818.* Grand Rapids: Eerdmans, 1975.

Scott, Annie V. "A History of Alamance Church." *State Normal* 18, no. 2 (1913) 82–98.

Sewall, Samuel. *The Selling of Joseph: A Memorial.* 1700. Repr., Amherst: University of Massachusettes Press, 1969.

Shanks, Carolina. "The Biblical Antislavery Argument of the Decade 1830–1840." *Journal of Negro History* 16 2 (1931) 132–57.

Shavit, Yaco. *History in Black: African Americans in Search of an Ancient Past.* London: Cass, 2001.

Shay, John Michael. "Antislavery Movement in North Carolina Princeton." PhD diss., Princeton University, 1971.

Sherlock, William. *A Discourse concerning the Divine Providence.* 1715. Repr., Pittsburgh: Read, 1849.

Skinner, Quentin. *The Foundations of Modern Political Thought.* 2 vols. Cambridge: Cambridge University Press, 1978.

"Slavery in the Church Courts." *Danville Quarterly Journal* 4 (1864) 516–56.

Smith, Goldwin. *Does the Bible Sanction American Slavery?* Cambridge: Sever and Francis, 1863.

Snay, Mitchell. *The Gospel of Disunion: Religion and Separatism in the Antebellum South.* Cambridge: Cambridge University Press, 1993.

Stanhope Smith, Samuel. *An Essay on the Causes of the Variety of Complexion and Figure in the Human Specie.* New Brunswick, NJ: Simpson, 1810.

———. *The Lectures Corrected and Improved which Have Been Delivered . . . in the College of New Jersey on the Subjects of Moral and Political Philosophy.* 2 vols. New York: Whiting and Watson, 1812.

Staudenraus P. J. *The African Colonization Movement, 1816–1865.* New York: Octagon, 1961.

Stephen, James. *New Reasons for Abolishing the Slave Trade: Being the last section of a larger work, now first published, entitled "The dangers of the country."* London: Butterworth, 1807.

———. *The Slavery of the British West India Colonies Delineated as It Exists Both in Law and Practice, and Compared with Other Countries Ancient and Modern.* 1824. Repr., New York: Cambridge University Press, 2010.

Stewart, James Brewer. "Abolitionists, the Bible, and the Challenge of Slavery." In *The Bible and Social Reform*, edited by Ernest R. Sandeen, 31–57. Chico, CA: Scholars, 1982.

Stott, John. *The Message of Ephesians.* Downers Grove, IL: InterVarsity, 1979.

Stroud, George M. *Sketch of the Laws Relating to Slavery in the Several States of the United States of America.* Philadelphia: Kimber and Sharpless, 1827.

Stringfellow, Thornton. "A Scriptural View of Slavery." In *Slavery Defended: The Views of the Old South*, edited by Eric L. McKitrick, 87–89. Englewood Cliffs, NJ: Prentice-Hall, 1963.

Sumner, Charles. *Emancipation!: Its policy and necessity as a war measure for the suppression of the rebellion: speech of Hon. Charles Sumner, at Faneuil Hall, Oct. 6, 1862.* Samuel J. May Antislavery Collection, Cornell University.

Sunderland, La Roy. *The Testimony of God against Slavery: A Collection of Passages from the Bible Which Show the Sin of Holding and Treating the Human Species as Property with notes. To which is added The Testimony of the Civilized World Against Slavery.* Boston: Knapp, 1836.

Swartley, Willard. *Slavery Sabbath War and Women: Case Issues in Biblical Interpretation.* Scottsdale, PA: Herald, 1983.

Symmes, Joseph Gaston. *National Thanksgiving: A Sermon, Preached in the First Presbyterian Church of Cranbury, New Jersey, on November 26, 1863.* Philadelphia: Martien, 1864.

T. R. "Observations on the Early History of the Negro Race." *African Colonial Journal* 1 (1825) 7–12.

Taylor, Clare. *British and American Abolitionists: An Episode in Transatlantic Understanding.* Edinburgh: Edinburgh University Press, 1974.

Thompson, George. *The Free Church and Her Accusers: The Question at Issue.* Edinburgh: Dalrymple, 1846.

Thompson, J. Earl. "Abolitionism and Theological Education at Andover." In *New England Quarterly* 47, no. 2 (1974) 238–61.

Thornwell, James Henley. *Ecclesiastical.* Vol. 4 of *The Collected Writings of James Henley Thornwell.* Richmond, VA: Presbyterian Committee of Publication, 1873.

———. "The Rights and the Duties of Masters." In *God Ordained This War.* Edited by David Chesebrough. Columbia: University of South Carolina Press, 1991.

———. *Theological.* Vol. 1 of *The Collected Writings of James Henley Thornwell.* Richmond, VA: Presbyterian Committee of Publication, 1873.

Tise, Larry. *Proslavery: A History of the Defense of Slavery in America, 1701–1840.* Athens: University of Georgia Press, 1987.

Tombs, David. *Latin American Liberation Theology.* London: Brill, 2002.

Torrance, James. "The Contribution of McLeod Campbell to Scottish Theology." *Scottish Journal of Theology* 26 (1973) 295–311.

———. "New Introduction." In *The Nature of the Atonement,* by James McLeod Campbell, 1–16. Repr., Stables, Scotland: Handsel, 1996.

Troxler, George. "Eli Caruthers: A Silent Dissenter in the Old South." *Journal of Presbyterian History* 45, no. 2 (1967) 95–111.

Turley, David. *The Culture of English Antislavery, 1780–1860.* New York: Routledge, Chapman, and Hall, 1991.

Union Antislavery Auxiliary No. 2. *Address of the Union Anti-slavery Auxiliary to the Congregation of the Western Presbyterian Church.* Ithaca: Cornell University Library, 1838.

Vail, Stephen Montford. *Overthrow of the Slave Power: A Sermon Preached Before the Students of the Methodist Biblical Institute, Concord, N.H., November 7, 1862.* Concord, NH: Hadley Fogg, 1862.

Van Groningen, Gerard. *Messianic Revelation in the Old Testament.* Grand Rapids: Baker, 1990.

Van Rensselaer, C. "Dr. Van Rensselaer's Reply to Dr. Armstrong." *Presbyterian Magazine* 8 (1858) 13–26.

———. "Dr. Van Rensselaer's Second Rejoinder." *Presbyterian Magazine* 8 (1858) 529–52.

Vos, Gerhardus. *Redemptive History and Biblical Interpretation.* Phillipsburg, NJ: Presbyterian and Reformed, 1980.

Walhout, M. D. "The Hermeneutical Turn in American Critical Theory." In *Journal of the History of Ideas* 57, no. 4 (1996) 683–703.

Walzer, Michael. *Exodus and Revolution.* New York: Basic, 1985.

Weld, Theodore Dwight. *The Bible against Slavery: An Inquiry into the Genius of the Mosaic System and the Teaching of the Old Testament on the Subject of Human Rights.* 1864. Repr., Detroit: Negro History, 1970.

Wheelock, Edwin M. *Harper's Ferry and Its Lesson. A Sermon for the Times.* Boston: Rand and Avery, 1859.

Whyte, Iain. *Scotland and the Abolition of Black Slavery, 1756–1838.* Edinburgh: Edinburgh University Press, 2006.

Williams, Harold P. "Brookline in the Anti-Slavery Movement." Unpublished paper. 1899. Brookline Historical Publication Society 18. Brookline, Massachusetts.

Wilkins, Steve, and DouglasWilson, *Southern Slavery as It Was.* Moscow, ID: Canon, 1996.

Wilson, Douglas. *Black and Tan: A Collection of Essays and Excursions on Slavery, Culture, War, and Scripture in America.* Moscow: Canon P., 2005.

Wilson, Jeremiah M. *Afrotopia: The Roots of African American Popular History.* Cambridge: Cambridge University Press, 1998.

Wilson, Joseph M. *The Presbyterian Historical Almanac.* Philadelphia: Wilson, 1866.

Witherington, Ben, III. *Conflict and Community in Corinth: A Socio-Rhetorical Commentary on 1 and 2 Corinthians.* Grand Rapids: Eerdmans, 1995.

BIBLIOGRAPHY

Wood, A. Skevington. "Ephesians." In *The Expositor's Bible Commentary*, edited by Frank Gabelein, 11:3–92. Grand Rapids: Zondervan, 1978.
Woods, Leonard. *The Works of Leonard Woods*. 4 vols. Andover, MA: Flagg, 1850.
Wright, N. T. *Paul for Everyone: The Prison Letters*. London: SPCK, 2004.
Yacovone, Donald. Review of *Black Soldiers in Blue: African Troops in the Civil War Era* by John David Smith. *The Pennsylvania Magazine of History and Biography* 128, no. 4 (2004) 413–14.

www.ingramcontent.com/pod-product-compliance
Lightning Source LLC
Chambersburg PA
CBHW051638230426
43669CB00013B/2358